D0425599

In Whose Interest?

A COUNCIL ON FOREIGN RELATIONS BOOK

In Whose Interest?
International Banking and American Foreign Policy

Benjamin J. Cohen

A COUNCIL ON FOREIGN RELATIONS BOOK

Yale University Press
New Haven and London

Designed by James J. Johnson and set in Aster
Roman.
Printed in the United States of America by
Vail-Ballou Press, Binghamton, N.Y.

Library of Congress Cataloging-in-Publication Data

Cohen, Benjamin J.
  In whose interest?

  "A Council on Foreign Relations book."
  Includes index.
  1. Banks and banking, International. 2. Banks
and banking—United States. 3. United States—
Foreign relations—1981–   . I. Title.
HG3881.C586 1986   332.1'5   86–9210
ISBN 0–300–03614–0 (alk. paper)

---

*The paper in this book meets the guidelines for perma-
nence and durability of the Committee on Production
Guidelines for Book Longevity of the Council on
Library Resources.*

---

10   9   8   7   6   5   4   3   2   1

For
Ch. Ch. Supply-Sider
("Spaghetti")

Contents

Acknowledgments

I wrote this book between September 1984 and September 1985, while on academic leave from the Fletcher School of Law and Diplomacy, Tufts University. Final revisions of the manuscript were completed in January 1986.

The book was commissioned by the Council on Foreign Relations in 1983. I conducted basic research during the academic year 1983–84, with additional background and ideas contributed by a series of six study group meetings convened at the Council, graciously chaired by the Honorable Nathaniel Samuels, former under secretary of state for economic affairs. Partially funded by a grant from the Ford Foundation (Grant No. 845–0385), the study group brought together a variety of experts from the financial community, universities, research institutions, governmental agencies, and journalism. (A complete list of participants is provided in an appendix.) During 1984–85, while the book was being written, I was resident at the Council's offices in New York as the Whitney H. Shepardson Senior Visiting Fellow.

I accumulated many debts of gratitude over the course of this project. I especially wish to express my deep and heartfelt appreciation to six key individuals at the Council on Foreign Relations: Winston Lord, former president of the Council, for his timely support and encouragement; Paul Kreisberg, director of studies, for his firm leadership and constructive criticism; William Diebold, former senior fellow (now retired), for his inspiration and unstinting assistance at every stage of the project; Helena Stalson, also now a retired senior fellow, for her unflagging enthusiasm and insight (and also, incidentally, for teaching me the true meaning of the phrase *lion's share*); David Kellogg, director of publications, for his sympathetic efforts to ensure that this book would eventually see the light of day; and Alice McLoughlin, for her incredible patience and fortitude in typing draft after draft of the manuscript.

While this book was being written, the Council organized two separate author's review groups to provide me with detailed and useful commentary on the manuscript in progress. One group, which was convened in New York, met in December 1984, April 1985, and May 1985. The members of the group included Michael Aho, Lawrence Brainard, George Clark, Charles Dallara, Carlos Díaz-Alejandro, William Diebold, James Drumwright, Charles Ganoe, Miles Kahler, David Kellogg, Paul Kreisberg, Roger Kubarych, Charles Meissner, Nathaniel Samuels, Robert Solomon, and Helena Stalson.

The second group was convened in San Francisco, with the cooperation of the World Affairs Council of Northern California, in June 1985. Members of this group included Paul Applegarth, William Bolin, Russell Burbank, Alexander Calhoun, Elaine Chao, Gary Christianson, Albert Fishlow, Philip Habib, Edward Hamilton, Bernard Hargadon, Robert Heller, Cordell Hull, Peter Jones, Thomas Layman, Angus MacNaughton, Robert Marcus, Jesun Paik, John Place, Paul Slawson, Richard Sutch, Peter Tarnoff, John Treat, Anton Tucher, and Stephen Wilson.

I am deeply grateful to the members of both groups for their invaluable assistance in this project.

Over the course of the project, I interviewed more than three dozen individuals in both the private and public sectors in this country and also in Argentina, Brazil, and Mexico. I wish to thank them all for their time and cooperation. I am especially indebted to Charles Dallara and Gregory Wilson for helping to arrange interviews in Washington, D.C. And I am indebted to Karin Lissakers for sharing interview materials with me that she had gathered for related research of her own.

In addition, I wish to express my sincere gratitude to a number of other friends and colleagues who were kind enough to read and comment critically on portions of this manuscript at various stages in its preparation. These included Karen Dawisha, Jeff Frieden, John Karlik, Robert Keohane, Susan Purcell, Dorothy Sobol, Andrew Spindler, Susan Strange, and Philip Wellons. Special thanks go to William Diebold, Roger Kubarych, Charles Meissner, Robert Solomon, Joan Spero, and Anton Tucher for their very detailed commentaries on the penultimate draft of the manuscript.

Finally, the usual caveat applies. All of the above are absolved of any guilt for blips, bleeps, or bloopers that may remain in what follows. I alone bear full responsibility.

Part I

CHAPTER 1

High Finance/High Politics

International banking used to be regarded not so long ago as a straightforward commercial activity in which tidy sums of money could be earned. Bankers compared opportunities in domestic and foreign markets, totted up the costs and benefits of alternative profit strategies, and allocated their resources accordingly. Even with formal political-risk analysis thrown in, financial decisions were ostensibly divorced from considerations of foreign policy. High finance, in principle at least, was kept separate from the "high politics" of international diplomacy.

That era is over. International banking has expanded dramatically in recent decades—and with that "internationalization," banking operations have become increasingly politicized, as involvements with foreign governments have rapidly multiplied in scores of countries from Argentina to Zaire, from Poland to the Philippines, from Libya to South Africa. Bankers today have no choice but to pay more attention to foreign policy issues in the ordinary course of their business. In practice, high finance can no longer be kept separate from high politics. Indeed, in the contemporary era, they are increasingly one and the same.

What does this mean for U.S. foreign policy? That is the question addressed by this book. With the growing interna-

3

tionalization and politicization of banking activity, financial decisions have come more and more to encroach on the traditional terrain of policymakers. When Americans were taken hostage in Iran in 1979, banking relationships turned out to be one of the key elements in their eventual release. When Poland suppressed the Solidarity trade union movement in 1981, Polish debt to Western banks seriously compromised U.S. efforts to retaliate with economic sanctions. And when bank loans in Latin America started to go bad in 1982, the U.S. government had to step in to keep the financial crisis from getting out of control. Today, high finance is much of what international diplomacy is all about. Is U.S. foreign policy better or worse off as a result?

The answer is not obvious. By supporting the spread of trade and investment links across national frontiers, international banking brings many broad economic benefits that serve America extremely well. An international commercial environment is facilitated that promotes growth and prosperity at home as well as abroad. More narrowly, banking relationships may also generate new foreign policy opportunities, as for example during the Iranian hostage crisis. But international banking can be disadvantageous as well, when seen from the perspective of the public authorities in Washington. Economic, or even political, costs may be threatened as a consequence of the sizable risks inherent in cross-border banking activity. And additional constraints may be imposed on policy in specific instances too, as in the Polish case and during certain stages of the Latin American debt crisis. The tidy sums that bankers earn can carry untidy implications for policymakers.

The essence of the problem is that the two sets of actors, bankers and policymakers, do not share all the same motivations or goals. While their activities have become increasingly intertwined and interdependent, a potential for conflicting interests exists—and such conflict could severely handicap the public authorities in their ability to formulate and implement an effective foreign policy. At a time in history when events in the world seem increasingly to be slipping beyond America's control, this is no small matter. It would not take much loss of policy effectiveness to trigger a major unraveling of diplomatic positions. The stakes are high.

The fundamental challenge is to articulate a coherent public policy on international banking for the contemporary era. Extensive cross-border banking relationships have become an integral part of the American economy's links with the outside world. Yet there is strikingly little awareness in the United States of the key role that banks now play in foreign affairs. Other economic aspects of U.S. diplomacy receive far more attention in policy debates. People may not agree on such matters as import barriers, energy trade, or exchange rates; but the relevance of questions like these to America's foreign policy is manifestly recognized and acknowledged. We are still very distant from a clear definition of the public interest in international banking.

From a foreign policy point of view, the urgent need is to minimize any adverse effects on U.S. government policy capabilities while at the same time protecting the legitimate interests of banks. Two levels of challenge can be distinguished. At the institutional level, we need a new structure of relations between policymakers and bankers that more effectively accommodates the interests of each. At the substantive level, we need new approaches to managing the potential economic or political costs of international banking, in order to maximize its many benefits. The growing interdependence of high finance and high politics must be explicitly acknowledged. Defining the public interest in international banking is what this book is about.

Specifically, the book is written in the hope of promoting better general understanding of the complex issues involved in bank–government relations in the foreign policy area. These relations have always been a subject of considerable controversy. Many people argue that the government has no business getting involved in private international finance; others, that the government has every right, given the alleged mistakes and malfeasances of bankers. To the first I would point out that, like it or not, the government is already involved. Public policy both shapes the environment for international banking and is shaped by it. To the second, I would point out that bankers, for all their human fallibility, perform an invaluable role in promoting the general economic welfare. This book is not intended to be a polemic against the banks, even if I do feel that banks must accept new responsibilities in the foreign policy process. The government, I shall argue, also must accept new responsibilities in relation to the banks. The aim of the following chapters is to develop practical proposals to enable both sides to perform their respective functions more effectively.

This book is an exercise in international political economy. Social scientists traditionally distinguish among three basic conceptions of political economy: Marxism, class-based analysis in which economics tends to dominate all politics and political structure; mercantilism (or "economic nationalism"), which reverses the sequence, assuming the subservience of all economic activity to the state and its interests; and liberalism, which takes as its starting point the presumption that politics and economics are relatively separable and autonomous spheres of activity. The perspective informing this book is eclectic, stressing the reciprocal and dynamic interactions between the two spheres of economics and politics. Banks and the government are assumed to act independently, motivated by different interests and intentions, but always within a relationship of close and mutual interdependence. Each side has its legitimate responsibilities and objectives; many interests are shared. Yet, like an old married couple, both sides must be prepared to make adjustments to changing times if they are to be able to go on living together. The problem posed by the internationalization of banking activity in recent years is, What should those adjustments be? Bankers and the makers of foreign policy have to find a new modus vivendi.

To begin, it is important to know what we are talking about, and why. What precisely do we mean by foreign policy? What do we mean by international banking? And what justifies a special study of the relationship between the two?

I

The first question is the easiest to answer. For my purposes, foreign policy must be understood in the broadest sense of the term—to encompass the full range of strategies and actions developed by the U.S. government in America's relations with the outside world. Foreign policy aims to achieve specific goals in terms of national interests. These goals naturally include the high politics of political and military concerns. Equally important, they include the low politics of economic relations—international trade, investment, finance, and the like. No aspect of America's overseas relations can be excluded from discussion a priori, neither issue areas nor geographic regions. To do so would be not only arbitrary; worse, it would risk neglecting some of the potentially most significant dimensions of our international diplomacy. Economics surely is as much a part of foreign policy as is politics.

To put the point differently: America's security in an uncertain world surely depends as much on the success of its national economy as it does on its political and military alliances overseas. And the success of its economy, in turn, depends as much these days on its commercial and financial links abroad as it does on developments closer to home. America is an insular economy no longer. Prosperity has become vitally dependent on sustained access to foreign markets for its exports and investments and to foreign sources of supply for energy and other essential imports. International capital movements have become a significant determinant of the overall availability of funds for borrowing domestically; external fluctuations of the dollar have come to have marked effects on its internal unemployment and inflation rates. The authorities in Washington have no choice but to count economic interests among the goals of its international diplomacy. Foreign policy necessarily includes foreign economic policy.

Moreover, in framing its economic goals, American policymakers have no choice but to include interests that go well beyond the narrow pursuit of national advantage alone (which is the popular understanding of national interests in international affairs). A systemic component must be included as well. Economics is by definition a matter of interdependence among nations—and this has extra special meaning for the United States, which, by virtue of its size and importance, has an inordinate influence on the overall network of international economic relations. Actions here can typically be expected to have major consequences for the world economy as a whole; and these consequences, in turn, can typically be expected to feed back to affect the U.S. economy as well. Like it or not, therefore, America has a vital interest in overall systemic stability and prosperity; equally, America's interests are affected directly by anything that impacts on the overall system, including its own actions. As the largest and most influential state actor in the world economy, America must go beyond its own parochial concerns to take account of questions of systemic maintenance—support and preservation of the external commercial and financial environment that contributes so much to its own, as well as others', economic welfare. The general evolution of the world economy, and not only America's specific place in it, must figure prominently in Washington's perception of policy goals. It can ignore the systemic component only at its peril.

Even if we agree on the broadest possible definition of foreign policy, however, a crucial issue remains: How are national interests (the public interest) to be defined? More precisely, by whom are they to be defined? From one perspective, national interests may be said to be defined by the apparatus of the state through command or bureaucratic negotiations; from another, by society as a whole through the domestic political process; from a third, they may be said to be transcendent, independent of the transitory and often volatile preferences of either state or society. Which perspective should be adopted here?

Given the central focus of this book on the government's foreign policy capabilities, it seems most appropriate to start with the first perspective—the public interest as interpreted by the public authorities themselves. Accordingly, in most of the analysis that follows, I will concentrate objectively on the various constraints and opportunities that are created by international banking for government officials in the pursuit of their policy preferences. Ultimately, however, it will be necessary to go beyond that perspective, to make judgments about some of those preferences; in other words, to take a normative view of the national interest in the international arena. Hence, in the concluding chapters of the book, I shall offer recommendations for public policy that rely most on the third perspective on America's foreign policy.

That is not to question Washington's exclusive responsibility for foreign policy. Identifying and promoting the public interest is, ostensibly, what government does. No other institution is formally mandated to perform that function. But it is possible to question specific policy preferences: Washington does not always know best. In practice, public officials are as fallible as the next person and often are unable even to articulate a convincing rationale for their own policy choices. Frequently domestic politics dominates decision making, in the sense that policy choices reflect little more than the relative bargaining strength of different political constituencies. Bureaucratic power struggles often blur the logic or consistency of key policy decisions. And frequently officials, with their diverse values and at times conflicting responsibilities and priorities, are unable to achieve any degree of policy consensus or coherence at all. Washington's policy process is anything but smooth or efficient. In such circumstances, the objective analyst has no alternative but to make an independent judgment of the public interest when attempting to frame practical proposals for policy.

II

What do we understand by international banking? To the uninitiated, banking can seem mysterious, yet it need hardly be so intimidating. Stripped to its essence, commercial banking is simply the business of taking deposits and making loans. Commercial banks are financial intermediaries, one of a class of institutions that perform the function of financial intermediation collectively reconciling the differing needs of savers and dissavers in society. The assets of financial intermediaries are the obligations of the ultimate users of funds (borrowers); their liabilities, the claims of ultimate suppliers of funds (depositors). Other financial intermediaries, in addition to commercial banks, include traditional savings banks and other so-called thrift institutions, investment banks, insurance companies, brokerage firms, and pension funds, each type with its own specialized brands of activity. They include as well the newly emerging "financial supermarkets," like Merrill Lynch, Sears Roebuck, Prudential-Bache, and Shearson Lehman-American Express, which combine under one roof a growing variety of financial services and operations. Commercial banks of course also provide a variety of services to their customers, for example, trustee and executor facilities, securities trading, leasing, and credit card accounts, among other things. But deposits and loans remain, at least for now, the central core of their business.

What distinguishes international banking from domestic banking? International banking comprises a range of transactions that can be distinguished from purely domestic operations by (a) the currency of denomination of the transaction; (b) the residence of the bank customer; and (c) the location of the booking office. A deposit or loan transacted in local currency between a bank in its home country and a resident of that same country may be termed pure domestic banking. Anything else, in one form or another, is international banking. The range of possible variations of international (or cross-border) banking is obviously considerable.

Finding suitable labels for all these possible variations is no easy task. One convenient approach is illustrated schematically in table 1.1.[1] While transactions in subset A represent pure domestic banking, those in subset B broadly correspond to what traditionally have been described as foreign banking operations—deposits from abroad or loans to customers abroad booked in local currency by a bank in its home country. Historically, until the development of what is today commonly called the Euro-currency market, that was the predominant form of international banking.

The Euro-currency market, also known as the foreign-

TABLE 1.1. Schema of Banking Transactions

Transaction with a		Resident	Nonresident
denominated in the domestic currency	booked in home country	A	B
	booked outside home country	D1	D2
denominated in foreign currency	booked in home country	C	
	booked outside home country	D3	D4

currency-deposit market or simply the offshore banking market, is conventionally defined to encompass all deposit and loan operations of a banking office transacted in a currency other than that of the nation in which the office is located. Euro-currencies are created whenever a national currency is deposited in a bank outside its country of issue (hence the alternative nomenclature of foreign-currency deposits). In table 1.1, Euro-currency (foreign-currency-deposit) transactions include subset C as well as much of those comprising subsets D1, D2, and D3.[2] Subset D4, comprising transactions in local currency with local residents, differs from subset A only in the fact that the booking office is not locally owned. The four subsets D1–D4 together are sometimes referred to as multinational or foreign-based banking transactions.

Alternative taxonomies are of course possible, involving yet other terminology.[3] But for my purposes, it seems most appropriate to use terms that are popular and familiar. No understanding is lost as long as clarity in their use is maintained.

III

What justifies a special study of international banking in relation to foreign policy? After all, other industries are also international in scope; nonfinancial multinational enter-

prises have foreign policy implications too. We need only recall the role of ITT in Chile in the early 1970s, for example,
or the activities of America's largest oil companies in the
Middle East even earlier. In such circumstances one also finds
considerable interdependence between the public and private
sectors; here too a potential for conflicting interests exists.
What makes banking different?

Banking is special for two reasons. First, it is a peculiarly
vulnerable industry, owing to the unique characteristics of
its core commercial operations. Lending money is not like
selling apples: after the loan transaction is consummated,
there remains the question of the borrower's ultimate ability
or willingness to repay. Moreover, the risks associated with
debt default are compounded both by the high degree of le-
veraging in bank balance sheets (that is, their low capital/
asset ratios) and by the remarkable ease with which banks
are able to manufacture new assets (that is, loans) when conditions seem to warrant. And second, banking is a peculiarly
influential industry, owing to the central role that banks play
in providing, through their credit and deposit facilities, the
means of payment for transactions of every kind—the oil, in
effect, that lubricates the interlocking wheels of commerce.
The indirect repercussions of any eruptions or failures in the
industry (its social externalities) are apt to be out of proportion to the size of the institutions directly involved. For both
reasons, banking is typically subject to more regulation than
other sectors of the economy. And this in turn dictates a more
active relationship with the public authorities than is the case
for most nonfinancial enterprises, not only at home but also
outside the nation's borders. Banks are different because the
risks of their activities, both to themselves and to others, are
greater.

But should analysis be restricted solely to the familiar
commercial-banking sector? In an era of rapidly accelerating
integration of financial services, it might be argued, such an
approach could run the risk of omitting potentially important
actors and activities. Today, the lines between traditional
commercial-banking operations and other financial services
(for example, investment banking, brokerage, insurance, leas-

ing, etc.) are rapidly dissolving. Merrill Lynch, Sears Roebuck, Prudential-Bache, and Shearson Lehman-American Express are already, in effect, among the biggest "bankers" in the country; while commercial banks like Citicorp, Chase Manhattan, and Bank of America are finding more and more ways to circumvent formal barriers to entry into the securities business and other fields of financial endeavor. Furthermore, the activities of these financial supermarkets as well as of more conventionally specialized institutions (investment banks, insurance and leasing companies, brokerage firms, pension funds) are becoming increasingly internationalized. Investment banks now not only underwrite international bond issues but also act as advisers to troubled sovereign debtors. Insurance companies do more and more of their business overseas, especially in the highly competitive commercial insurance and reinsurance fields, as do leasing companies. Brokers are now making markets abroad, particularly in Europe, to deal in U.S. government securities outside New York trading hours. And pension funds now invest a rising share of their portfolios in foreign assets. Moreover, growing numbers of foreign financial institutions of all kinds are coming to the United States to do business. An argument might be made, therefore, that it is not just with traditional commercial banking alone that we should properly be concerned, but rather with the internationalization of financial activity in general. Analysis, accordingly, would encompass all institutions with significant cross-border operations.

But that would be going too far. An increase in the geographic diversification of pension fund investments, the spread of insurance and leasing business, and the organized trading of U.S. government securities overseas are not unimportant in quantitative terms; but they are not qualitatively new. In effect, they merely reinforce the trend toward integration of national financial markets that has been in progress for over a quarter of a century, steadily adding to the volume and speed of international capital movements. The issue of capital mobility, however, is something that Washington (like other governments) has had to live with for many years. If that were all that were implied by the expansion of international banking in recent decades, there would be little justification for yet another book on the subject. There are already many studies of the policy consequences of cross-border financial integration. What justifies this book is the belief that, with banks, much more is involved than just the issue of capital mobility—issues that touch on other dimensions of what we understand as foreign policy.

In fact, banks still are clearly distinguishable from other internationally active financial institutions in this context. Not only do they play a central economic role through the means of payment they provide to facilitate transactions of every kind, both domestically and internationally. Even more important, they have come to play a key political role as well, through their ever-widening array of interactions with the public sector both at home and abroad. Internationalization of banking activity has brought with it a degree of functional involvement with sovereign governments far greater than that for any other class of financial institutions; moreover, this involvement increasingly has taken on an explicitly strategic, and therefore politicized, dimension. It is these growing strategic interactions that justify concentrating my analysis specifically on the commercial-banking sector. With banks, uniquely, we go well beyond merely financial issues, to enter the realm of foreign policy in its fullest sense. That is the realm to be explored in this book.

IV

My central focus is on the impact of international banking on the government's foreign policy capabilities—the constraints and opportunities that are posed for policymakers. My purpose is not to analyze the process by which policy is actually made or the role of various players in the traditional policy establishment, but rather to highlight the key implications of foreign policy's increasing interdependence with the private banking sector. Many interests are shared by the two sides. Banks benefit from a diplomacy designed to maintain a peaceful and open international system; the national interest, in turn, is served insofar as banks, in pursuing their own commercial interests, promote widespread growth and prosperity as well. To this extent, international banking is obviously advantageous from the perspective of public policy. But circumstances exist too where interests may come into conflict, hampering Washington's ability to realize its foreign policy preferences. Cross-border banking can also be disadvantageous from the government's point of view. To move toward a coherent definition of the public interest in international banking, it is necessary to gain a firmer understanding of what these circumstances might be. Are any generalizations possible?

I intend to highlight two critical factors: (1) the immediate source of any significant challenge to U.S. foreign policy; and (2) the net balance-sheet position of U.S. banks. The first factor distinguishes between challenges to U.S. foreign policy that arise directly in the area of financial relations (what may be called intrafinance issues) and those that originate in other issue areas (extrafinance issues). Intrafinance issues involve the economic dimension of our international diplomacy—threats to our national economy or to the international economic system that helps make the success of our national economy possible. Extrafinance issues involve the more traditional high politics of political and military concerns. The second factor distinguishes between circumstances in which U.S. banks are either net creditors or net debtors vis-à-vis relevant countries or regions. In combination, as we shall see, these factors tend to be particularly decisive in determining impacts on U.S. foreign policy capabilities.

The two factors, each binary in nature, yield a matrix of four possible foreign policy contingencies, as illustrated schematically in table 1.2. Subset A includes situations where foreigners' net claims on American banks could conceivably become a source of leverage on other instruments or issues of interest to the U.S. government. An obvious example was the inflow of Arab bank deposits in the 1970s, which many thought at the time might put a money weapon into the hands of potentially hostile governments. Subset B, conversely, comprises circumstances where a possible threat to America's interests arises owing to foreigners' net debts to U.S. banks;

TABLE 1.2. Schema of Possible Foreign Policy Contingencies

	Source of challenge to U.S. foreign policy	
	Intrafinance issues	*Extrafinance issues*
Net balance-sheet position of U.S. banks — Net liabilities	A Example: Arab deposits	C Example: Iran
Net claims	B Example: Latin America	D Example: Poland

here the recent loan troubles of many Latin American countries quickly come to mind. In subset C we have occasions where a challenge to U.S. foreign policy originating outside the financial area could become joined to banking issues at a time of net liabilities to foreigners, such as occurred during the Iranian hostage crisis. In subset D we have occasions where an extrafinance issue comes up at a time of net claims on foreigners, as in Poland after the suppression of Solidarity. These four contingencies define the agenda for the discussion to come.

CHAPTER 2

The Incredible Quarter Century

Over the last quarter century, few developments in international economic relations have been as dramatic as the spread of banking and other financial activities across national frontiers. The phenomenon started slowly. In the first years after World War II, most banks deliberately limited their aspirations largely to their home markets—a legacy of the financial collapse of the 1930s, when virtually the entire structure of international debt fell into default. Apart from trade financing and some foreign-exchange operations, there was little interest in international business. U.S. institutions, in particular, recalling their searing interwar experience, were loath to expose themselves again to the risks of cross-border lending. Just two decades ago, at the time of the reissue of his classic Council on Foreign Relations study, *Europe, the World's Banker*, Herbert Feis wrote, "The American people and financial community vowed that never again would they trust their fortunes abroad or respond to the requests of recreant foreign governments."[1] But memories fade—who would have guessed how quickly?—and today those words seem nothing less than ironic. Already by the time Feis wrote them, such vows were being forgotten by a new generation of bankers. During the go-go years of the 1960s and 1970s, fortunes once again were trusted abroad—enormous fortunes—as banking activity throughout the world moved beyond trade financing to project financing and eventually even to the financing of balance-of-payments deficits. In retrospect, the quarter century seems incredible. And in that Incredible Quarter Century, American banks played, as they continue to play, a leading role.

I

The phenomenal spread of international banking over the Incredible Quarter Century can be measured in many ways. Perhaps it is best illustrated by the growth of the Euro-currency market, since that is in fact where the bulk of cross-border business has come to take place. Thirty years ago, an organized market for foreign-currency deposits did not even exist. Today the Euro-market, despite its regional ("Euro-") label, is a truly global system with banking centers in operation on or off the shores of almost every major continent and with participating institutions numbering in the thousands. In less than three decades, Euro-banking has surpassed traditional foreign banking operations (see chapter 1) as the predominant form of international banking.[2]

The "Euro-" label reflects the system's origins rather than its current geographic locale. The market got its start in 1957 when the government of Great Britain, faced with yet another of its incessant balance-of-payments crises, imposed tight new restrictions on foreign-trade financing denominated in pounds sterling. In response, British banks sought to preserve their sizable overseas business by actively soliciting and lending U.S. dollar deposits instead (taking advantage of the comparative regulatory freedom traditionally accorded foreign-currency banking in London). Although dollar deposits had been accepted even before 1957, these normally had simply been repatriated to the U.S. money market and invested there. Only in 1957 did banks begin to take the initiative in attracting dollars for use in trade credits and other forms of international lending. Once started, a regular market for foreign-currency deposits quickly developed, first in London, then in other European financial centers—and thus was the Euro-market born. Subsequently the market grew, both within Europe and beyond it, at a truly phenomenal rate.

Partly because of the rapid rate at which Euro-currency operations have expanded over the years, no single, overall statistical series is available to trace the development of the market from its inception straight through to the present day. For the early years, we have only informed guesses to rely on—and these, understandably, tend to vary widely. For example, in 1960, while one source was estimating the size of the Euro-market at around $1 billion,[3] another was suggesting a figure two-and-one-half to three times as large.[4] Not until 1964, in fact, did consistent series of data begin to be published by the Bank for International Settlements (BIS), which today is acknowledged to be the primary source of statistical information on the Euro-currency market as well as on other forms of international banking activity.[5] Two alternative measures of the Euro-market's size and growth, as estimated by the BIS, are reproduced in table 2.1. These data are presented at two levels of aggregation—"gross" and "net." Either way, the numbers are staggering.

At the gross level, the BIS data include all foreign-currency assets reported by banks in a group of key European countries—the so-called European reporting area. These figures clearly demonstrate the phenomenal rate at which the market has grown since its inception. By 1964, volume had already risen to the neighborhood of $12 billion. Two decades later, gross claims were in excess of $920 billion—an increase of more than 7,500 percent, far faster than the rate of expansion recorded by world production, foreign trade, or any other relevant measure of international economic activity. At the net level, Euro-market size has been measured by estimating the net sources and uses of funds for reporting banks in the European area.[6] This series was discontinued after 1982. But up to that date, as can be seen in the table, the phenomenal growth of the net market was as evident as in the gross data. From a mere $9 billion in 1964, the net size of the market skyrocketed to $702 billion by 1982—also an increase of more than 7,500 percent.

In more recent years, the BIS has supplemented its data

TABLE 2.1. BIS Estimates of the Size of the Euro-Currency Market in the European Reporting Area, 1964–84 (in billions of dollars)

	"Gross"[a]	"Net"[b]
1964	12.0	9.0
1965	15.1	11.5
1966	19.9	14.5
1967	24.5	17.5
1968	37.7	25.0
1969	58.2	44.0
1970	78.2	57.0
1971	100.1	71.0
1972	131.8	92.0
1973[c]	187.6	132.0
1974[d]	215.2	177.0
1975	258.1	205.0
1976	305.3	247.0
1977I	373.8	300.0
1977II	384.9	300.0
1978I[e]	502.0	375.0
1978II[e]	502.0	377.0
1979	639.7	475.0
1980	751.2	575.0
1981	847.3	661.0
1982[f]	872.4	702.0
1983I[f]	882.0	—
1983II[f]	903.3	—
1984I[f]	920.5	—
1984II[f]	921.3	—

Source: Bank for International Settlements (BIS), *Annual Reports* (from 1968 only: for earlier years, as reported in Geoffrey Bell, *The Euro-Dollar Market and the International Financial System*, p. 20); and BIS, *Quarterly Report* on "International Banking and Financial Market Developments" (October 1985).

[a]As measured by the total external foreign currency claims of banks in the European reporting area. Up to December 1977 (1977I), the European reporting area covered Belgium-Luxembourg, France, Germany, Italy, Netherlands, Sweden, Switzerland, and the United Kingdom. From 1977 (1977II) it also includes Austria, Denmark, and Ireland. In 1983 (1983II), Finland, Norway, and Spain were added.

[b]As measured by net sources and uses of funds estimated for banks in the European reporting area. From 1964 to 1968, the figures include dollars only.

[c]As of 1973, the figures no longer include the Euro-currency positions of the

on the European reporting area by adding the foreign-currency assets of banks in key financial centers outside Europe—specifically, in Canada, Japan, the United States, and the principal offshore branches of U.S. banks. These totals for the BIS reporting area, reproduced in table 2.2 (column 1), constitute a more accurate measure of the gross size of the global Euromarket. By this broader measure, market size reached almost $1.6 trillion in 1984. The BIS also compiles the total external claims in domestic currencies (traditional foreign loans) of these same banks within and outside Europe (column 2 of table 2.2). The sum of domestic and foreign-currency claims gives a rough measure of the overall volume of international banking activity (column 3).[7] Deducting interbank transactions yields a measure of net international bank lending during these years (column 4). At the end of 1984 net bank lending (claims on final borrowers) stood near $1.3 trillion, representing nearly a sixfold increase in just one decade.

A glance at the BIS data suggests that over the course of the Incredible Quarter Century three phases of growth may be distinguished. These correspond roughly to the 1960s, the 1970s, and the first half of the 1980s.

The decade of the 1960s, the period of takeoff, reflects a number of factors connected with changes in the international economic environment, the evolution of demand for financial services, and the spread of new technological facilities. Of key importance was the completion of postwar reconstruction in

---

BIS (previously reported under the figures for the Swiss banks) but do incorporate certain long-term positions not previously reported.

[d]As of 1974, the figures include certain long-term positions not previously reported by some of the banks as well as some minor changes in the coverage of the statistics.

[e]As of December 1978, a change was made in estimating procedures for sources and uses of funds: the partial netting-out of interbank assets and liabilities, previously limited to the growth of the reporting European banks within their own area, was extended to cover their positions vis-à-vis the United States, Canada, Japan, and the offshore centers.

[f]Certain breaks occur in the series for 1982, 1983, and 1984 due to changes in reporting and institutional coverage.

TABLE 2.2. External Domestic and Foreign Currency Claims of all BIS Reporting Banks[a] and BIS Estimates of Total Net International Bank Lending, 1973–84 (in billions of dollars)

	Foreign Currency Claims (1)	Domestic Currency Claims (2)	Total Claims (1 + 2) (3)	Net International Bank Lending[b] (4)
1973	247.6	49.0	296.6	—
1974	282.5	78.4	360.8	220.0
1975	342.9	99.4	442.4	260.0
1976	418.4	129.6	549.5	330.0
1977I	503.1	153.9	657.1	405.0
1977II	514.3	175.5	689.8	435.0
1978	659.7	233.5	893.2	530.0
1979	828.9	282.1	1,111.0	665.0
1980	980.0	341.9	1,321.9	810.0
1981	1,124.8	425.4	1,550.2	945.0
1982	1,135.9	558.6	1,694.5	1,020.0
1983I	1,186.7	570.4	1,757.1	1,085.0
1983II	1,527.3	570.6	2,097.9	1,240.0
1984I	1,565.1	586.4	2,151.5	1,280.0
1984II	1,573.9	586.5	2,160.4	1,280.0

Source: Bank for International Settlements (BIS), *Annual Reports*; and BIS, *Quarterly Report* on "International Banking and Financial Market Developments" (October 1985).

[a]Includes banks in the European reporting area, Canada, Japan, and the United States, and offshore branches of U.S. banks in the Bahamas, Cayman Islands, Panama, Hong Kong, and Singapore. Austria, Denmark, and Ireland are not included in the European reporting area until 1977 (1977II); Finland, Norway, and Spain are not included until 1983 (1983II); offshore branches of non-U.S. banks are not included until 1983 (1983II).

[b]Column 3 minus BIS estimates of interbank deposits: equals net outstanding claims on final borrowers.

Europe and Japan as well as restoration of currency convertibility and liberalization of capital movements at the end of the 1950s. Not only did international trade greatly expand as a result, stimulating renewed growth in traditional documentary-type trade financing and foreign-exchange activities. More important, a massive increase of foreign direct investment was encouraged, leading to the emergence of the new multinational corporation with its own special financing requirements. To keep up with the increasingly global operations of their giant industrial clients, larger banks found it convenient to move abroad as well, establishing integrated networks of branches and affiliates to provide MNCs with a broadened range of financial services. Bank strategies became more internationally oriented, with emphasis shifting increasingly to direct participation in large-scale project financing; and gradually this process of internationalization gave rise to a variety of new lending techniques—most significant were so-called syndicated credits, which were highly attractive to customers because of their ability to raise large sums of money through a single operation. A single bank or a very small number of banks would act as manager in assembling a larger group of institutions (a syndicate) that were prepared to participate in or underwrite a joint loan. Partly as a result of such new techniques, external banking claims increased over the course of the decade at a rate in excess of 20 percent a year.

Not surprisingly, the most rapid growth was recorded in the Euro-currency segment of the market, which expanded at a rate in excess of 30 percent a year. Banks were initially attracted to the foreign-currency-deposit business by perceived profit opportunities arising from the comparative regulatory freedom accorded such activity; for American banks in particular, the offshore market offered an irresistible opportunity at the time to bypass domestic reserve requirements and interest-rate limitations as well as the widening array of capital controls imposed by Washington in the 1960s to cope with the U.S. balance-of-payments problem. (These controls and most interest-rate limitations were eliminated for American banks in the 1970s; in addition, marginal reserve requirements have since been imposed by the Federal Reserve on Euro-deposits repatriated from abroad.) In addition, bankers in the United States and abroad soon found that they were able to exploit contemporary improvements in communications facilities to develop sophisticated techniques for the management of both assets and liabilities denominated in foreign currency. By the end of the 1960s, the Euro-currency market was fully established not just in London, where it had begun, but in many other centers as well, all linked together by a flourishing global interbank market for foreign-currency deposits.

The decade of the 1970s witnessed a further acceleration in the internationalization of banking activity, especially after the first oil shock in 1973, which triggered unprecedented imbalances in the pattern of global payments. The distinctive feature of this phase was the banks' large-scale involvement in what came to be known as the petrodollar recycling process. On the deposit side, banks faced a massive inflow of surplus dollar revenues (petrodollars) from a number of the newly enriched oil-exporting countries; while on the loan side, they were confronted with rising demands for financing by deficit-ridden oil importers. After a hesitant start, banks soon became the principal source of balance-of-payments financing for a wide range of countries, not only in the industrial world but in Eastern Europe and the Third World as well. And this process was given further impetus by the second oil shock in 1978–79. Innovative lending arrangements were introduced that seemed suitable to longer-term projects and general-purpose financing on the necessary scale (for example, rollover credits, package deals connected with government-guaranteed loans, parallel loans); and a widening number of institutions was drawn into the business on both sides of the market. During these years new bank lending grew at a rate of nearly 25 percent a year.

In the process, many banks sharply increased their dependence on international activity on both sides of their balance sheets. For banks in the twenty-four member countries of the Organization for Economic Cooperation and Development (OECD), the share of foreign business in total activity roughly doubled between 1970 and 1981.[8] Foreign deposits as a proportion of total deposits rose from 11.3 percent to 23.4 percent. Foreign loans as a proportion of total loans rose from 12.1 percent to 23.7 percent.

The third phase of the Incredible Quarter Century, coinciding with the onset of the global debt crisis, has been a period of severe retrenchment marked by a pronounced deceleration of international banking activity. The turnaround was swift and sizable. At the end of the 1970s, net external bank claims were expanding by more than $130 billion annually (table 2.2). In 1982 new lending dropped to $75 billion, mostly in the first half of the year, and to an average annual rate under $50 billion in 1983–84, mainly because of greatly increased market perceptions of risk. The sudden difficulties of several key international debtors after mid–1982 and the rising specter of default put a decided chill on bank psychology. Managers became far more cautious about adding to their institutions' foreign exposure, particularly in the Third World and Eastern Europe, where virtually no new lending took place. Whether, or for how long, that retreat from the international market might persist is not now clear. I shall have more to say on that question below.

II

First, however, let us take a closer look at the major players in the game—the suppliers of funds (depositors), the users of funds (borrowers), and those who intermediate between them (the banks).

Thousands of institutions participate in the business of international banking, but of these, a handful account for the bulk of activity. In fact, the market is heavily tiered, and only the world's largest banks can aspire to the top rank. In the top tier are two to three dozen large money-center banks based in OECD countries, including the following:

United States: Bank of America, Bankers Trust, Chase Manhattan, Chemical, Citibank, Manufacturers Hanover, Morgan Guaranty

United Kingdom: Barclays, Lloyds, Midland, National Westminster

Germany: Commerzbank, Deutsche Bank, Dresdner Bank, Westdeutsche Landesbank

Japan: Bank of Tokyo, Dai-Ichi Kangyo Bank, Fuji Bank, Industrial Bank of Japan, Sumitomo Bank

Canada: Bank of Montreal, Canadian Imperial Bank of Commerce, Royal Bank of Canada

Switzerland: Crédit Suisse, Swiss Bank Corporation, Union Bank of Switzerland .
France: Banque Nationale de Paris, Crédit Lyonnais, Société Générale
Belgium: Société Générale de Banque
Netherlands: Amsterdam-Rotterdam Bank

These giant banks enjoy certain key advantages in relation to other market participants, including large capital positions, well-developed international customer relations, and diversified asset portfolios. They have sufficiently broad deposit bases at home to support traditional "foreign" lending in domestic currencies. And they have sufficiently extensive international networks of branches, subsidiaries, and correspondents to attract substantial foreign-currency deposits as well. In fact, these few intermediaries take in the vast majority of all cross-border deposits. Large international depositors prefer the safety of well-established name institutions. This gives the giants the capacity to be simultaneously the main participants in credits to final borrowers and the main suppliers of funds, through interbank placements, to other banks in the market. In recent years, as few as twenty large money-center banks have accounted for about half of all lending to ultimate users; at the same time, they have also typically redeposited about 60 percent of their deposits in other banks.[9]

Below the giants are at least three thousand other banks of every size, description, and nationality. The process of internationalization was initiated by the giants in the 1960s. But gradually, especially during the second phase of growth in the 1970s, involvement in the market spread to more and more institutions operating either from their own home base or via foreign outlets. These included local and regional banks from the United States and other OECD countries, so-called consortium banks (representing groups of banks with similar characteristics or interests), commercial banks from the Third World and Soviet bloc, and even some savings and investment banks and other financial institutions. Some of these players were drawn into the game by the need to provide trade-related services to their traditional customers, especially medium- and small-sized firms entering the export field for the first time. Others were eager to take up shares in the profitable new syndicated loans being managed by the giants, even for borrowers with whom they had no direct customer relationship. Since few of these institutions have much direct access to cross-border deposits, many rely on interbank borrowing to fund their participation in international lending. Indeed, they are a principal channel through which the large foreign-currency deposits collected by the leading money-center banks (and not used by them directly) are lent onward to final borrowers.

The wholesale interbank market is crucial in the linking together of this heterogeneous collection of institutions. In all, approximately two thousand banks participate regularly in the interbank market, which accounts for roughly 40 percent of total international bank lending (compare columns 3 and 4 of table 2.2). The interbank market, in fact, is the heart of the international banking business. Just as they do in domestic systems, banks operating internationally need ready access to some kind of efficient market mechanism that will allow them to manage their asset and liability positions on a flexible and continuous basis. (In the United States, this function is performed by the federal funds market.) Without the global interbank network, a viable market for the placement and lending of foreign-currency deposits (the Euro-market) could never have developed. With it, ultimate suppliers and users of funds can be effectively brought together on a global scale through the intermediation of banking institutions.

Among these myriad institutions, American banks have always played a leading role. Indeed, until the early 1970s international banking was very much the province of the largest American banks, for two principal reasons. First was the predominance of the U.S. multinational enterprise during the 1960s. This was the era of *le défi americain*, the heyday of U.S. business expansion overseas, when American corporations seemed to be going everywhere and doing everything. American banks enjoyed a key competitive advantage in financial markets by virtue of their long-established customer relationships with these industrial giants. Wherever the U.S. multinationals went, American banks were sure to follow. And second was the predominance of the U.S. dollar in financial markets, reflecting both its long-established role among central banks as the main reserve and intervention currency and its persistent popularity in international trade as the main currency for invoicing. As compared with banks elsewhere, U.S. banks thus had another advantage owing to their "natural" dollar deposit base as well as their privileged ability to borrow from the Federal Reserve System. British banks may have started the Euro-currency market in the 1950s, by attracting and lending dollar deposits, but U.S. banks, through branches in London and later elsewhere, rapidly took over the bulk of the business in the 1960s.

In the 1970s, inevitably, the ascendancy of U.S. banks was eroded by the suspension of the dollar's gold convertibility in 1971 and the abandonment of fixed exchange rates in 1973. Widening exchange-rate movements and the spreading international use of currencies other than the dollar as well as the growing ranks of multinational corporations from countries other than the United States created profit opportunities that attracted other banks to the game. In the seventies the larger European, Canadian, and Japanese banks moved into international business in a big way. Yet even now American banks continue to stand out, in part because of their still considerable advantages in management expertise, entrenched positions in overseas markets, and specialist skills. U.S. institutions benefit as well from the enduring popularity of the dollar, which continues to account for roughly 70–75 percent of all international banking transactions. Between a quarter and a third of all international deposit and loan activity is still handled by U.S. banks.[10]

American banks led the way during the Incredible Quarter Century, not only in pioneering new financial techniques and services for their customers, but also in establishing integrated networks of offices overseas. In 1960, only 8 U.S. banks operated a total of 131 branches in foreign countries. By 1982, the numbers had grown to 162 banks operating 900 branches.[11] The main concentrations of offices, not surprisingly, were to be found in London and the major offshore centers in the Caribbean and Far East, reflecting the desire of many institutions to gain access to the then bourgeoning Euro-currency market. Many of the offshore offices were really no more than "shell" or "brass-plate" operations set up for booking purposes; that is, simply a brass nameplate on a door and a receptionist to answer the phone, to provide a legal haven from regulation or taxation for transactions that were in fact handled elsewhere. But at least as many foreign branches were established as genuine full-service facilities. In all, between 1960 and 1982, the total assets of overseas branches soared from $3.5 billion to $390 billion,[12] although more recently growth of foreign offices has slowed a bit as a result of the amendment of Federal Reserve regulations in 1981 authorizing creation of International Banking Facilities (IBFs) in the United States, where external deposit and loan transactions can be booked directly, free of domestic reserve requirements.[13] IBFs reduce the incentive for using the subterfuge of a shell abroad.

The largest number of foreign branches, of course, was established by the largest U.S. banks. Bank of America, Chase Manhattan, and Citibank—America's three biggest banks—account for nearly one half of the total; and just nine other large money-center or regional institutions have maintained overseas networks of any size (Bankers Trust, Chemical, Bank of Boston, First Chicago, Continental Illinois, Manufacturers Hanover, Marine Midland, Morgan Guaranty, Security Pacific, and Wells Fargo). Other, smaller banks have only one or a few offices each, and fully 99 percent of the nearly 14,000 commercial banks in the United States keep none at all. International banking remains a specialized activity dominated by a handful of giants.

In turn, international banking now dominates the giants, who have grown strikingly dependent on their cross-border activity for profits. At the start of the 1970s, America's largest banks generally derived less than a fifth of their total revenues from overseas operations. Toward the end of the decade, as table 2.3 illustrates, foreign income was accounting on average for half or more of total earnings. Of course, since the onset of the global debt crisis, foreign earnings growth has decelerated somewhat, reflecting the retrenchment of inter-

TABLE 2.3. International Earnings of Ten Leading U.S. Banks, 1979–83 (in millions of dollars and percentage of consolidated earnings)[a]

	1979		1980		1981		1982		1983	
	Amount	Percentage	Amount	Percentage	Amount	Percentage	Amount	Percentage	Amount	Percentage
Citibank	355	(65.3)	323	(63.7)	346	(62.3)	508	(68.0)	468	(54.8)
Chase Manhattan	146	(46.9)	179	(49.1)	247	(55.6)	215	(64.7)	181	(43.3)
Bank of America	225	(37.4)	287	(44.4)	282	(63.1)	247	(62.7)	185	(49.7)
Manufacturers Hanover	103	(48.7)	113	(49.1)	128	(49.9)	147	(49.6)	164	(51.7)
Morgan Guaranty	150	(55.2)	216	(59.3)	259	(68.0)	283	(64.0)	250	(54.2)
Chemical	43	(31.7)	68	(38.4)	74	(34.2)	104	(38.7)	129	(42.7)
Continental Illinois	32	(16.6)	63	(28.1)	73	(28.1)	51	(60.4)	8	(8.0)
Bankers Trust	59	(51.6)	104	(48.6)	116	(60.4)	113	(45.3)	101	(39.2)
First Chicago	4	(3.6)	–6	(–9.1)	20	(16.7)	40	(27.5)	22	(12.1)
Security Pacific	18	(10.9)	24	(12.9)	53	(25.4)	74	(31.6)	46	(17.4)
Total/Composite[b]	1,136	(42.4)	1,370	(46.0)	1,598	(51.9)	1,782	(55.8)	1,554	(44.0)

Source: *Salomon Brothers, A Review of Bank Performance, 1984 Edition.*

[a]Earnings shown on a net income basis. Banks ranked by total assets.

[b]Weighted average.

national banking activity. Still, could there be any better indicator of the degree to which the business of the largest American banks has become internationalized?

Significantly, a very large share of this business is with official institutions, including governmental agencies and other public-sector entities, rather than with the private sector (business firms and individuals). And this is of course true for non-American banks as well. On both sides of the international banking market, official institutions have come to play a key role, both as suppliers and as users of funds. To a considerable extent, international banks today function as intermediaries between national sovereignties.

On the supply side, official institutions have always been an important influence. Among the very first suppliers of Eurocurrency deposits, for example, were government-controlled banks in communist Eastern Europe anxious to disguise the ownership of their dollar balances by redepositing them with banking offices in Western Europe. Not wishing to leave their dollars in banks in the United States, where they might be hostage to shifts of U.S. foreign policy, they preferred to take advantage instead of the presumed security offered by deposit facilities in Europe. They were soon joined, especially toward the end of the 1960s, by other, noncommunist official institutions, whose motivations were more economic than political (that is, they were attracted by liquidity and high interest rates). In part, these new inflows reflected widening payments surpluses in Europe and Japan; in part, the growing awareness of central banks in many developing nations (particularly in Latin America and the Middle East) of the attractions of foreign deposit facilities. And then came the two oil shocks of the 1970s, which led to large inflows of petrodollars from the governments of a number of oil-exporting countries. Between 1973 and 1981, deposits of member countries of the Organization of Petroleum Exporting Countries (OPEC) increased tenfold, to a total of $157 billion in 1981, before falling off to $120 billion at the end of 1983.

Geographically, as can be seen in table 2.4, more than three-quarters of all deposits have originated from within the core group of industrial countries, and a small amount from

TABLE 2.4. Geographic Pattern of International Bank Flows (Sources and Uses of Funds), end 1984 (in billions of dollars and percentages)

	Liabilities (Sources)		Claims (Uses)	
Total	2,129.4	(100.0)	2,160.4	(100.0)
BIS reporting area[a]	1,663.7	(78.1)	1,497.9	(69.3)
Offshore banking centers[b]	45.2	(2.1)	47.0	(2.2)
Other developed countries	29.0	(1.4)	88.2	(4.1)
Eastern Europe	22.1	(1.0)	48.2	(2.3)
OPEC countries[c]	147.0	(6.9)	106.1	(4.9)
Non-OPEC developing countries	169.0	(7.9)	330.9	(15.3)
(of which: Latin America)[d]	(68.1)	(3.2)	(212.0)	(9.8)
Unallocated[e]	53.4	(2.5)	42.1	(1.9)

Source: Bank for International Settlements (BIS), *Quarterly Report* on "International Banking and Financial Market Developments" (October 1985).

[a]Includes the European reporting area, Canada, Japan, the United States, and the offshore centers of Bahrain, Bahamas, Cayman Islands, Hong Kong, Netherlands Antilles, and Singapore.

[b]Includes Bermuda, Lebanon, Liberia, Panama, Vanuatu (formerly New Hebrides), and other British West Indies.

[c]Includes, in addition, Brunei, Oman, and Trinidad and Tobago.

[d]Includes those countries in the Caribbean area that are not offshore banking centers.

[e]Includes international institutions other than the BIS.

other OECD economies. Of the remainder, the origin of a good share is obscured by being channeled through offshore financial centers, where banking offices act as fiduciaries for assets held in nominee or custody accounts. Tracing the ultimate beneficial ownership of such deposits is not easy. But even taking this fact into account, it is clear that—two or three OPEC nations apart (see chapter 5)—nonindustrial countries have not been a major force on the supply side of the market.

The borrowers' side of the market is also heavily influenced by official institutions, though that was not always the case. In the early years of the Incredible Quarter Century, in fact, governmental entities were comparatively insignificant as users of funds. Public-sector borrowing was largely limited to certain local authorities (mainly in Britain) and public utilities. The greatest part of borrowing was by private business firms and individuals, who found the international market a convenient and relatively inexpensive source of financing for domestic as well as foreign operations. Not until the late 1960s did the market's attractions begin to interest public entities on a large scale as well, including now not just local authorities but also central governments and their agencies. National governments (mainly, at first, in the industrial world) began to borrow from banks for balance-of-payments purposes, supplementing scarce foreign-exchange reserves. Loans either were used to help sustain the governments' own spending levels or were sold to private users to finance imports or other activities. After 1973 sovereign borrowing became the principal force on the demand side of the market.

Geographically, a little more than two-thirds of all bank lending has gone to industrial nations and about one-fifth to non-OPEC developing countries and Eastern Europe (table 2.4). Undoubtedly, the key influence on the market since the first oil shock has been the critical need of many non-OPEC governments for massive balance-of-payments financing. From 1973 to 1984, borrowing by the principal categories of oil importers (non-OPEC developing countries, Eastern Europe, and smaller OECD countries) expanded by some $400 billion, to more than $460 billion. One result of this extraordinary rate of borrowing, as we know, has been the so-called global debt crisis of the 1980s.

In fact, the conventional label "global" is something of a misnomer. The crisis is global only in its implications (see below). In terms of actual borrowing, the accumulation of debt by nonindustrial countries was highly concentrated in a handful of resource-rich and newly industrializing economies (table 2.5) that were considered most creditworthy by the markets. Of total bank claims on Eastern Europe and the Third World at the end of 1984, nearly one-third ($149 billion) was accounted for by just two countries, the big Latin debtors of Brazil and Mexico; and another one-quarter ($129 billion) by just ten others: Argentina, Chile, Colombia, Egypt, Israel,

TABLE 2.5. Bank Debt Owed by Principal Third World and East European Borrowers, end 1984 (in billions of dollars)

All Third World and Eastern Europe	478.3
Principal borrowers	367.1
Principal non-OPEC borrowers	278.2
Argentina	26.1
Brazil	76.9
Chile	13.7
Colombia	7.1
Egypt	7.0
Israel	6.2
Korea	30.9
Malaysia	11.2
Mexico	72.1
Peru	5.7
Philippines	13.8
Thailand	7.5
Principal OPEC borrowers	55.1
Algeria	7.8
Indonesia	14.2
Nigeria	8.1
Venezuela	25.0
Principal East European borrowers	33.8
East Germany	8.3
Hungary	6.9
Poland	8.9
Yugoslavia	9.7

Source: Bank for International Settlements (BIS), *Quarterly Report* on "International Banking and Financial Market Developments" (October 1985).

Korea, Malaysia, Peru, the Philippines, and Thailand. Moreover, most of the remainder was highly concentrated in four East European nations (East Germany, Hungary, Poland, and Yugoslavia) and four members of OPEC (Algeria, Indonesia, Nigeria, and Venezuela). Altogether, this score of borrowers accounted for just under $370 billion of claims, equal to nearly four-fifths of all bank loans outside the industrial world.

Many of these same borrowers are among the most prominent of the countries lately experiencing serious debt-service difficulties. For most of them, in the 1970s, banks were virtually the only source of external finance available to private or public-sector borrowers. And since bank credits typically tended to have higher interest rates than loans from official sources, as well as shorter maturities, debt-service burdens naturally accelerated in relation to scarce foreign-exchange resources. In 1982, overall debt service (interest plus amortization) for a number of major Third World borrowers—including the three largest: Argentina, Brazil, and Mexico—actually exceeded total exports of goods and services. Interest payments alone in that year for these three debtors ate up 35 to 45 percent of export revenues.[14] Small wonder, then, that so many countries (including even many minor borrowing nations) fell into arrears on their debts—nearly three dozen in all in 1982 and 1983. Without adequate foreign exchange available, even a country's commercially viable private debts could not be serviced on time. All borrowers in these countries—private and public alike—found themselves caught in the same vise.

With so many debtors seemingly on the brink of default, debt reschedulings have become increasingly commonplace, involving ever-larger sums of money. The 1970s saw no more than three or four reschedulings annually, involving on average $1–2 billion in any single year. Over the eighteen months from January 1983 to June 1984, by contrast, nineteen countries reached rescheduling agreements involving a total of some $95 billion, equal to nearly one-quarter of all external bank debt then owed by nations of the Third World and Eastern Europe.[15] Rescheduling agreements are negotiated by small ad hoc steering groups of banks organized for that purpose. These steering groups, usually comprising at most a dozen or so of a country's largest bank creditors, negotiate on behalf of all banks with exposure to the debtor. Negotiations are normally conducted with governments, even where much of a country's debt may be owed by private firms or individuals. By necessity, the entire nation becomes involved when debt-service difficulties are caused by a general foreign-exchange constraint. All of the country's debt then becomes a matter of sovereign concern.

Because of their preeminence in the international market, American banks—mainly the big money-center and regional institutions—have been among the most seriously exposed to such sovereign debt-service difficulties. As table 2.6 indicates, overall U.S. bank claims in the Third World and Eastern Europe at the end of 1984 added up to some $135 billion (out of total U.S. foreign bank claims of $323 billion). This represented just over one-quarter of all bank loans outside the industrial world at the time. Nearly 85 percent of the U.S. total was accounted for by just the two dozen largest American banks (65 percent alone by the nine biggest institutions). The U.S. banks involved like to point out that less than 10 percent of their total assets have been at risk to foreign borrowers in trouble. But the figures loom much larger when compared instead with the banks' own capital, which comprises their shareholders' equity, capital reserves and other provisions for loan losses, and certain notes and debentures. A bank's capital represents the difference between the book value of its assets and liabilities. Essentially it can be thought of as what banks would have left after paying off their depositors and creditors. Loans to the ten largest sovereign borrowers by American banks amounted to 155 percent of total U.S. bank capital in mid–1982; for America's nine biggest banks, loans to their three largest borrowers (Argentina, Brazil, and Mexico) alone amounted to 140 percent of capital. Overall, the aggregate exposure of America's nine biggest banks in the Third World and Eastern Europe stood in excess of 350 percent of capital.[16] Against this, these same banks had set aside loan–loss reserves totaling only some $3.6 billion.

Some financial institutions have managed to find a silver lining in the dark clouds of troubled debt. Investment banks such as Salomon Brothers and Shearson Lehman-American Express have developed a lucrative line of business advising sovereign governments on their loan reschedulings and providing other financial services. And of course commercial banks have compensated themselves for the inconvenience of debt arrearages by charging higher interest rates and profitable renegotiation fees when debts are rescheduled. Nevertheless, the degree of exposure is undeniably high. There can be no question that the remarkable spread of banking activity during the Incredible Quarter Century served the world econ-

TABLE 2.6. Geographic Pattern of International Claims of U.S. Banks, end 1984 (in billions of dollars)

	All U.S. Banks	*Nine Largest U.S. Banks*	*Next Fifteen U.S. Banks*
Total	323.3	194.3	62.4
OECD nations	148.9	88.5	27.7
Non-OPEC developing nations	105.8	66.4	21.7
Of which:			
Argentina	8.0	5.1	1.8
Brazil	23.9	15.8	4.7
Chile	6.7	3.8	1.4
Colombia	3.0	2.2	0.4
Egypt	1.3	0.8	0.3
Israel	2.1	1.3	0.3
Korea	10.0	5.6	2.7
Malaysia	1.7	1.3	0.3
Mexico	26.5	14.7	5.3
Peru	2.4	1.3	0.7
Philippines	5.5	3.8	1.2
Thailand	2.2	0.8	0.6
OPEC nations	24.1	17.4	4.2
Of which:			
Algeria	1.1	0.7	0.3
Indonesia	3.4	2.8	0.5
Nigeria	1.5	1.1	0.2
Venezuela	10.8	7.5	2.0
East European nations	4.8	3.2	0.8
Of which:			
East Germany	0.4	0.2	0.1
Hungary	0.8	0.5	0.2
Poland	0.7	0.5	0.1
Yugoslavia	2.4	1.5	0.5
Offshore banking centers	38.8	18.3	7.7
International and regional organizations	1.0	0.6	0.3

Source: Federal Financial Institutions Examination Council, *Country Exposure Lending Survey: December 1984* (April 19, 1985).

omy, for the most part, extremely well. In effect, international financial intermediation by commercial banks helped to underwrite an expansion of global production, trade, and investment that was itself remarkable in historical terms. But neither can there be any question that the period also had a downside. As the Incredible Quarter Century drew to a close, the major international banks found themselves with what looked like a lot of questionable paper on their hands. The question naturally arises: How could these presumably prudent institutions have made such a large number of apparently dubious loans? While this book is not another treatise on the debt crisis—international banking involves more than just debt—a look here at the roots of that crisis can be instructive. Much can be learned about the dynamics of international banking by examining some of the reasons why banks could have allowed themselves to become as deeply involved as they did. Explanation could aid greatly in the framing of an appropriate public policy on international banking for the future.

III

The primary impetus for the loans came from the two oil shocks of the 1970s. OPEC's first price hike in 1973 created enormous financing problems for many oil-importing Third World countries, who could maintain their domestic economic growth in the face of massive foreign deficits only by increasing their borrowing from abroad. Meanwhile, the banks themselves were awash in liquidity, owing in good part to the rising tide of OPEC surplus revenues that were being reinvested in the international financial markets. Looking back, we can see that the matchup seems to have been inevitable (as well as mutually beneficial). The banks needed customers, and the oil importers needed loans. Moreover, the growth prospects of many of the potential borrowers appeared to promise excellent returns to investors. The process of petrodollar recycling began: funds flowed from oil exporters through the intermediation of international banks to oil-importing countries and back again. Recycling was universally regarded as vital to keeping the world economy afloat. By the time the second oil shock hit, toward the end of the decade, the process was routine. The growing debts of the Third World (and also of the East European nations) seemed a part of the natural order of things.

But this does not explain why the debts were allowed to grow as much as they did. Why did the banks get in so deep? Bankers themselves offer three explanations, each attributing responsibility, in effect, to circumstances beyond their control. Unfortunately, none of the three explanations is overly persuasive.

In the first place, bankers argue, they loaned so much because they were encouraged to do so by Washington and other Western governments, as a matter of public interest. There is some truth to this, of course. After all, someone had to do the recycling. Official agencies could have taken on the responsibility but were loath to do so—mainly because it would have added to public-sector borrowing requirements at a time of already unpalatably high budgetary deficits. So banks were prompted to assume the crucial intermediary role instead. In the words of the American Bankers Association in testimony before the House Banking Committee, "There was no government directive that the banks act to recycle the funds, but clearly, it was expected."[17]

The argument, nonetheless, is disingenuous. Are we to believe that these proud institutions were so meekly submissive to the will of public officials? Would they have gotten in so deep had they not thought that something was in it for them? Bankers are not indifferent to signals from the government sector (see chapter 3), but ultimately bank managements must answer to their investors and shareholders; they can never take their eye off the bottom line. It is not unreasonable to assume, therefore, that if they were so ready to recycle petrodollars, it must have been because they believed that there was money—perhaps lots of money—to be made from it. No one forced them to do it. Governments may have given them the green light, but they alone chose to put the accelerator to the floor and keep it there. Profit, not the public interest, was their main driving force.

The banks' second explanation runs in terms of information gaps. To hear bankers tell it, their biggest problem at the time was lack of access to all the relevant facts about the financial conditions and activities of potential customers. There is some truth to this charge too. Third World nations seldom have good data on their finances, and most East European countries refuse to furnish many details at all. How could lenders at the time intelligently assess the risks of prospective credits, bankers now ask, if they had no idea of how much a country was borrowing until well after the fact? Multilateral agencies like the World Bank and the International Monetary Fund were repeatedly criticized for their refusal to share confidential data obtained from member governments.

More recently, bankers have taken an initiative of their own to close these information gaps. In January 1983, leading banks from North America, Europe, and Japan formed a private organization, the Institute of International Finance, to do the job for them. Headquartered in Washington, the institute is mandated to collect pertinent data on the financial position of borrowing nations, conduct periodic country reviews, develop regular channels of communication with the IMF and World Bank, and provide a forum for the banks to exchange experience on international lending issues. Membership, which in early 1985 stood at 185 banks from 40 countries, is open to all institutions active in the international loan market. Information is disseminated to members through a linked computer network using international telecommunications lines.

But the question may legitimately be raised whether an inadequacy of information is enough to absolve banks of responsibility for their own actions. Indeed, one might ask why the banks lent at all if they knew so little about their customers. Some bankers, in their franker moments, admit that information gaps existed as much within their own institutions as in the system at large. Frequently, the left hand did not know what the right hand was doing. Consider the response of one European banker to a recent survey by the Group of Thirty, a New York–based private research body. The banker insisted that he would never have sanctioned a further growth of short-term credits to Mexico in the spring of 1982 had he been informed of the extent to which they were building up. Closer questioning revealed, however, that the numbers were in fact known to his subordinates but had not been passed upward. "If the figures had been brought to my attention, I would surely have acted differently," he said.[18] Another banker is quoted as stressing the need not for more statistics but for better judgment: "Banks would not have acted differently had quicker detailed information been available to them. What is important is not only information, but how we react to it."[19] Perhaps not even improved data would have slowed the banks in their determined drive to expand foreign lending in the 1970s.

Finally, there is the explanation that the banks were overtaken by adverse events in the world economy that were unforeseen—and unforeseeable. These events included not just the second oil shock, which again created serious financing problems for oil-importing countries, but also the prolonged global recession and record rise of interest rates that followed it. Global recession cut into debtors' export earnings and depressed commodity prices. The escalation of world interest rates added greatly to debt-service burdens. Typically, rates on private international credits are set at an agreed margin or spread over the banks' own cost of funds (most often using, as a proxy, the London Interbank Offered Rate— LIBOR), the margin ostensibly representing the banks' assessment of the risk of individual loans. Rates themselves float, that is, are subject to periodic revision to reflect movements of LIBOR. As market rates took off after the end of 1979, debtors found themselves being called upon to pay far more interest than had been expected, and at precisely the worst possible moment, when their terms of trade were already deteriorating (owing to the second round of oil-price increases) and their export revenues were drastically shrinking (owing to the global recession). Hit by such a remarkable confluence of events, it was only a matter of time before countries would start falling into arrears, as they did in 1982. Today bankers ask: Who would have guessed that all these things would go wrong at once? It was not their loans that were questionable, they insist. Rather, it was the quality of international economic management, which failed to prevent this unprecedented triple whammy of shocks to sovereign debtors.

There is some truth here as well. Before the end of the decade, the pace of lending in the aggregate did not look imprudent. On the contrary, in most of the major capital-importing countries, growth prospects were fully realized. High rates of expansion were achieved in both domestic income and investment, and exports grew on average as rapidly as debt, indicating little immediate erosion of borrowers' capacity to service foreign loans. In 1980, the overall debt-service ratio of non-OPEC developing nations (that is, the ratio of interest and amortization payments to total exports of goods and services), at 17.3 percent, was scarcely changed from the average of 15.4 percent recorded in 1973–77. Only after the three shocks at the end of the decade did their debt-service ratios begin to deteriorate sharply, reaching a level near 24 percent in 1982 for the group as a whole (and far worse, as indicated above, for a number of individual countries). Likewise, if we consider interest payments alone in relation to export revenues, the overall ratio for non-OPEC developing nations remained essentially flat, below 8 percent, for most of the decade, before escalating to a peak in excess of 13 percent in 1982.[20] Bankers do have a point. Such a combination of events could not have been easily foreseen.

Yet here too the argument is disingenuous. Even if the specific events were unforeseen, bankers ought to have suspected that something might happen to jeopardize their overseas positions. Something always does. If economic history teaches anything, it is that booms never last forever: major exogenous shocks do occur from time to time to expose frailties in the economic system. Life is like that. The probability of such shocks may be low; their specific nature and timing may be quite unpredictable. Yet bank managements have an obligation to be on guard against them, if they are to protect the interests of their investors and shareholders. That important point was forgotten in the go-go years of the 1960s and 1970s. Banks neglected to develop adequate defensive strategies to cope with the hazards of occasional economic or political disasters. Their foreign exposure, as a result, was allowed to become dangerously high by the time debtors were hit by the triple whammy of the 1980s. The question remains: How could they have let it happen?

IV

For a more persuasive explanation, it is necessary to go directly to the decision-making processes of the banks themselves. Governments may have urged bankers to lend; their information may have been imperfect. Still, in the end, it was they who made the decisions, not others: the risks were knowingly assumed. Banks have to accept their share of responsibility.

The key lies in the banks' failure to plan adequately for the possibility of major exogenous shocks—"disaster myopia," to use the phrase of the economists Jack Guttentag and Richard Herring.[21] Decision making under uncertainty, Guttentag and Herring point out, is often characterized by a tendency, over time, to discount the risks associated with potentially high-cost calamities of unknown probability. The longer the interval since the last disaster, the more people behave as if it could never happen again; caution gradually yields to increasingly excessive—and unrealistic—optimism. As a result, decision makers make themselves more and more vulnerable to exceptionally heavy losses should some new adverse shock hit the system. Such behavior is well documented in, for example, the insurance decisions of homeowners in floodplains or earthquake zones. It also seems to describe accurately the lending pattern of international banks in the 1970s. Few bankers who had personally experienced the financial collapse of the 1930s were still around. A new generation of financiers let it happen because they chose to ignore economic history.

In fact, what happened was not at all unfamiliar to students of financial behavior: lenders saw a good thing and got carried away by their animal spirits. Indeed, petrodollar recycling looked like a bonanza to the banks. The loan–loss record on foreign loans was better than that on domestic loans; the average rate of return, significantly higher. And so cross-border lending grew increasingly frenzied, as more and more institutions fought to share in an attractive, expanding market. International league standing became a key strategic objective for many banks in the 1970s, measured by overall asset growth, and this in turn tended to weaken internal restraints (such as credit committees) designed to safeguard against lending excess. In such an environment caution became, if anything, a hindrance, since more prudent lenders were bound to lose business to others who were prepared to disregard the hazards of possible adverse shocks. In effect, therefore, tendencies toward disaster myopia were fed by the intensity of competitive forces.

Witness, for example, what happened to interest rates. As the competition for borrowers grew more fierce, spreads narrowed almost to the vanishing point. In 1976 the average margin on loans to developing countries was 2.25 percent. By 1979 spreads had dropped as low as 0.75 percent on average, and even lower for prime borrowers. As late as the spring of 1982, just months before the worst financial crisis in its history, Mexico was able to obtain funds at no more than one-half of one percent over LIBOR. It would hardly be an overstatement to suggest that over the course of the decade, there was indeed some erosion of restraint in the assessment of international risk.

Disaster myopia was worsened by the incentive systems and high job mobility then prevailing within lending institutions. For one thing, foreign lending was exciting. "The international side looked glamorous," said one bank executive. "Bankers like travel and exotic locations. It was certainly more exciting than Cleveland or Pittsburgh, and an easier way to make money than nursing along a $100,000 loan to some scrap metal smelter."[22] For another, foreign lending was highly rewarding, especially as a loan officer's performance was usually evaluated over relatively short periods of time in relation to specific current earnings targets or loan quotas. This encouraged an inclination to discount low-probability future hazards. Indeed, cognizant that their salaries and career prospects were at stake, the last thing loan officers wanted to worry about was long-term risk. They knew that no one ever got a bonus or a promotion for turning down a loan application. They also knew that they probably would not be around to bear the consequences of any possible disaster in years to come. As one of them admitted, "It was always tempting to sign up a loan.... By the time the problems began, you'd moved on somewhere else and the chairman had retired."[23] The profits were taken up front, the residue of potentially bad debt being left for someone else to cope with.

Most important, the bank's contagious enthusiasm made their disaster myopia even more acute. In their ebullience bankers demonstrated a prodigious gift for self-deception, persuading themselves by a series of unexamined, self-serving arguments that there was little to worry about. Most of these arguments hold little water. The wonder is that anyone believed them at the time.

For example, there was the argument that countries cannot go bankrupt. Unlike corporations, sovereign borrowers cannot be eliminated by insolvency. So why worry? This was a favorite theme of former Citibank chairman Walter Wriston, a leader in the internationalization of banking throughout the Incredible Quarter Century: "Countries do not fail to exist."[24] For precisely that reason, however, governments could not always be relied upon to exercise prudential self-restraint in their borrowing. Faced by the exigencies of budget demands and balance-of-payments deficits, many were bound at some point to succumb to the temptation of easy credits from abroad, becoming overcommitted in the process. If anything, the argument ought to have put banks *more* on their guard, not *less*. There was always an element of illusion in it. As one New York banker now ruefully admits:

> The problem with all of this was that the ... capital markets lacked any real anchor. Rather than impose discipline on countries in payments disequilibrium, the system rewarded non-adjustment in the name of growth promotion....

> The only effective constraint on sovereign borrowing was the willingness of the banks to grant new credits.... Judgments tended to become self-validating: New loans confirmed a country's creditworthiness and this perception generated even more loans.[25]

More pointed are the words of British financial expert Harold Lever. "I call Walter Wriston the Peter Pan of bankers," Lever says, "because he still believes in fairies."[26]

Then there was the argument that countries could be relied upon to honor their debts, no matter how troubled their economies, since it was so clearly in their own interest to do so. Default would shut a nation out of the financial market for years and could make its assets and exports subject to seizure anywhere in the world. No country would ever voluntarily suspend payments of interest or principal due. The flaw in this logic is the assumption of pure economic rationality in a context in which complex political or even personal considerations might well take precedence. Economic rationality did not dissuade Fidel Castro, after his successful revolution, from repudiating Cuba's foreign debts in 1961. It might prove equally irrelevant in other countries at other times. The issue was clearly drawn by one U.S. expert:

> Imagine you are a Latin dictator deep in debt. If you cut back on imports, you get riots in the streets. If you default, you are ostracized by the world capital markets. Now if the first approach leaves you swinging from a tree branch, you know you are going to go the default route.[27]

Furthermore, even if countries want to keep up the service on their debt, they might not be able to. As recent experience has amply demonstrated, circumstances can force borrowers into arrears whether they like it or not. Technically, such countries are already in default. But since legally only a creditor can declare a formal default, banks prefer to finesse the situation for as long as possible by rescheduling the debt. The advantage from the banks' point of view is that they can thereby avoid marking down or writing off some of the paper on their books. The disadvantage is that they find themselves locked into positions for far longer periods of time than they may have originally intended. Of course, even in the best of circumstances, borrowers (public or private) rarely reduce their debt in the aggregate; more normally, maturing loans are rolled over or refinanced, affording creditors individually an opportunity to get out. But getting out is impossible when the same debts are simply rescheduled each time they come due, as has been happening to much sovereign debt since 1982. At first only medium- and longer-term loans were rescheduled, but more recently short-term debts and even interest arrears have been included in restructurings. More significant, the whole process has become increasingly routine as the same countries fall into arrears time after time. Repeated often enough, the process comes to represent default in all but name—default by attrition, as it were. For individual creditors, debts are formally honored but never repaid.

A third argument was that any risks in international lending could be safely limited through diversification. Spreading loans across a large number of countries would minimize vulnerability to problems in any single nation or region. The banks' eggs would not all be in one basket. But this overlooked gathering world economic difficulties, especially after the second oil shock, that threatened prospects for all sovereign borrowers, wherever they might be located. These common problems, as I indicated above, included low commodity prices and stagnant export markets, which reduced the debtors' ability to service their obligations, as well as record high interest rates, which added greatly to the cost of their floating-rate debt. Such disasters could not be diversified away. The whole basket of eggs was in danger of breaking. Banks were optimistic in believing that they could protect themselves so easily.

Likewise, the banks were optimistic in believing that they could easily protect themselves by shortening the maturities of new credits, as they began to do after the second oil shock. During most of the 1970s, short-term loans accounted for no more than about 12–13 percent of total debt of non-OPEC developing countries. By 1982 that share had doubled, to almost one-quarter. According to one estimate, fully one-half of all new bank lending to these countries in 1981–82 was at short term, as compared with only 40 percent on average in the three preceding years.[28] The banks' idea was to position themselves to get their money out quickly, should something go wrong—certainly a rational policy for one lender acting alone. Unfortunately, other banks tended to follow suit, reducing their credit lines as well (the so-called herd effect). The practice of shortening maturities, therefore, added to the risks of lending and to the potential for liquidity crises by greatly increasing the aggregate amount of sovereign debt that repeatedly had to be rolled over. At work was the fallacy of composition. What was good for any single bank was far from healthy for the market as a whole.

Finally, there was the argument—more an unspoken assumption—that in the last resort banks could count on help from official sources, either in the form of emergency loans to troubled debtors or as liquidity or solvency backing for the banks themselves. Governments, they reasoned, considered the banking system too vital to be allowed to fall. Lenders would ultimately be sheltered from their own mistakes by the umbrella of taxpayer money. In fact, they were not far wrong. Governments have indeed come to their aid—in early 1982, for instance, when the Reagan administration chose to repay several hundred million dollars' worth of Poland's overdue debt to U.S. banks, under existing loan-guarantee programs, rather than countenance formal default (chapter 7); or later the same year, when official rescue packages were quickly arranged for Argentina, Brazil, and Mexico, the Third World's three biggest sovereign borrowers (chapter 8). But as was demonstrated by the 1983 congressional debate over the administration's proposed increase of IMF funding, such support need not come without a price (chapter 8). Lawmakers and their constituents, irritated over the possibility that fund credits might be used in effect to bail out imprudent lenders, insisted on a pound of flesh in the form of mandated increases of loan–loss reserves and ceilings on renegotiation fees in debt reschedulings. A public umbrella, the banks discovered, is not necessarily cheap. A major theme of this book, developed in subsequent chapters, is that there is little reason to assume that such an umbrella should be cheap.

V

Bankers now understand that they did indeed deceive themselves—that there really was much to worry about. That explains, of course, why international lending slowed down so strikingly once the debt crisis erupted. Excessive optimism was transformed into exaggerated caution as banks attempted to correct for their former myopia by reining in their foreign exposure as quickly as possible. The question is: What does this mean for the long-term future of international banking? Is the current retreat from the market temporary or permanent?

In the opinion of many market experts, it is permanent.[29] The age of internationalization, it is said, is over. Having ignored the history of the interwar period, a new generation of bankers was condemned to repeat it. But now, supposedly, they have learned their lesson; they too vow never again to "trust their fortunes abroad or respond to the requests of recreant foreign governments." Once again management aspirations in many of the capital-market countries will turn inward, to focus more on home markets, as they did before what is seen as the aberration of the Incredible Quarter Century. A more domestically oriented strategy may not be as exciting as foreign lending, but at least it holds out the promise of less risk. In the words of one U.S. regional banker, "Our capital is ploughed back into the region. Nobody here is chasing thin margins on Mars."[30]

Powerful forces are driving American bankers, in particular, to focus more on the home front. First and foremost is the battering that bank stock prices started to take after the onset of the debt crisis. Many of the most active international banks found their equity severely depreciated, which in turn hampered their ability to raise the capital they needed for future earnings growth. Of course, troubled foreign loans were not the only reason for investors' loss of confidence in bank shares. As the experiences of Penn Square, Continental Illinois, and others testify, many dubious loans were made domestically as well. Lending at home is not necessarily less risky. But the problems of Mexico, Brazil, and other Third World debtors were more sensational and received wider attention. Many investors questioned, in particular, the banks' practice of carrying rescheduled debt on their books at 100 percent of value, despite its dubious quality. "The market is telling us they want a definition of the cost of the less developed country problems," conceded one New York banker.[31] In effect, investors did the discounting for the banks by writing down the value of their shares instead. To many bank managers, the conclusion seemed obvious. If capital positions were to be strengthened, banks would have to reduce their commitment to risky international business as compared with operations closer to home.

And then there are the positive attractions of a more domestic orientation. Banks are being impelled not just by the push of potential losses abroad but also, in many countries, by the pull of improved profit prospects at home. Particularly in the United States, new horizons are opening up in the 1980s that could be every bit as glamorous as the foreign lending of the 1970s. Partly as a result of regulatory changes, partly owing to technological advances, a virtual revolution is occurring in what is now called the financial services industry. Commercial bank managers find themselves confronted with new and fascinating challenges to their skills and imagination.

On the one hand, for American banks, is the challenge of new geographic horizons brought on by the accelerating dissolution of regulatory barriers to multistate banking. For decades after passage of the McFadden Act in 1927, U.S. banks were prevented from establishing branches or subsidiaries in more than one state. Recently, however, loopholes have emerged that have led to a widening movement of operations across state lines. One big breakthrough originated in the so-called Douglas amendment to the Bank Holding Company Act of 1956, authorizing banks to operate subsidiaries in states that allow reciprocal privileges. In the 1980s, more and more

states are enacting the legislation necessary to permit inter-
state banking on a regional or national basis. The constitu-
tionality of regional banking pacts was upheld by the
Supreme Court in June 1985.[32] Another possible breakthrough
was the debut in 1980 of the so-called limited-service facility,
or nonbank bank. The legal definition of a bank, spelled out
in the 1956 Bank Holding Company Act, is any institution
that both takes demand deposits and makes commercial
loans. Banks eventually realized that any operation not per-
forming both of these functions—even if they conduct other
banking business, like accepting consumer deposits or making
consumer loans—might therefore be set up across state lines.
At first a trickle, the flow of applications to the regulatory
authorities for charters for nonbank banks soon became a flood.
By the spring of 1985, some 368 applications had been filed
by bank holding companies around the country, with more
expected, despite opposition from the Federal Reserve and
continuing questions about the loophole in both Congress and
the courts.[33]

On the other hand is the challenge of new product horizons brought on by the accelerating dissolution, mentioned
in chapter 1, of the lines between traditional commercial-
banking operations and other types of financial services. Under the Glass–Steagall Act of 1933, for instance, banks were
formally barred from public underwriting of bond or equity
issues. But here too, in recent years, loopholes have been found
to permit banks to become more involved in investment banking, for example, by acting as agents for new issues while
placing them privately with institutional investors or by
transforming existing bank loans into tradable securities ("se-
curitization"). Says one New York banker, "Glass–Steagall is
important—but for the biggest banks it is becoming increasingly irrelevant."[34] Banks are also finding ways of getting
more heavily into other kinds of sophisticated financial activity, including brokerage, leasing, cash and investment
management, and even such esoteric fields as barter trade
and venture capital.

One motive for getting more heavily into such activities
is that, since they are mostly fee-based, they can generate

substantial earnings for banks without a major commitment of new financial resources. Any obligations instead normally take the form of contingent liabilities—for example, standby letters of credit, overdraft and note-issuing facilities, bank-issued guarantees, and the like—that have the advantage of never even showing up on a bank's balance sheet. Asset growth, so prominent in bank aspirations in the 1970s, can be conveniently de-emphasized in management strategies as a source of profits in the 1980s and 1990s. Equally important, however, is the growing competition from other financial institutions, which have been increasingly encroaching on the banks' own traditional areas of specialization—taking deposits and making loans. Brokerage houses, insurance companies, credit card agencies, and even retail department store chains have all begun to perform certain banking-type activities. Some provide the equivalent of a checking account through money market mutual funds; others engage in consumer lending through credit card facilities or cash management accounts. Indeed, as mentioned in the previous chapter, the financial supermarkets such as Merrill Lynch, Sears Roebuck, Prudential-Bache, and Shearson Lehman-American Express are now, in effect, among the biggest "bankers" in the country. Commercial banks feel the need to meet the competition on its own turf.

Last, behind all these developments is an even more profound force for change, the contemporary revolution in information-processing and communication technologies, which has been rapidly eroding conventional distinctions between different providers of financial services and virtually changing the face of the industry.[35] Technological change is swiftly transforming the way financial services are defined, packaged, and delivered; and commercial banks are eager to exploit the attractive profit opportunities that are opening up as a result.

But does all this add up to an end of internationalization? Not at all. For all the forces driving bankers to focus more on the home front, the pull of the international market remains fundamentally strong. There are still all those multinational corporate clients out there to be serviced, still plenty of opportunities for asset diversification through trade and project financing, still the attractions of a broader and potentially less expensive funding base, still the allure of expanding foreign-based banking operations in many countries. Says the president of Chemical Bank, "We want to retain that sense of balance on both sides of the accounts and both functionally and geographically."[36] In the words of the chairman of Security Pacific, "I wouldn't want all my eggs in California, even if it is the greatest market in the world."[37] Some bankers even foresee an eventual return to straightforward balance-of-payments financing on a sizable scale, despite the specter of the debt problem. "We are not very far away from a return to normal," predicted a Citibank vice-president in late 1984. "The perception is that bankers are going to get out of the sovereign lending business permanently. I don't believe that—I think they will return."[38]

In fact, the retreat that began in 1982 was probably more tactical than strategic—a shaking out of the market rather than a fading away. After the excesses of the 1970s a period of consolidation was inevitable, as banks reconsidered their options; and some of the more peripheral players were bound to get out of the game. For many smaller institutions, participation in syndicated credits had seemed a shortcut to prestige, high earnings, and asset growth. Now they know better: without significant direct customer relationships abroad, a shift of emphasis back to the domestic market really makes much more sense. Many are closing offices abroad and dismantling consortium banks that had been optimistically set up during the land-rush years of the previous decade.[39] For larger players, however, with more extensive international commitments, a continued presence remains essential, even if at the margin there may well continue to be some reorientation of operations to reduce dependence on overseas earnings in relative terms. Such an adjustment was evident as early as 1983 (see for example, table 2.4). Overall, a thinning of the ranks seems rational. But that, by itself, is hardly likely to slow down the momentum of the market over the longer term.

Indeed, even during the worst days of the retrenchment

after mid–1982, interest in international activity had not really waned. Almost all of the deceleration of new lending was concentrated in countries experiencing debt-service difficulties, where worry was indeed justified. Loans to more highly regarded borrowers, particularly in the OECD group of countries and the rapidly growing nations of eastern Asia, continued to expand at rates comparable to earlier years.[40] Foreign branches and subsidiaries are still being set up, deposits are still on the rise, and new product lines are still being developed.[41] The same technological revolution that is changing the face of the domestic industry is transforming international banking as well. And here too banks are eager to exploit emergent profit opportunities. The international market developed in the first place precisely because it serves the most basic interests of all its participants, the ultimate suppliers and users of funds no less than the banks themselves. No one wants to kill the goose that lays the golden egg (even if she did get rather carried away with herself in the 1970s).

The internationalization of banking was no aberration. In all likelihood, the present period of consolidation will one day be seen as no more than a temporary pause in the unfolding of a fundamental and probably irreversible historical process. From almost purely domestic institutions not so long ago, banks have evolved into truly international actors. That fact was not altered by the debt crisis. First came traditional foreign banking; then, more and more, offshore and foreign based operations. Gradually, banks became multinationals in their own right, with vested interests of their own. The two or three dozen largest money-center banks here and abroad that are capable of providing a full range of financial services to customers have every incentive to continue developing into genuinely global "universal" banks. For smaller institutions, lower down on the scale, selective opportunities abound for specialization in a variety of market niches, for example, investment banking, corporate financial services, securities trading, or data processing. Plenty of room exists for expansion. The business will go on.

CHAPTER 3

Private Interests/Public Interest

If the internationalization of banking was no aberration, then some critical issues are raised for the foreign policy of the United States. The central issue is clear. By becoming truly international actors, banks have entered as full participants into the realm of foreign policy. High finance and high politics are now closely interdependent. Yet there is no assurance at all that the banks' interpretation of their private interests in the marketplace will necessarily converge with the public interest as interpreted by government officials in Washington. A potential for conflicting interests exists. As one astute observer has commented, "U.S. foreign policy actions and the overseas activities of the private banks have come increasingly to overlap. The interests of the two sides do not always coincide and indeed may at times be contradictory."[1] Or, to quote Ronald Reagan's first under secretary of state for economic affairs,

> There are areas of shared interest . . . as well as areas of potential friction. . . . The bankers must be guided by the interests of their stockholders. . . . Governments, on the other hand, are guided by a mix of political, humanitarian, strategic and economic objectives. . . . Banks may dif-

fer with government in their assessment of political factors.[2]

This is not to deny the many benefits of international banking. On the contrary, the key role played by banks in promoting widespread growth and prosperity is an essential element of the public interest, as I stressed in chapter 1. Much of foreign policy is necessarily concerned with preserving the positive contribution that banks make to the achievement of our nation's economic goals. The problem, however, is that these are not the only goals of foreign policy: the business of the United States is not just business. Diplomatic and security interests also matter; and it is because of these additional concerns of policymakers that the possibility of conflict between the two sectors unfortunately arises. As broad as the "areas of shared interest" are, there may indeed be areas of potential friction as well. And these areas of potential friction can only grow in extent and intensity so long as banks continue to expand their manifold overseas activities. That is the reason why a coherent public policy on international banking is now so urgently needed in the United States.

I

In formal terms, the overlapping bank–government relationship that has emerged in recent years corresponds closely to the paradigm of world politics labeled "complex interdependence" by the social scientists Robert Keohane and Joseph Nye.[3] In contradistinction to the older "realist" tradition of foreign affairs scholarship, which focused exclusively on the dominant role of nation states in international relations, complex interdependence acknowledges the presence as well of other important actors on the world stage, including private organizations of all sorts (both profit and nonprofit) and various multilateral institutions. These so-called transnational actors, Keohane and Nye write, "are important not only because of their activities in pursuit of their own interests, but also because they act as transmission belts, making government policies in various countries more sensitive to one another."[4] Transnational actors multiply both the channels connecting societies and the issues of relevance to foreign policy. In effect, therefore, they generate new linkages in world politics, joining otherwise unrelated policy issues or instruments. And this in turn reduces the utility of pure military force as a means for achieving state goals. In a world of complex interdependence, foreign policy must be pursued through a multilevel political bargaining process in which the ability to realize policy preferences is very much a function of a government's linkage strategies—that is, how well it can make use of instruments or issues where its bargaining position is relatively strong to promote or defend interests where its position may be weaker.[5] The participation of transnational actors in the foreign policy process, with their own interests to pursue, can significantly affect outcomes in the relations between states.

Banks have come to number among the most important of such transnational actors today. In the United States the major money-center institutions, through their international activities, have already increased the mutual sensitivities of America and other countries and complicated considerably Washington's pursuit of its foreign policy objectives. Think of Iran or Poland. Think of the Latin American debt crisis and America's relations recently with Mexico, Brazil, or Argentina. High finance obviously does now impinge on high politics. Strategic interactions between governments—the traditional focus of foreign policy analysis—increasingly are linked with strategic interactions between the public sector and private financial institutions both here and abroad. The foreign policy process has become very complex indeed.

These strategic interactions are the heart of the matter. Insofar as there really are "areas of potential friction" between the government and banks as well as shared interests, the key question for analysis becomes evident. What is the potential for reciprocal influences between the public and private sectors? Who influences whom, and how?

Curiously, there have been few attempts in the formal

scholarly literature to explore this question systematically in a foreign policy context.[6] But a useful start may be made by distinguishing for analytical purposes between direct and indirect forms of influence or impact. Direct influence refers to deliberate attempts by one actor or group of actors to alter the behavior of another; indirect influence, to the effects that one actor or group of actors may have on another by unintentionally altering the decision-making environment of the latter. The internationalization of banking brings with it the possibility that both kinds of influence may be exerted by either group of actors, banks or policymakers, namely:

1. Banks may have become self-conscious political actors, deliberately attempting to sway the foreign policy of the U.S. government on behalf of their own commercial interests.
2. Policy makers, conversely, may self-consciously attempt to shape the commercial decisions of banks to suit foreign policy considerations.
3. Banks may have become more sensitive to noneconomic (political) considerations and influences and increasingly factor these into their ongoing commercial decisions.
4. Banks, conversely, through their ongoing commercial decisions, may have impacts on the general foreign policy environment that alter the issues of salience for policy and/or the nature and scope of policy options available to government officials.

Direct influences (1) and (2) are the strategic interactions that generally first come to mind in popular thinking about the connections between high finance and high politics. But as we shall see in the following discussion, what comes to mind first is not necessarily what is most germane. In fact, there is good reason to believe that indirect influences (3) and (4) are really far more important to the actual formulation and implementation of foreign policy by the government. Indirect influences are more likely to determine the basic constraints and opportunities posed for policymakers, by way of their crucial impact on the linkages between various policy issues and instruments. Ultimately at issue is the government's ability to adapt its linkage strategies to radically altered circumstances.

II

Direct influences like (1) or (2) are the stuff of which conspiratorial social theories are made. Political polemicists find it easy to see manipulation or control when domains of interest come to overlap. Since banks and policymakers increasingly find themselves dealing with the same sets of issues and actors, some commentators, inevitably, perceive sinister efforts by public officials to make banks a political arm of the government or alternatively by banks to cynically subordinate public policy to their own private ends.[7] Such theories, risible though they may be, have a superficial appeal for many. What they lack in subtlety or hard evidence they more than make up for in color and drama—hardy grist for the mills of novelists, filmmakers, and sensation-seeking journalists. They have little intellectual or empirical substance, however. Cut from whole cloth, they belong to the realm of fantasy, not fact, and can hardly be taken seriously as a portrayal of the real world.

But neither can they be wholly ignored. Even if caricatures, they do tend to underscore a real issue. It is one thing to discount systematic conspiratorial theories as such; it is quite another to deny any reciprocal attempts at all to alter behavior. The relationship between bankers and public officials is far more complex than that. Neither group may be the puppet of the other, but both manifestly do on occasion try to pull strings. The dynamic is common to most market economies, as one American banker has pointed out:

> At...times...some governments have perceived in commercial banks' international activities a means of advancing specific policy objectives of the state....In other instances, banks have sought and obtained the assistance of their home government in furthering commercial objectives abroad....Whether the prevailing direction of influences runs from government to banks or banks to government, commercial outcomes in these cases are likely to be determined by nonmarket factors.[8]

The essential question for U.S. public policy is the extent to which this sort of influence is or should be exercised in either direction. Given the continuing trend toward internationalization of American banking activity, would the public interest be served by more such direct contacts between banks and Washington? Or, alternatively, would we be better off with greater insulation between the two?

Consider, first, government attempts to influence banks. In principle, the international operations of American financial institutions are totally independent of politics. In practice, however, Washington has long had an arsenal of policy instruments available to use, when deemed appropriate, to shape bank decisions to suit foreign policy considerations, including loan-guarantee programs, restrictions, and outright prohibitions as well as prudential supervision, general monetary policy, and "moral suasion." During the years of the Cold War, for instance, loans to some communist governments were strictly prohibited on political grounds (and still are to Cambodia, Cuba, North Korea, and Vietnam), a policy that was to be reversed with the coming of détente. At their summit conference in 1972, President Richard Nixon and Soviet leader Leonid Brezhnev declared that "the USA and the USSR regard commercial and economic ties as an important and necessary element in the strengthening of their bilateral relations and thus will actively promote the growth of such ties." Quite clearly this was to include encouragement of credits from American banks. By mid–1982 U.S. bankers had built up an exposure in Soviet bloc countries in excess of $7 billion.

Other examples can be cited. Prohibitions on lending were employed in support of United Nations sanctions against Rhodesia, for instance, during the years of that colony's Unilateral Declaration of Independence as well as in support of Washington's economic sanctions against the revolutionary government of Iran during the months of the hostage crisis. Conversely, expansion of credits has sometimes been encouraged when it seemed to serve broader foreign policy objectives, for example, in Poland in the summer of 1980, when the State Department openly pressured American banks to keep a substantial refinancing loan from failing. Likewise, in early 1982 State went out its way to make plain its hope that banks would keep open their credit lines to Yugoslavia, lest that nation be driven closer to the Soviet Union.[9] And even more recently, as we shall see in chapter 8, great stress has been placed on easing the debt-service difficulties of some major friendly governments in Latin America.

Such political interventions by Washington—whether to encourage or discourage lending, to individual countries or in general—have not been without controversy. Quite the opposite, in fact. Public debate has been quite heated. For some observers, the only problem is that the government has not gone far enough to link foreign policy and the lending practices of American banks. Argues one source, "This step must be taken to preserve not only the financial integrity of the banking system but also the discretion of the Government in the formulation of foreign policy."[10] For others, the problem is precisely the opposite: "It would seem better to keep public policy and private investment at arm's length to the extent possible.... Injecting foreign policy considerations into private bank decision making . . . seems likely to exacerbate both the problems of foreign policy and bank soundness."[11] Unfortunately, the heat of the debate has not shed much light, largely because protagonists have been too busy arguing among themselves to clarify the main issues involved.

In fact, at least four distinct issues are involved. Call them the four *e*'s—*effectiveness, efficiency, equity,* and *external relations.* Assume, for instance, that in some situation or other public officials are indeed resolved to make use of available policy instruments to influence bank behavior on foreign policy grounds. The first issue is how to assure maximum effectiveness. That is no simple matter. For one thing, the government does not always speak with one voice. As I stressed in chapter 1, different agencies with differing responsibilities often disagree over policy priorities and objectives, a situation whose confusion is compounded by bureaucratic struggles for turf; and banks, as a result, frequently find themselves receiving distinctly mixed signals over just what it is that constitutes the public interest (for example, if the classification of country loans by bank regulators comes into conflict with foreign policy goals as defined by the Department of State). How can they respond to political interventions, bankers complain, if the government cannot get its act together?

Besides, with the internationalization of banking over the last quarter century, much of the overseas activity of U.S. banks now takes place beyond the government's direct jurisdictional reach in a comparatively unregulated business environment. Moreover, the evolution of the Euro-currency market has blurred the strictly national identity of many banking institutions, further limiting Washington's leverage. Most big bank credits today are the product of syndicates of indeterminate nationality. Not that Washington is without any leverage at all. After all, national identity may have become blurred, but it has certainly not been forgotten. As Herbert Feis wrote in *Europe, the World's Banker*, "Bankers are subject to the forces of national feeling as are their fellow men."[12] Those who run America's largest banks can still be moved by moral suasion when the national interest appears to be at stake. Furthermore, despite the extent of their overseas operations, they are still ultimately dependent on a domestic financial base and subject to the influence of domestic policy and regulation. But it does suggest that the effectiveness of political interventions is apt to vary considerably, depending on circumstances, as we shall see in part II.

Then there is the question of the cost, in economic terms, of any such interventions (the second *e*: efficiency). Advocates of an arm's-length relationship between foreign policy and the banks rest their case primarily on efficiency grounds. The key assumption here is that international banking activity is on balance beneficial for the American economy. From this the inference seems to follow that any intervention by the public sector will most likely result in efficiency losses, not only for banks but for the economy as a whole. All intrusion of politics, therefore, should be resisted. Only in extreme circumstances, it is argued, should policymakers be able to impede banks in their competitive pursuit of profit.

However, in practical terms neither the assumption nor the inference is necessarily beyond question. Economists still debate the overall costs and benefits of international banking for the American economy, so far without any consensus. No doubt the competitive pursuit of profit does produce genuine efficiency gains, promoting economic growth and prosperity. But exceptional risks are also involved, as I emphasized in chapter 1. Markets do not always work perfectly; financial markets in particular have a well-known tendency at times to get carried away with themselves (see chapter 2), potentially endangering not only the solvency of individual institutions but also the stability of economic conditions in general. Hence the case for regulation differentiating finance from most other sectors of the private economy. In the words of Charles Kindleberger: "Markets generally work, but occasionally they break down. When they do, they require government intervention."[13] For banks that intervention, justified by the public interest, takes the familiar forms of *prudential supervision*, which is concerned with the internal health of individual institutions and the stability of financial markets; and *monetary management*, which is concerned with such key macroeconomic variables as the price level, employment, and real income and output. In other words, the potential economic costs of international banking must also be weighed in the balance as possible intrafinance challenges to public policy—at the level of prudential supervision, possible threats to bank safety and soundness; and at the level of monetary management, the risks of undue unemployment or inflation. These costs may not outweigh the efficiency gains of international banking, but they may not be trivial either.

Furthermore, even granting that net economic gains are most likely to be positive, it does not necessarily follow that all intrusion of politics into international banking should thus be resisted. Economics, I have said, is only a part of the public interest. Diplomatic and security concerns also matter; and this means that a rational foreign policy must countenance tradeoffs among all of the government's multiple international objectives. To be sure, that is no easy task. Since by definition noneconomic costs and benefits cannot be reduced to numbers—and even economic costs and benefits are difficult to quantify with any precision—the overall policy calculus can never be anything but subjective. But it must be made. Indeed, that is what the responsibility of governance is all about.

Difficult questions of equity are also raised by this debate (the third *e*). We know, for instance, that banks do not all respond uniformly to political interventions from Washington. To take just one recent example: after eruption of the global debt crisis in 1982, many smaller, regional banks tried desperately to find ways to back out of syndicated credits to major sovereign borrowers, even as the larger banks responded positively to government (and IMF) calls for continued lending. Differentiated responses of this sort could well have had adverse effects on the competitive position of cooperating institutions vis-à-vis not only other U.S. banks but also foreign banks. The question therefore arises of what obligation, if any, the authorities should have assumed to differentiate their own policies in return. Did banks that cooperated with the government have any special claim to official assistance or other compensatory treatment had they run into trouble as a result? Conversely, should noncooperating institutions have been subject to disciplines of any sort? Would that have been fair? Similarly, we know that in some cases banks abroad receive favorable treatment from their governments in return for cooperation with foreign policy guidelines. Political links between financial institutions and the public authorities in most countries are a good deal closer than they are in the United States, including not just developing nations but also many of the main capital-market countries of Western Europe and Japan.[14] Such favorable treatment also could affect competitive positions, putting U.S. banks at a disadvantage in selected foreign markets. What obligation, if any, does that prospect impose on the American government?

Finally, the closeness of those links raises the question of potentially negative impacts on our external relations (the fourth *e*). What diplomatic costs might there be, in terms of our interests in other countries—particularly our European and Japanese allies—of politically motivated attempts by Washington to influence international banking activity? It is easy to imagine serious frictions arising out of conflicting signals by different governments.

Any attempts by banks to influence the government raise parallel issues. Unlike public officials, bankers have relatively few direct instruments available to sway foreign policy decisions. But like all other private citizens, they do have the power of persuasion and, probably more than most interest groups, a variety of formal and informal channels of communication through which to try to exercise it—Congressional hearings, the print and electronic media, public and private meetings, "old-boy networks," and the like. To what extent these channels are actually used is difficult to say with precision, since inevitably most efforts at private lobbying tend to go on behind the scenes and slip by unrecorded. However, as we shall see in part II, such evidence as exists suggests that bankers do not hesitate to express their views, often quite vigorously, on issues they care about. Indeed, contacts apparently occur virtually all the time and at every level. This too poses serious questions regarding the public interest.

Most important, it poses the question of the extent to which, if at all, lobbying efforts by banks now go beyond strictly economic issues, with which they have traditionally and legitimately been concerned. Has the spreading internationalization of financial activity led them to attempt to relate broader political or security policies to their own commercial interests? To be sure, there is little evidence that bankers regularly or intentionally promote profits knowingly at the expense of broader national objectives; they are not so crudely venal as that. But even if narrow self-interest does not consciously dominate their thinking, it must be acknowledged that at a deeper level—the level of unconscious perception—some impact could indeed be felt. As their cross-border commitments grow, it does not seem unreasonable to presume that commercial interests could subtly bias their views of political or security issues, thereby altering the positions they take in formal or informal contacts with public officials. For example, bankers with a heavy concentration of Saudi Arabian or Kuwaiti deposits might gradually—and quite sincerely—grow more inclined toward an Arab perspective on Middle East issues and come to lend it greater support in foreign policy discussions. Similarly, banks with major loan exposure in specific countries or investment bankers with important sovereign clients might gradually come to revise the positions they take with respect to other relevant regional conflicts. Bankers, like anyone else, need not be conscious of their motivations in order to be persuaded of the correctness of their views, and to try to persuade others. The basic issue is not one of intent but of propriety. How much such persuasion, and what kind, should be regarded as legitimate?

Beyond that, again, are the four *e*'s—the same questions of effectiveness, efficiency, equity, and external relations. How effective are the banks in promoting their preferences, either negatively (for example, preventing certain government actions) or positively (promoting certain actions)? What are the costs of their lobbying, in economic terms and in terms of U.S. diplomatic interests in other countries? And what impacts might there be on relative competitive positions within the banking community? We know that banks do not speak with one voice either. Indeed, available evidence suggests that larger banks, especially the giant money-center institutions, have far easier access to the corridors of power in Washington, when it comes to international issues, than do local or regional institutions. Prominent money-center bankers also have many more opportunities to attempt to sway U.S. official policy by practicing their own brand of "private" diplomacy abroad, forging transnational coalitions with private or public-sector actors in other countries. Walter Wriston or David Rockefeller, as heads of large New York banks, could deal directly with foreign government leaders; the president of a local or regional institution cannot. Informed public policy must take all these considerations into account in assessing the evolving relationship between banks and government officials. Reciprocal attempts to alter behavior are bound to continue, if not grow; mutual accommodations are inevitable. One practical challenge for policymakers is to find the most appropriate institutional form for these ongoing direct contacts.

III

Direct influences, however, are only part of the story—and as suggested at the outset of this chapter, not even the main part at that. Reciprocal attempts to alter behavior are just the surface manifestation of the strategic interaction between banks and the government. Much more fundamental are indirect influences that arise from the growing overlap of their respective domains of interest. Inevitably, if unintentionally, each side has an impact on the decision-making environment of the other through the ongoing pursuit of its own legitimate responsibilities and objectives. For both sides, issues of salience and options for behavior are perforce continually being altered. The two are locked in a perpetual embrace, a ceaseless dialectic between the public and private sectors—between "politics" and "markets"—to which each side contributes and to which each side reacts. Indirect influences are subtle, in that they operate at the level of general incentives and disincentives for action. But for that very reason they are also more pervasive and potent, in practical terms, than individualized direct attempts at influence. As important as the latter may be for public policy, the challenge of the former, ultimately, is even more daunting for officials. Can Washington manage the dialectic in a manner that satisfactorily balances the interests of both the banking community and U.S. foreign policy?

In the immediate postwar period, Washington attempted to achieve such a balance by promoting an open and liberal environment for international capital movements. Scholars today speak of international regimes, defined as arrangements of principles, norms, rules, and decision-making procedures around which actors' expectations converge in a given issue area.[15] A regime is akin to a constitutional structure, a substitute form of authority in international relations where, by definition, no formal government exists. At Bretton Woods in 1944, the United States was largely responsible for creating a regime for the issue area of monetary relations which, it was hoped, would eventually lead to a revival of international financial markets from their collapse of the 1930s. Certain monetary responsibilities were reserved to governments—

most important, decisions affecting exchange rates and nations' access to the international liquidity needed to finance balance-of-payments deficits. Exchange rates were to be maintained by governments within the context of a "par-value" system; access to liquidity was to be set by strictly limited borrowing rights at the newly established International Monetary Fund. But otherwise the markets were to be encouraged to determine the international allocation of financial resources, for example, by a return to free convertibility of currencies. In effect, after the disasters of the Great Depression and World War II, the decision-making environment of the private sector was to be radically altered in favor of more active cross-border involvement.

As I indicated in the previous chapter, the private sector was not slow to respond once currency convertibility was at last restored and then capital movements began to be liberalized, starting at the end of the 1950s. In the Incredible Quarter Century that followed, banks took advantage of the opportunities presented them to establish themselves firmly on a global scale. The incentives they responded to were economic. But what permitted the process of internationalization to evolve to the extent it did was a political environment that was essentially benign for bank interests. The Euro-currency market in particular owed its remarkable vitality to the virtual absence of regulatory restraints on foreign-currency banking in London and other financial centers. More broadly, international banking benefited from the continuing commitment of the United States and other major governments to an open and liberal world system.

Ironically, the very success of international banking eventually undermined the regime that had helped to get it started in the first place. The dialectic between politics and markets took its toll on both the par-value system and the role of the IMF. As capital mobility accelerated, the private sector began to play an ever greater role in determining both exchange rates and access to liquidity. The move to floating rates among the major currencies in 1973 was, in effect, a surrender to market forces: governments acknowledged that they could no longer maintain official parities against the weight of speculative sentiment. Likewise, reliance on the financial markets to recycle petrodollars after each of the two oil shocks effectively conceded to the private sector a share of control over access to liquidity as well.[16] In the words of one former central banker, "The private banking system took over the functions proper to an official institution possessed of the power to finance balance-of-payments disequilibria through credit-granting and to create international liquidity.... The function of creating international liquidity has been transferred from official institutions to private ones."[17] The regime, in short, became to a significant extent "privatized."

It is also ironic that as the regime became increasingly privatized, banking inevitably became more and more politicized as well, in the sense of heightening awareness on both sides of the dialectic to the growing connections between high finance and high politics. Banks and the government alike, not to say many other interested parties—including public opinion at large—had their level of consciousness raised by events like the Iranian asset freeze and the Latin American debt crisis. Each side has been forced to think more about the indirect influences of the other.

Banks certainly have grown more sensitive to political considerations in their thinking. We saw in chapter 2 the extent to which, in their international activities, they have come to function largely as intermediaries between national sovereignties. Today, bankers acknowledge, they have no choice but to pay more attention to foreign policy issues in the ordinary course of their business.

Of course, banks have long engaged in formal political-risk analysis. Particularly in the 1970s, with the growth of large-scale sovereign lending, institutions endeavored to develop practical techniques for integrating political factors systematically into their ongoing commercial decisions. Approaches vary, depending on the needs and resources of individual institutions. Some banks rely primarily on qualitative assessments employing checklists of various kinds; others seek greater mathematical rigor in quantitative or even econometric ranking systems. Some depend on inputs from officers in the field, while others rely mainly on the evaluations of analysts in the head office. But whatever the approach employed, the main objective is to arrive at "country limits" that will presumably balance perceived risks and returns by constraining a bank's exposure in various ways, for example, by ceilings on short-term and long-term lending, letters of credit, and the like. Some of the formal evaluation systems currently in use in the United States, especially in major money-center banks, have achieved a notably high order of sophistication.

In most approaches, the primary focus has always been on domestic political factors in borrowing countries—variables that might affect either the ability or the willingness of a government to continue servicing foreign debt without delays or default. Key social indicators are tracked that might highlight potential sources of political instability or upheaval. But increasingly, as their dealings with national sovereignties have grown, banks have begun explicitly to factor in external political considerations as well—the potential for instability or upheaval in a country's foreign relations, especially with Washington. These considerations too affect the calculus of prospective financial risks and returns. Bankers need no instruction in the perils of doing much business with nations that are at odds politically with the United States. Intergovernmental tensions not only threaten a nation's economic prospects but could translate into tensions between Washington and the banks as well. Nor is it irrational for banks to favor greater involvement in countries where the United States is clearly committed to protecting its diplomatic interests; that may simply be financial wisdom. The foreign policy environment, through such considerations, has come to play a key role in bank decision making, both on a day-to-day basis and in terms of broader operational strategies.

Certainly evidence for such influence exists. We know, for example, that U.S. banks tend to be most involved in Western alliance countries or elsewhere where America may be said to have special political or security relationships (for example, Turkey and Yugoslavia in Europe, Israel and Egypt in the Middle East, Korea and the Philippines in the Far East). There also seems to be an accelerating tendency for the level of

lending in individual countries to correlate more closely with
movements of the diplomatic barometer. An early illustration
occurred in 1970, when Salvador Allende was elected president of Chile and relations with Washington began to deteriorate. Credits from U.S. banks rapidly dried up, whereas
three years later, when Allende was overthrown by pro-U.S.
generals, the pattern quickly reversed itself. "As soon as we
heard that Allende had been overthrown," one banker said,
"I got on a plane and went straight back in."[18] There is no
evidence that any of this was the result of overt manipulation
by the U.S. government. More recently, such examples have
multiplied. In the late 1970s, lending to Jamaica dwindled
under "democratic socialist" Michael Manley, a sharp critic
of U.S. "imperialism," only to resume immediately when his
government was replaced by a conservative, pro-Western
administration in late 1980. Similarly, business picked up
smartly in Egypt in the late 1970s after Anwar Sadat threw
out his Soviet military advisers and promoted a diplomatic
tilt toward the United States. And even more recently, all new
lending to Nicaragua was effectively halted after the successful Sandinista revolution. Conversations with bankers
suggest that such sensitivity to foreign policy considerations
today is by no means exceptional.

The question, from a public-policy point of view, is how
bankers arrive at their understanding of these foreign policy
considerations. How accurate are their perceptions of the
present or future diplomatic environment? Essentially, this
becomes a question of how effective the public authorities are
in communicating their policy programs and priorities to the
banks. Even apart from any direct political interventions in
the marketplace, commercial decisions may be affected in-
advertently by the flow of information (or misinformation)
from Washington, as we shall see in part II. Put differently,
public officials today—whether they intend it or not—have a
growing indirect influence on international banking behavior.
Whether they like it or not, therefore, they have a growing
responsibility to ensure that their foreign policy intentions
are neither misperceived nor misunderstood. Improved communication would not remove all risk of conflicting interests

between the public and private sectors; the divergences of the two sides' underlying motives and goals are too fundamental for that. But insofar as areas of potential friction could be reduced, the chances for a satisfactory balancing of interests should be enhanced. The immediate challenge, once again, is a practical one—to find the most appropriate institutional means for achieving that improved communication.

IV

Do banks have a corresponding responsibility to the government? That depends in large part on one's view of just what it is that banks contribute, from their side, to the continuing dialectic with the public sector. Through their commercial decisions, financial institutions do have an impact, even if unintentional, on the general foreign policy environment. But is that impact disadvantageous to the government? Is it significant? Therein lies the ultimate issue for analysis.

For some observers, there is no question that the impact of international banking is disadvantageous to the government, particularly in the Third World and Eastern Europe, where the volume of private lending in recent years greatly exceeded official flows of funds. By their ongoing decisions affecting sovereign borrowers—to lend or reschedule debt? for which countries? how much? when? on what terms? and under what conditions (if any)?—banks establish priorities among capital-importing nations that amount, in effect, to foreign aid decisions. And since these decisions may depart substantially from the recognized goals and priorities of official policy, they could in turn hamper significantly the effectiveness of existing foreign policy instruments in specific instances. Washington could find it more difficult to support or reward its friends, or thwart or punish its enemies. Generous debt assistance to countries with poor human rights records, for instance, or to regimes that support international terrorism could easily undermine government efforts to exercise influence through the withholding of public moneys; states deemed vital to U.S. security interests could be seriously destabilized if they were suddenly to be "red-lined" by the financial community. Contends one U.S. Congressman, "The large money center banks are the true foreign aid policymakers of the United States." [19]

Clearly, there is some truth in this charge. As *The Banker* has commented, "Bankers assume a political role ... through the mere act of lending on any large scale. The provision of finance to sovereign borrowers ... immediately involves financial intermediaries in passively helping to determine priorities." [20] But equally clearly, it is an exaggeration to thus argue, as one source does, that "private banks are effectively making United States foreign economic policy." [21] Public officials still make policy. What has changed is the nature of the constraints and opportunities that now confront those officials in the international arena. What is not at all clear is that these changes are, on balance, necessarily disadvantageous for foreign policy in the broadest sense of the term.

In the first place, it is necessary to keep in mind the economic dimension of foreign policy. Whatever negative impacts there may be on the government's policy capabilities, we must remember that banks also make a positive social contribution insofar as they help to promote the success of our national economy. International banking brings with it many broad economic benefits. I have already stressed the need to include these gains, as well as noneconomic considerations, in the overall foreign policy calculus.

Second, there is an empirical question. How serious is the problem? The fact that banks may establish priorities that are at variance with the goals of official policy does not mean that they inevitably will do so. As I indicated above, banks today increasingly pay attention to foreign relations in the ordinary course of their business and, to some extent at least, tailor their commercial decisions accordingly. It should be obvious that insofar as flows of funds correlate positively with movements of the diplomatic barometer, rather than negatively, bank decisions may actually enhance, not diminish, the effectiveness of existing foreign policy instruments in specific instances. The Nixon administration's campaign against Salvador Allende after his election was undoubtedly strengthened by the drying up of private credits to Chile. U.S. government support of such strategic allies as Korea and Thailand is undoubtedly reinforced by a continued high level of private bank lending. Sometimes private and public interests converge, sometimes they do not, as we shall see in part II.

Furthermore, even where bank decisions do not appear to conform closely with official priorities, the resulting impacts on policy effectiveness could turn out to be little more than trivial. This applies as much to the funding operations of banks as to their lending activities. To say that foreign policy could be affected is not to say that any such influences are necessarily significant. That remains to be seen.

Finally, and most important, any such impacts will depend on the linkages that are generated as a result of international banking operations, that is, the extent to which otherwise unrelated policy instruments or issues are now explicitly joined for bargaining purposes. Connections may be compelled between different instruments or issues that might not otherwise have been felt necessary; opportunities for connections may be found that might not otherwise have been thought possible. The outcome will be disadvantageous to the government only if the additional constraints imposed on policymakers by these linkages tend to outweigh any new opportunities created for more effective linkage strategies.

Scholars distinguish between two kinds of foreign policy linkages—those that advance the interests of the "linker" at the expense of the "linkee" (what might be called, borrowing from the language of game theory, zero-sum linkages), and those that are mutually advantageous (positive-sum linkages).[22] The former are more familiar in popular discussions and are a customary ingredient in bilateral relations among governments; but the latter are also important, particularly in multilateral negotiations on international regime issues. Each type advances the interests of the linker. The difference between them lies in their impact on the linkee. In zero-sum linkages, the linkee is coerced or threatened into adopting a course of action that would not otherwise have been freely chosen. Leverage is used in one issue area to obtain concessions in another. Positive-sum linkages, by contrast, promote the interests of the linkee as well as those of the linker through mutually beneficial cooperative arrangements. Leverage is used to move both actors toward a superior policy outcome.

For the United States, the internationalization of banking activity has generated linkages of both kinds. Whether they constitute a net plus or minus for U.S. interests, however, is not as obvious as it might seem. For example, the substantial amount of Arab investment in the United States in the 1970s, mostly concentrated in the hands of Saudi Arabia and Kuwait, sometimes used to be said to threaten a potentially dangerous leverage over U.S. foreign policy—a "money weapon," in effect, to pressure Washington on Middle East issues. But such influence can also work the other way, as demonstrated by the Iranian asset freeze of November 1979, which ultimately proved quite instrumental in gaining release of our hostages in Tehran. Likewise, the global debt crisis may be a fertile breeding ground for linkages, such as in the case of Poland, where American bank exposure apparently complicated Washington's efforts to retaliate against the imposition of martial law in December 1981. However, whether in the end U.S. influence over the course of events in that sad country was weakened or strengthened by concern for U.S. banking interests is difficult to say without further careful analysis. Nor is it yet obvious whether the severe debt-service difficulties of Mexico, Brazil, and other Latin American borrowers since 1982 will in the end enhance or diminish U.S. policy interests in that region of the world.

When key sovereign borrowers get into trouble, Washington often feels obliged to respond, however reluctantly, with some sort of support—in effect, to alter tradeoffs among current foreign policy objectives by underwriting the debts in some way. This may be because the borrowers are considered too crucial for U.S. interests to ignore. As the Senate Foreign Relations Committee staff has written, America "has important security interests in other debtor countries....It can hardly afford to stand by and watch the economies of these countries collapse, or to have their governments undermined politically by financial difficulties."[23] Or it may be because of concerns about possible repercussions on the health and stability of American banks or the wider financial or economic system. Either way, debtors gain a new degree of leverage to extract concessions from the U.S. government that might not otherwise be obtainable. These concessions may be financial, trade, or even political.

Financial concessions are the most familiar. In 1979, for example, at a time when it was near bankruptcy, Turkey was able to exploit its strategic position within NATO to persuade the United States and other Western allies to come to its rescue with pledges of special assistance totaling nearly $1 billion. Subsequent aid packages for similar amounts were pledged for 1980 and 1981 as well. Likewise, temporary financial assistance more recently was arranged for several major Latin American debtors that had trouble meeting their obligations to foreign creditors.

There may also be trade concessions. Despite strong domestic protectionist pressures, policymakers have been forced to acknowledge the obvious linkage between trade and finance—that import liberalization could be the only way to enable major borrowers to earn their way out of their debt morass. In the words of one former official,

> We must face the interdependence of the financial and trading systems. External debt only makes sense if the borrower has a reasonable prospect for servicing the debt by exporting goods and services to the lenders.... Ultimately, we, the lenders, will be confronted with a decision—either to open our markets in order to provide outlets to the borrowers for their exports, thus generating revenues in the borrowing countries for debt repayment, or to yield to protectionist pressures and be forced to deal with resultant financial failures.[24]

Finally, even political concessions might be felt necessary. In 1977 the Senate Foreign Relations Committee staff worried that "there appears to be a direct correlation between economic hardship and political repression in many countries. The Carter administration may therefore have to choose between pressing its international human rights effort, and supporting creditor demands for drastic austerity programs that can only be achieved at the expense of civil liberties in the countries that undertake them."[25] One example the committee staff evidently had in mind was the Philippines, Asia's second largest debtor to the banks, where a choice seems to have been made after Ferdinand Marcos's declaration of martial law in 1972 to maintain support of his authoritarian New Society regime on broad foreign policy grounds. Strict domestic controls, including the stifling of political opposition, were justified at the time by the need to preserve the financial viability of an important strategic ally. Later, of course, after the assassination of opposition leader Benigno Aquino in 1983, U.S. policy toward the Philippines shifted significantly in favor of support for greater domestic reform and political liberalization; this was especially evident during the election campaign that brought Corazon Aquino to power in early 1986. Nonetheless, the dilemma outlined by the committee staff continues to confront Washington in a wide range of countries around the world, from Mexico and Chile to Zaire and even South Africa. I shall have more to say about both the Philippines and South Africa in chapter 10.

Concessions, however, may run the other way too. Debt-service difficulties also create opportunities for exerting leverage on borrowers. As we shall see in chapter 8, evidence exists to suggest that at least for a time, the financial problems of some of the major Latin debtors tended to make them more amenable than previously to U.S. influence and more accommodating of Washington's policy preferences. Furthermore, opportunities for positive-sum linkages may have been generated by the debt crisis, through consideration of various ideas for mutually advantageous reforms of the international monetary regime (see chapter 11). All of these would have to be counted as pluses for U.S. foreign policy, to be balanced against the disadvantages of any concessions made to troubled debtors.

In short, there are no absolutes here. International banking may or may not be disadvantageous to the government: bankers are not automatically the villain of the piece. But neither are they mere innocent bystanders, free of accountability of any kind. They too are a source of indirect influence in their continuing dialectic with the public sector. Therefore, they too bear some responsibility for outcomes of the process. If the makers of foreign policy have an obligation to ensure that their intentions are not misperceived or misunderstood, bankers for their part have an obligation to take the fullest possible account of those intentions in their own decision making, so as to make their own contribution to minimizing areas of potential friction. As before, the immediate challenge is practical—to find the most appropriate institutional means for achieving that objective.

V

Many more questions are posed for public policy by the growing interdependence between high finance and high politics than can possibly be addressed systematically in the course of a single book. Parallel to the analytical issues already outlined in this chapter, any number of additional questions can be identified. Economic questions are raised about how to relate international banking issues generally (not just debt) to national trade policy or to overseas investment concerns. Legal questions are raised regarding the taxation of cross-border activity, the extraterritorial application of U.S. financial controls and regulations and, indeed, even the basic issue of the increasingly blurred national identity of banking institutions with widespread foreign operations. And diplomatic questions are suggested by the nature of bank–government relations in other countries and how these should or do relate to banking policy in the United States. What might be the significance of the fact that many banks abroad are state-owned rather than private? What should the U.S. attitude be toward the further establishment of foreign-owned banking offices in the United States? And what role, if any, ought foreign-owned banks to play in the determination of purely domestic U.S. banking policy?

In the interest of analytical coherence, however, none of these additional questions will be taken up in detail here. The essence of the problem is still the same—the potential for conflict of interest between U.S. banks and the government.

This therefore must remain our principal focus. The discussion in this chapter has demonstrated clearly the extent to which the scope for strategic interactions between the public and private sectors has been increased by the internationalization of banking activity: the potential for reciprocal influences, direct as well as indirect, has now become quite considerable. The overriding challenge for public policy today, as indicated earlier, is to manage the relationship in a manner that satisfactorily balances the interests of both the banking community and U.S. foreign policy. Bankers and policymakers must find a new modus vivendi. At the institutional level, to repeat, this calls for appropriate means for achieving mutual accommodation between the two sides. At the substantive level, it calls for new approaches to the potential economic and political costs of international banking, in order to maximize its many benefits. Can these needs be met? That of course is the question that this book aims to answer.

Part II

CHAPTER 4

So What's New?

"There is nothing new under the sun," says the Old Testament book Ecclesiastes. And so it might seem to anyone at all familiar with the history of global finance. International banking did not begin with the Incredible Quarter Century. It was not the internationalization of banking activity after 1960 that was the aberration, but rather the period of retreat and insularity that preceded it. Following the disasters of the 1930s, bankers, quite simply, became intimidated. But it was not in the nature of bankers to remain intimidated for long. Their competitive instincts, their drive for profits are too relentless for that. Repeatedly, over the longer course of history, new generations of financiers have restlessly thrust outward in search of fresh horizons, forgetting—or conveniently ignoring—any setbacks of the past. Falling prey to disaster myopia, they have time and again, despite recognized hazards, allowed themselves to become intimately involved with governments both at home and abroad. High finance has often been closely linked with high politics. There is nothing new about that.

So what *is* new? The answer, obviously, lies in the details. Ecclesiastes did not get it quite right. History does have a frustrating tendency to repeat itself—yet never in precisely the same way. The form is theme and variations, not rondo;

and the variations, too, are important. Between earlier epochs and the contemporary era there are broad similarities but also profound differences. To gain a fuller appreciation of the issues for policy today, it is necessary to comprehend both.

I

International banking normally tends to be an attractive and profitable business. Moreover, as a historical phenomenon it has usually been socially beneficial as well, promoting the spread of economic growth around the globe, often for decades on end, via flows of capital from areas of surplus savings to regions of high investment opportunities. The world today would undoubtedly be a far poorer place had there been no international intermediation by the private financial markets over the centuries. Unfortunately, international banking also tends to be an exceptionally vulnerable business, particularly when lenders become too intimately involved with governments. Economic or political disasters occur from time to time, causing traumatic losses or even ruin for investors. Long periods of remunerative activity alternate with briefer episodes of calamity and collapse. Such a recurrent pattern has been evident in high finance ever since systematic banking records began to be kept in the early years of the Renaissance.

Although no adequate documentation exists prior to the thirteenth century, it is known that international banking goes back at least to the second millennium before the common era, when Babylonian temples under the code of Hammurabi safeguarded the idle funds of the wealthy and extended loans to merchants to finance the movement of goods. Likewise, during the period of Greek ascendancy in the ancient world (roughly 500 to 300 B.C.), "banks" regularly advertised interest for deposits and loans and routinely handled foreign money payments. And under the Roman Empire a variety of financial instruments were legalized, such as bills of exchange, to help promote regional (international) trade. During the Dark Ages, most such activity disappeared. But with the coming of the Renaissance, international banking again emerged as a powerful force on the landscape.

The earliest documented banks originated in the various city-states of Italy, as a result of the revival of European trade in the twelfth and thirteenth centuries. Although medieval laws forbade the practice of usury, newly emergent merchant houses found that profits could be made from dealing in currencies as well as goods, particularly through the use of bills of exchange providing for remittance of money and settlement of accounts at a distance. Such services could be performed without shipping any actual coins because many merchants, having international business, held assets at a number of points on key trading routes. For a consideration, instructions could be accepted to pay out money through an agent or correspondent elsewhere to a named party, the amount of the bill being debited by the agent from the merchant-banker's own account. Since there was always the possibility of a loss in such transactions (for example, if the drawer of the initial bill would not pay, or if the correspondent failed to make the funds available), they were not regarded as usorious by church authorities. From such activities, it was only a short step to start accepting deposits and making loans as well. By the fourteenth century, merchant-banking dynasties had sprung up in most of the Italian city-states.

Formally, these dynasties were merchants first and bankers second. Their origins and principal interests lay in trade, selling goods on consignment, or investing for their own account in the manufacture and shipment of such commodities as alum, silk, spices, and wool. But once drawn into the realm of currency dealing, they found the temptation to expand banking-type operations difficult to resist. Deposits from the clergy and wealthy noblemen were a convenient way of supplementing their own narrow capital base; credits to customers, initially in the form of simple overdraft facilities, were a natural extension of their mercantile activities. Moreover, given their often extensive networks of branches, subsidiaries, and representative offices in trading centers throughout Italy and elsewhere (for example, Antwerp, Bruges, London, and Lyon), their banking operations were inevitably international in character. The Italian term for them was *banchi grossi* (great banks)—the multinational banks of their day.[1]

The strength of the *banchi grossi* lay in the wide range of financial services they could provide to customers, not unlike today's multinational banks. Like today's multinationals, also, they came increasingly to function as intermediaries between different sovereign entities (including the clergy and nobility). For many of the *banchi*, this politicization of operations ultimately proved fatal.

For example, in fourteenth-century Florence, the leading banking center of the Renaissance, the most powerful houses were the Bardi and the Peruzzi. Both, however, collapsed following defaults on extensive loans to monarchs such as Edward I and Edward II of England and Robert of Anjou, king of Naples. One source describes these loans as "the first instance of international lending by the forerunners of modern banks to the forerunner of modern governments."[2] In principle such loans, which were made on a fixed-rate basis, were fully secured by collateral consisting of crown jewels or other saleable valuables, customs or tax receipts, or the proceeds of sales of products from royal monopolies. But as a matter of practice, little recourse was possible in those days once a ruler fell into arrears. Instead, the *banchi* found themselves in a dilemma that any international bank today, mired in Latin American sovereign debt, will find disturbingly familiar:

> Instead of being repaid, the lender was willy-nilly forced to lend more and to throw good money after bad in the hope of saving what he had already lent. Once engaged in making advances to princes, it was impossible to pull out and to retrench without courting disaster. Inevitably the lender was sucked deeper and deeper into the whirlpool.... And a banker who had been pressed dry was mercilessly dropped like an orange whose juice had been squeezed out.[3]

A fate similar to this befell the famous Medici Bank in the fifteenth century. Founded in Florence in 1397 by the legendary Cosimo de' Medici, the Medici Bank quickly grew to become the largest banking house of its time, with branches in Britain and all across the continent of Europe. Initially, all loans to princes were forbidden; Cosimo had no desire to be pressed dry like his predecessors. But even before his death in 1464, this prohibition was being gradually relaxed at the behest of ambitious branch managers eager to expand their lending activity, even at the risk of being sucked deeper into the whirlpool. Not surprisingly, one branch after another soon got into trouble and ultimately had to be liquidated or reorganized. Finally, in 1494, the house itself came to grief, as the new republican regime in Florence confiscated its assets and drove the Medici family into exile.

Typical was the experience of the Medici branch in London, which foundered as early as 1464, the year of Cosimo's death, owing to excessive loans to Edward IV. The loans were the quid pro quo demanded by King Edward for permission to export English wool to Italy; eventually they grew to a sum equal to more than four times the branch's own capital. In the end, the cost of borrowing funds to carry these nonaccruing loans, coupled with periodic defaults caused by the War of the Roses, exhausted all of the branch's profits. In similar fashion, the Bruges branch was ultimately ruined by large-scale lending to Charles the Bold of Burgundy, who died in battle in 1477, and to his successors, Mary of Burgundy and her impecunious husband, Archduke Maximilian of Austria. Charles's reckless military campaigns and Maximilian's spendthrift ways made default on these loans inevitable, leading directly to the branch's failure.

Perhaps most interesting, from this book's point of view, is the story of the Milan branch, which became heavily embroiled in loans to the Ducal Court of Francesco Sforza, largely for reasons of state. In this case, involvement with the duke was undertaken with the full support and encouragement of Cosimo, who at the time was actively promoting an alliance of Florence with Milan aimed at preventing Venice from disturbing the balance of power in Italy. Politically, the policy worked—though only with calamitous financial results for Cosimo's Milan branch. As the historian of the Medici Bank has pointed out:

Everything went well with the Milan branch for a few years, during which loans to the Sforza court were kept within bounds. Nonetheless, the policy adopted ... with Cosimo's approval led to a slippery path. ...

Instead of financing business ventures, such loans encouraged conspicuous consumption or helped to finance the exploits of condottieri. From the point of view of the banker, they involved dangerous immobilization of funds because rulers tended to pay off maturing obligations by contracting new loans without ever extinguishing the debt.[4]

Nor were Italian houses alone in risking the "slippery path" of sovereign lending. Half a century after the Medici Bank's demise, the south German Fugger family became similarly mired in loans to princes, mostly to various members of the Hapsburg dynasty. Starting with a few advances to monarchs such as Charles V and his brother, the king of Rome, the Fuggers gradually grew to become, in effect, bankers to an empire. Loans for political purposes became increasingly common, and risk became increasingly concentrated. By the middle of the sixteenth century, Hapsburg loans amounted to more than twice the Fugger Bank's total capital. As time went by, the Fuggers too found themselves sucked into the whirlpool, forced to lend more and more in a frantic effort to protect their existing investment. Collateral, in the form of pledged tax receipts, often proved worthless, particularly with the waning of Hapsburg political fortunes in Spain and the Netherlands. Finally, in 1650, after a series of agreed moratoria, the bulk of the loans were written off, in effect wiping out most of the bank's earnings over the whole of the previous century.[5]

Why did the Renaissance banks so often risk the slippery path? To recall the question posed in chapter 2: How could they have let it happen? Raymond de Roover offers one explanation—needs of commerce. "Such loans were a perennial threat to the solvency of medieval companies. Yet [they] always became involved in them, probably because it was difficult to avoid doing business with courts, a major outlet for the luxury products in which they were dealing."[6] In this respect they were quite unlike modern banks, which do not have such mercantile interests. Being traders as well as bankers, the medieval companies had little choice but to seek sales where they could find them—though, of course, once they did become financially committed, their plight became remarkably similar to that of the large international banks today. Politics became crucial to their continued solvency.

Another reason was that, like modern banks, the medieval companies engaged in a certain amount of self-deception—in this instance, convincing themselves that by securing their sovereign loans with collateral of various kinds, they could protect themselves against default. In fact, the collateral proved to be no shelter at all. About 1480, Archduke Maximilian pledged a costly jewel, the rich fleur-de-lys of Burgundy, as security for his loans from the manager of the Medici's Bruges branch. De Roover wryly comments, "Crown jewels are a poor substitute for cash, especially when interest charges are piling up."[7] Likewise, when push came to shove, promises of customs or tax receipts turned out to be of remarkably little value. The Bardi and Peruzzi initiated their lending to the English kings, beginning with Edward I, only in return for a claim on England's tax on wool exports. As foreigners, however, they were in no position to collect the tax themselves, should the need arise. Hence when Edward III, upon ascending the throne in 1327, repudiated the debts of his predecessors, the Italian houses could do little about it. Nor could the Fuggers do much when assigned tax revenues declined because of the political reversals of the Hapsburgs. Although Renaissance bankers were not without a certain measure of influence, ultimately they were at the mercy of the whims or welfare of their princely clients.

Perhaps the principal reason for the medieval companies' hazardous commitment to sovereign lending, however, was their need to employ idle financial resources. Once having begun to accept deposits—at a price, of course—they had no choice but to lend the money out again, hopefully at a better price. Just like the major international banks after 1973, they needed customers to absorb their excess liquidity; and like

contemporary banks, they found a ready market in the vo-
racious needs of national rulers, sometimes with fatal consequences. Again to quote the Medici Bank's historian,

> Rather than refuse deposits, the Medici succumbed to the
> temptation of seeking an outlet for surplus cash in making
> dangerous loans to princes. This policy proved to be their
> undoing as it had caused the ruin of the Peruzzi in the
> fourteenth century and later brought the Fuggers to the
> brink of bankruptcy.... The case of the Medici is no ex-
> ception.[8]

II

Throughout the Renaissance, one of the most tempting of all
markets for excess liquidity seemed to lie directly to the north,
across the English Channel. In the words of Anthony Sampson, "To these Italian bankers England was a wild developing
country on the edge of their world, a kind of medieval Zaire."[9]
With the coming of the Industrial Revolution, however, England's economy was transformed dramatically into the greatest commercial and financial power of the world. From
peripheral borrower, the country grew into the biggest exporter of capital the world had ever seen, with of course great
economic benefits for the English themselves. Over one-
quarter of England's national wealth came to be held in foreign assets, and on average about half of all domestic savings
was exported annually. The City of London took over as the
center of global finance, and British financial institutions
dominated the market for international lending. The only serious competition came from France, Germany, and, after the
turn of the century, another "wild developing country on the
edge of their world"—America.

Overall, the scale of lending in the nineteenth century
was unprecedented. England's dominance is well illustrated
by table 4.1, which summarizes the positions of the main
creditor countries on the eve of World War I. [10] Of the estimated $45 billion of foreign long-term investment then out-
standing, the British alone accounted for nearly half (44

percent)—more than twice France's total claims and more than three times Germany's. The United States in 1914 was still a net debtor nation (with foreign liabilities of $7.1 billion more than offsetting its $3.5 billion of assets). Other international creditors, like Belgium, the Netherlands, Sweden, and Switzerland, were relatively minor players in the game.

As can be seen in the table, England's investments were widely dispersed geographically. As Herbert Feis wrote, "There were few governments in the world to which the English people did not make a loan, few corners in which some enterprise was not financed from London."[11] This followed naturally from the irresistible spread of British commerce throughout the world as well as the global reach of an empire on which the sun never set. The greatest share of the lending, not surprisingly, was directed toward the empire itself, including the self-governing dominions, and toward English-speaking America. But large sums were invested as well in Latin America and even in China and Japan. Earlier in the nineteenth century, London had also been the main source of finance for continental European borrowers. But after the rise of competing financial centers across the Channel, in Paris, Berlin, and elsewhere, British holdings on the Continent went into relative decline, dropping to only about 5 percent of total claims by 1914. The continental centers, by contrast, focused well over half of their lending within Europe itself, particularly to czarist Russia, the Mediterranean and Balkan states, and to Turkey, which then was of course still very much regarded as a European power. The relatively small amount of U.S. foreign lending was concentrated almost exclusively in Canada and Latin America.

Led by British institutions, banks in the nineteenth century promoted two distinctly different types of international lending—trade financing and investment banking. The former, short-term commercial lending on the traditional basis of bills of exchange (also referred to as acceptance credits), was typically used to finance commodity exports and imports or to deal in foreign exchange. The latter, a pioneering development of the era consisting of the placement of long-term funds in fixed-interest securities on an agency or underwriting

TABLE 4.1. Geographical Distribution of Foreign Investments of Leading Capital-Exporting Countries, 1914 (in millions of dollars)

To	From	U.K.	France	Germany	U.S.A.	World[a]
Europe	Total	1,050 (8.75%)	4,700 (39.2%)	2,550 (21.25%)	700 (5.8%)	12,000 (100%)
North America						
U.S.A		4,250	400	900	—	7,100
Canada		2,800	100	200	900	3,850
	Total	7,050 (63.5%)	500 (4.5%)	1,150 (10.4%)	900 (8.1%)	11,100 (100%)
Latin America						
Mexico		500	400	n.a.	850	2,200
Cuba		150	—	—	350	500
Argentina		1,550	400	200		2,950
Brazil		700	700	500	} 450	2,200
Chile		300	50	n.a.		
Peru		150	—	100		} 1,000
Uruguay		200	50	n.		
Rest		100	n.	n.	—	100
	Total	3,700 (41.8%)	1,600 (18.1%)	900 (10.2%)	1,650 (18.5%)	8,900 (100%)
Oceania						
Australia		1,700	100	—	—	1,800
New Zealand		300	—	—	—	300
Rest		200	—	—	—	200
	Total	2,200 (95.7%)	100 (4.3%)			2,300 (100%)
Asia						
Turkey		100	650	450	—	1,200

India and Ceylon	1,850	—	—	—	1,850
Indo-China	—	200	—	—	200
Straits Settlements	150	n.	n.	n.	200
Dutch East Indies	300	150	250	n.	1,950
China	600	700	250	50	1,600
Japan	500	200	200	50	1,000
Rest	150	n.	n.	150	300
Total	3,550 (50.0%)	1,250 (17.6%)	700 (9.9%)	250 (3.5%)	7,100 (100%)
Africa					
Egypt	200	500	—	—	700
British West Africa	200	—	—	—	200
South Africa	1,550	100	—	—	1,650
Rhodesia	250	—	—	—	250
British E. and Cent. Africa	150	—	—	—	150
French North Africa	—	200	—	—	200
French Africa (So. of Sahara)	—	100	—	—	100
German Colonies	—	—	400	—	400
Belgian Congo	—	—	100	—	300
Rest	100	—	—	—	100
Total	2,450 (60.5%)	900 (22.2%)	500 (12.3%)	—	4,050 (100%)
World	Grand Total	20,000 (44.0%)	9,050 (19.9%)	5,800 (12.8%)	3,500 (7.8%)	45,450 (100%)

Source: William Woodruff, *Impact of Western Man* (New York: St. Martin's Press, 1967), chapter 4, based on estimates from a variety of published sources.

n.a. = not available   n. = negligible

[a]Estimates for the world as a whole include a total of $7,700 million of claims attributed to other net capital-exporting countries (Belgium, the Netherlands, Sweden, and Switzerland) and net debtors (Japan, Portugal, and Russia).

basis, was used more for infrastructural and industrial investment. Both types of activity tended to bring banks into intimate involvement with governments; and as during the Renaissance period, the resulting politicization of their operations sometimes proved hazardous to them in the extreme.

Typical of the trade-financing type of activity were the operations of Baring Brothers, a London company established in the mid-eighteenth century by the sons of a German immigrant cloth merchant.[12] On the strength of long-standing commercial links in the United States, Barings offered lines of credit to American commodity exporters and trading houses interested in drawing sterling bills in London, even functioning for a time, in its capacity as London correspondent of the Bank of the United States, as semiofficial banker to the U.S. government. (It was to Barings that Thomas Jefferson turned to find the $15 million he needed to finance the Louisiana Purchase in 1803.) Through prudent lending policies and good economic intelligence, the company was able to weather a series of public and private defaults through the early part of the nineteenth century and maintain a good profit record. In 1837, during a particularly severe crisis, it was the only Anglo-American financing house to survive without assistance from the Bank of England (which by then, although still privately owned, had already begun to function as the equivalent of a central bank, acting as a lender of last resort to other banks in distress). By the middle of the century, Barings had become one of the largest and most respected private banks in London, increasingly prominent in investment banking as well as trade financing.

However, from success grew complacency, and as the century wore on the company's lending policies became increasingly risky. Driven, like the medieval companies before it, to find outlets for excess liquidity, Barings tied up more and more of its funds in Latin America, especially in Argentina, which the directors of the house regarded as a kind of special business preserve. To quote again the colorful words of Anthony Sampson, "They had not reckoned with the ability of the Argentinians to wreck their own country."[13] In the late 1880s, in particular, at a time of market weakness for long-term Argentine securities, Barings felt obliged to lend heavily to the authorities in Buenos Aires through an ever-larger accumulation of short-term acceptance credits—much of which, it turned out, went to line the pockets of corrupt politicians. The turning point came in the summer of 1890, when the Bank of England privately warned Barings to limit the level of its exposure. Unfortunately, the warning came too late. The company was too deep into the whirlpool, holding more than £30 million of questionable bills. By November of that year rumors began sweeping the city that Barings was about to collapse.

A failure of Barings, however, was the last thing that the Bank of England wanted. Just as during the Latin American debt crisis of our own day, priority during the Baring crisis was placed first and foremost on preserving investor confidence. Just as occurred in 1982–83, an international rescue operation was mounted to keep the company in business. A total of £17 million, enough to cover most of Barings's own liabilities, was raised from the Bank of England, the Bank of France, the British Treasury, other London banking houses, and even the new American bank of J. P. Morgan; and a special Argentine Committee, was organized under the leadership of the Rothschild Bank to supervise a restructuring of Argentina's foreign debt. The role played by the committee, which included imposing economic policy conditions on the Argentine government, was closely parallel to that played by the International Monetary Fund in Latin America and other debtor regions today. As for Barings itself, its reputation being irreversibly damaged, the house was reconstructed as a limited company and eventually faded to the ranks of the also-rans. Once again, a bank had risked all and lost on the slippery path of sovereign lending.[14]

III

Trade financing, however, was only a relatively small part of the story in the nineteenth century. Far more important—and certainly most characteristic of the age—was the development of investment banking, which accounted for the great bulk of

the international lending recorded in table 4.1. In this business, financial houses acted primarily as agents or underwriters for the placement of long-term debt or equity issues with
the broader investing public, rather than as lenders on their
own account—intermediaries in the truest sense of the term.
Risk was borne by the tens of thousands of individual savers
who invested in the capital market, rather than directly by
the shareholders or partners of banks themselves.

In institutional terms, practices differed from country to
country. In England, a clear dividing line generally was maintained between, on the one hand, the commercial banks and
similar institutions (for example, so-called overseas banks—
British-owned companies operating exclusively in foreign
countries), which concentrated mostly on short-term trade
financing, foreign-exchange dealing, and the like; and on the
other hand, the various underwriters, brokers, and investment
companies that collectively "made" the longer-term issues
market, headed most prominently by powerful private banks
like Rothschilds, Barings, Brown Shipley, and Schroders. Occasionally the line might be crossed, as Baring Brothers did
in the run-up to the crisis of 1890, substituting short-term
acceptance credits for Argentina when longer-term bonds
could not be sold. Conversely, commercial banks might also,
on occasion, by their loans or purchases, indirectly facilitate
capital-market operations. But only rarely did the latter participate actively in the spread of new securities among the
British people. On the Continent, by contrast, it was much
more common for the two types of activity to be combined
in a single institution, for example, the Crédit Mobilier in
France or the Great Banks of Germany (most notably, the
Four D's—Deutsche, Diskonto, Dresdner, and Darmstadter).
And in the United States too, the two types of activity were
often merged (until the Glass-Steagall Act of 1933).

Whatever the specifics of each country's institutional arrangements, though, they all tended to share one characteristic—an enormous appetite for foreign lending, particularly
sovereign loans or their close equivalent. Most international
lending in the nineteenth century was accomplished through
purchases of fixed-interest government bonds or railway

TABLE 4.2. Growth of Foreign Investment of Leading Capital-Exporting Countries, 1825–1914 (in millions of dollars)

	1825	1840	1855	1870	1885	1900	1914
United Kingdom	500	700	2,300	4,900	7,800	12,100	20,000
France	100	300	1,000	2,500	3,300	5,200	9,050
Germany	—	—	—	—	1,900	4,800	5,800
United States	—	—	—	—	—	500	3,500

Source: William Woodruff, *Impact of Western Man* (New York: St. Martin's Press, 1967), chapter 4, based on estimates from a variety of published sources.

shares (railways, although mostly private, being treated in effect as quasi-governmental entities, owing to the close political and financial support they received). In 1913, according to Feis, fully 70 percent of all British overseas investments were in railways or government bonds; likewise, though documentation is scarce, it appears that "well over half" of France's investments consisted of sovereign loans, and "substantially more than half" of Germany's.[15]

As table 4.2 indicates, lending got started early in both England and France, almost as soon as the Napoleonic Wars ended, and continued to accelerate right up to the outbreak of World War I, with Germany joining the game after Bismarck's unification of the empire in 1870, and the United States coming in around the turn of the century. Periodically, uncontrolled speculative frenzies led to widespread defaults and losses to investors. Charles Kindleberger, a leading student of financial history, identified major international crises in 1819, 1825, 1828, 1836–38, 1847–48, 1857, 1864, 1866, 1873, 1882, 1890, 1893, and 1907, each followed by a temporary "revulsion" against new overseas lending.[16] Yet never for long: such was the enthusiasm of investors for the higher yields and glamour of foreign securities that very soon the process would pick up again more or less where it had left off. Disappointment tended to yield quickly to renewed euphoria in nineteenth-century capital markets.

This was especially true in the London market. In the words of one noted historian, "No country was so willing as

England to expand credit beyond the limits of commercial prudence."[17] Wrote another, "Any government which claimed sovereignty over a bit of the earth's surface and a fraction of its inhabitants could find a financial agent in London and purchasers for her bonds."[18] During the early 1820s, for example, following the breakup of the Spanish and Portuguese colonial empires in the New World, London was swept by a mania for loans to the new republics of Latin America. Not for the first time were investors badly burned as a result:

> The young republics had not yet succeeded in establishing internal order or settled government, while they were so feeble and impoverished that even their ability to maintain their independence was still in doubt; nevertheless, they all succeeded in their quest. In rapid succession issues were floated on behalf of Colombia, Chile, Peru, Buenos Aires, Brazil, Mexico, and Guatemala. The houses ... which undertook the bulk of this business issued prospectuses, circulated news and disseminated pamphlets, all representing the political situation, economic resources and potentialities of the borrowing states *couleur en rose*. The English investor ... was inexperienced, eager for high yields and in a feverishly speculative temper. Throwing discretion to the winds, he readily swallowed these puffed and highly colored descriptions.... The proceeds ... the borrower quickly expended on armaments, or otherwise wastefully dissipated, with little regard to the quite different purposes for which, in many instances, the loan had been ostensibly raised.... When these were exhausted, the debtor country, with only one or two exceptions, found itself utterly unable to make any payments out of its own resources, and default inevitably and promptly ensued.[19]

Nonetheless, London's enthusiasm for foreign issues persisted. In the 1830s, a new mania developed for the bonds of American states borrowing to finance canal and railway construction—almost all of which went into arrears in the early 1840s, after a collapse of cotton prices. Though most states subsequently did resume interest payments, eventually reaching a settlement on all or part of their loans, a few did not. To this day, Mississippi is still listed in London as a bad debtor. And then in the 1850s and 1860s there was yet another wave of interest in Latin American issues, followed once again by collapse after a sharp downturn in the world economy in the early 1870s. Carried away by their own fervor, investors put money down on flagrantly fraudulent or even imaginary offerings. In one famous case a Scottish adventurer named Gregor MacGregor persuaded a London house to market a £200,000 loan to the State of Poyais, an imaginary republic on the Mosquito Coast of Nicaragua; and despite the death of colonists who actually tried to go out and find Poyais, he was able to accomplish the same feat again, for another imaginary kingdom, just two years later. In 1873–74 alone, the governments of Bolivia, Costa Rica, Guatemala, Honduras, Paraguay, Peru, Santo Domingo, and Uruguay all defaulted on their English bonds.

Nor were the English alone. Continental investors too exhibited a periodic impulse toward madness in the markets. Though British savers suffered most, in absolute terms, from state insolvencies over the course of the century, considerable losses were experienced in Paris and Berlin as well, particularly during the era's closing decades. As indicated, the bulk of lending by the continental centers was focused within Europe itself. French and German bondholders were repeatedly burned by defaults, at various times, by the governments of Spain (on seven separate occasions), Portugal (four times), Turkey (three times), and Greece (twice) among others. The high (or low) point was reached in 1880 when, according to one estimate, fully 54 percent of all foreign government obligations outstanding in major capital markets were in default.[20] But debt-service problems also kept cropping up in subsequent years: for German investors in the Balkans in the 1890s, for instance, and for French investors in North Africa in the early 1900s. And of course there were the spectacular losses incurred by French *rentiers* in 1917 after repudiation of their czarist bond holding by the new Soviet revolutionary government. At a stroke, one quarter of all French foreign investments were wiped out forever.

Periodic frenzies of international lending are nothing new, of course. Such manias are a common theme in financial history, from the bankers of the Renaissance to the South Sea bubble of 1720 to the Incredible Quarter Century of our own age. Once again investors, competing to find outlets for excess liquidity, fell prey to disaster myopia. Risks were discounted: problems of political instability, wasteful expenditures, corrupt administration, and uncollectable collateral were conveniently ignored or underrated. And so once again they gambled—and often lost—on the slippery path of sovereign loans. However, two variations in the nineteenth-century experience deserve particular emphasis here—one at the technical level, one at the political level.

At the technical level, the big difference was the reliance on investment banking in the nineteenth century for the bulk of international lending, shifting most of the direct risk of sovereign exposure from financial houses to the broader investing public. This meant that when debt-service problems arose, or even when whole waves of default broke over the markets, there was relatively little threat to the solvency of financial intermediaries themselves or to the banking system as such. Individuals, not institutions, took the hit. The markets survived to lend another day.

Not that banking institutions were completely immune. Many financial houses did indeed fail in this period, having put too large a portion of their own assets at risk. At midcentury, dozens of banks were established in London and Paris to specialize in the export of capital to selected regions of the developing world. Most closed their doors within a few years owing to massive investment losses. Similarly, France's Crédit Mobilier foundered in 1867 owing, at least in part, to a large loan to finance the emperor Maximilian's disastrous expedition to Mexico. Nor can we forget the Baring crisis of 1890. No small number of companies followed the Bardi and Peruzzi, the Medici and Fuggers into the whirlpool.

Still, these were the exceptions, not the rule. More generally, it was bondholders at large that bore the brunt of state insolvencies. The attractions of sovereign loans were obvious: high yields, liquidity, glamour. But there was also a major disadvantage: lack of effective direct recourse when a foreign government fell into arrears. Claims on a sovereign debtor could not be easily settled through standard court procedures. Rather, investors had to rely mainly on often protracted negotiations with delinquent foreign states. To protect their interests and coordinate bargaining efforts, bondholders banded together in special associations or committees in each of the major creditor countries—not unlike the ad hoc bank steering groups organized to deal with sovereign-debt problems today. Britain's Council of Foreign Bondholders was the first, initially established in 1868 to negotiate with the State of Mississippi over its defaulted bonds dating from the 1830s. (The council still writes regularly to the governor of Mississippi about these bonds, which were formally repudiated in 1875—and is as regularly ignored.) Before the end of the century similar organizations were in operation in all of the continental financial centers. The principal laggard was the United States, where the Foreign Bondholders Protective Council was not formally created until 1933.

Although their bargaining power was limited, bondholder associations turned out to be remarkably successful in salvaging at least a part of their members' investments. Complete repudiation of sovereign debt was comparatively rare in the nineteenth century (unlike the Renaissance period, when creditors could engage in negotiations with defaulting princes only at their peril). More typically, arrears were settled on terms that preserved, at a minimum, some fraction of the interest and/or principal of the original claims, based on a revised evaluation of the debtor's capacity to pay. Terms varied widely, from consolidation and reduction of the face value of existing debt or refinancing at substantially lower rates of interest, to cancellation or capitalization of arrears on more liberal terms. Though payments were often delayed, most issues were in fact eventually redeemed, even if at a loss. The reason was simple. Under existing rules, the leading stock exchanges of Europe refused to list or permit trading of any new issue proposed by a defaulting state. Governments needing to raise fresh funds, therefore, had a strong incentive to reach some form of agreement with creditors about outstanding old debt. This threat of exclusion from the markets gave bondholder associations a not insignificant degree of leverage over debtors—similar, in practice, to the leverage wielded by the large international banks today over debtor countries anxious to preserve their external creditworthiness.

In reality, the pattern was a recurrent one. Countries experiencing debt-service difficulties would typically resort to a suspension of payments for a time. And then, when access to the capital markets was needed again, some kind of settlement would be sought through negotiations with bondholder associations. Bondholders, in turn, anticipating a possible repetition of such difficulties, might demand a considerable "risk premium" on new issues, in the form of steep discounts from face value and/or high interest rates, so that they could afford to take another hit on their earnings should similar problems arise in the future. As compared with net yields on less risky domestic claims, in fact, foreign investments more often than not still came out ahead, even after renegotiation of terms. It was this expectation, most fundamentally, that induced investors to keep lending abroad despite the evident hazards. Few risks seemed serious if the prospective profits were set high enough.

At times, however, negotiations on this pattern proved insufficient. Satisfactory new terms could not be agreed on, despite the mutual interest of creditors and debtors alike in some kind of settlement. Sometimes sovereign borrowers, with even the best of will to meet their obligations, might find themselves overwhelmed by circumstances beyond their control, for example, war, global depression, adverse terms-of-trade shocks, or failed investment schemes. And sometimes they were overwhelmed simply by their own administrative inefficiencies, corruption, or domestic political weaknesses. In such instances, bondholders would often use their bargaining leverage to take charge of a borrower's finances themselves, putting the country in effect into a sort of receivership. A control committee would be set up to restructure the government's debt, administer its revenues, and generally put its financial house in order. The Argentine Committee, formed during the 1890 Baring crisis, was by no means exceptional in this respect. Other similar IMF-type operations were organized elsewhere, for example, in Bulgaria, Greece, Serbia, Persia, and most famous of all, Ottoman Turkey.[21] Under the Decree of Mouharrem of 1881, foreign creditors formally took responsibility for management of the Ottoman government's debt service through a Public Debt Administration run by a seven-member Council of the Public Debt. The members of the council, just as in bank steering groups today, were appointed to represent all major holders of Turkish debt. By the end of the century, the administration effectively controlled as much as one-quarter of all the Ottoman government's fiscal revenues.

Occasionally, even this approach proved unworkable. Debtors became uncooperative, recalcitrant, or worse. At such times, bondholders were not loath to appeal to their home governments for support of their foreign claims; and quite frequently, home governments were not loath to respond in one manner or another—introducing a new degree of politicization into international financial relations. For the first time, the foreign policies of creditor countries, not just debtors, became systematically involved. (Earlier cases, like the Medici Bank's politically inspired loans to the duke of Milan, were isolated episodes; more generally, Renaissance banks were on their own when lending to princes.) This was the big difference in the nineteenth-century experience at the political level.

What explains the willingness of creditor countries to become systematically involved? Home governments took an interest at this time for the same reason that people worry about a bull in a china shop. Given the sheer scale of lending during the nineteenth century, financial relations could hardly be ignored. Policymakers felt they had little choice. The many economic benefits of international investment were recognized, of course, and even encouraged. To recall the language of the previous chapter, the wide range of shared interests between the public sector and private investors was fully appreciated at the time. But policymakers came to understand that there were areas of potential friction as well. The scope for reciprocal influence became evident. Like the

United States today, they were confronted by a need to forge a new relationship with financiers.

Attitudes differed from government to government. The British government, not surprisingly, given its traditional policy of laissez-faire in economic matters, was generally unsympathetic to appeals for support from bondholders. Whitehall preferred to remind investors that they had purchased their bonds voluntarily, at their own risk. Yet the authorities could hardly remain altogether indifferent to the treatment of British nationals by a sovereign elsewhere. At the least, the government encouraged bondholders' representatives to keep it informed on the progress of negotiations with delinquent foreign states. On occasion, it permitted its own diplomatic representatives to perform, on an unofficial basis, various services for investors. And from time to time, it did see fit to provide assistance on an official basis as well. In Whitehall's view, political intervention could be justified in instances where specific revenues that had been pledged as collateral to bondholders were willfully diverted for other purposes. Such behavior, to the Victorian mind, was simply bad faith. In a number of instances, diplomatic pressures were formally brought to bear on debtors to honor their financial commitments. And, in extremis, military force was resorted to, most often in the form of a naval blockade—the origin of the term *gunboat diplomacy*. In one famous incident in Venezuela in 1902 the Royal Navy was successfully used, together with units from Germany and Italy, to force the local dictator, General Cipriano Castro, into a settlement with his foreign creditors. Intervention was justified on the grounds that the Venezuelans had broken existing international agreements regarding the payment of assigned tax revenues.

The French and German governments, by contrast, were far more sympathetic to the claims of their nationals against delinquent debtors. But as one source points out, "In most or all of these cases the intervening powers were motivated more by political considerations than by solicitude for the bondholders."[22] For both countries, in a variation on Clausewitz's famous dictum, private international finance was regarded simply as an extension of diplomacy by other means. Not only were Paris and Berlin quite willing to back their investors with diplomatic pressures or armed intervention, should political interests seem to warrant. More significantly, they were prepared even to push the flow of new lending explicitly in directions that would reinforce national policy priorities. High finance, as a result, became more entangled with high politics than ever before. Herbert Feis summarized the era well in *Europe, the World's Banker*:

> The uses which the spared capital of western Europe found were often determined by political circumstance rather than by economic or financial calculation.... In the lending countries international financial transactions were supervised in accord with calculations of national advantage.... Peoples and governments exerted themselves to direct the capital to those purposes which were judged likely to strengthen the national state ...Capital was called upon to abstain from investment in the lands of potential enemies. It was urged or commanded into the service of allies.... It became an important instrument in the struggle between national states.[23]

Inside Europe, the struggle was particularly keen. It is no accident that the bulk of both French and German loans were focused within Europe itself. France and Germany were the main protagonists in the balance-of-power game, and Europe was their main playing field. The extensive investments of French *rentiers* in czarist Russia, for example, were a direct consequence of national political calculations and encouragement by the Paris government. Anxious to find an effective counterweight to the rising German Empire under Bismarck, Paris successfully used the lure of access to the French capital market in the late 1880s as an inducement to cultivate amicable relations and eventually a military alliance with Russia's rulers, who had previously been undisposed to associate themselves with republican France. The first czarist loans were floated on the Paris Bourse in 1888. The Franco-Russian Entente was signed three years later. Likewise, German investments in Austria-Hungary and Italy were actively promoted as a means of cementing the Triple Alliance at the center of Europe—though in the Italian case at least, without much lasting success. After the turn of the century, Italy turned increasingly to Paris for its financial needs, presaging its later political switch of sides. And of course there was also much financial competition in the Balkans and in Turkey, similarly motivated by diplomatic considerations.

Nor was the struggle confined only to Europe. This was also the era of the New Imperialism, one of the most singular events in modern history. From about 1870 onward, within a span of less than two generations, the major states of Europe, later joined by the United States and Japan, extended their colonial empires to virtually all of the peripheral regions of the Eastern Hemisphere—bringing under their control roughly one-fifth of the world's land area and perhaps a tenth of its population. In this process, high finance once again played a prominent role, particularly in North Africa, where France's protectorates over Tunisia (1881) and Morocco (1912) were both publicly justified by an ostensible need to safeguard the claims of French bondholders. And in the process even Britain got involved, despite its more general scruples about mixing private finance and politics. Exceptions could be made. The best known example was Egypt, nominally a province of the Turkish Empire, which gradually came under de facto English control in the late 1870s as a result of a default by the Egyptian Khedive in 1875–76. Initially London came in simply to take receivership of customs and other revenues that had earlier been assigned as security for the Khedive's foreign loans. But by 1882 the British had maneuvered to become the real governing power in Egypt, motivated in good part by a desire to safeguard their new Suez Canal route to India. An Egyptian protectorate was formally proclaimed in 1914.

The struggle even lapped over into the Western Hemisphere, though with a somewhat different outcome—largely because of the attitude of the United States government. Washington shared many values with the British government—on the one hand, it was generally unsympathetic to appeals for support from investors; on the other, it was concerned to ensure the sanctity of international agreements. But in addition Washington was also determined, on foreign-policy grounds, to prevent any recolonization of the New World through political or military interventions by the Old. The 1902 Venezuelan episode, in particular, raised fears of new annexations by European powers. President Theodore Roosevelt responded by announcing, as a corollary to the Monroe Doctrine, that henceforth the United States itself would assume the responsibility of seeing to it that "backward" states in the hemisphere fulfilled their financial obligations. In subsequent years Washington intervened forcibly in a number of Caribbean and Central American states, including the Dominican Republic, Haiti, Honduras, and Nicaragua, to ensure collection of foreign debts. Liquid assets were seized, and receivers were appointed to administer customs receipts and other fiscal revenues. Although in no instance was any of these nations formally annexed as a colony, the Roosevelt Corollary did help to establish the United States as the de facto hegemonic power of the region.

From the creditor countries' point of view, there seemed many advantages to be gained from this sort of mixing of finance and politics, whether inside Europe or beyond it— new opportunities, in effect, for linkage strategies to cement alliances and extend formal or informal colonial empires. But as matters turned out, there were also distinct disadvantages—most directly, the constraints that were imposed by the problems of foreign debtors. To cite just one example: France's loans to Russia may have been successful in drawing the czar into an anti-German entente. But once committed, the French found that they, too, were onto a slippery path, where diplomatic accommodations as well as new money were needed to protect earlier investments. Concern about possible losses to French *rentiers* led Paris to back new loans to the czar even after his international credit standing was virtually destroyed by Russia's defeat at the hands of the Japanese in 1905. It also led the French authorities, against their better judgment, to back the czar's pan-Slavic aspirations in the Balkans. As Feis described the situation,

Once the sums loaned had grown great they strengthened the necessity of making French foreign policy conform to Russian aims, a further cause of unwillingness to risk the rupture of the alliance. Debtor and creditor were firmly bound to each other, but debtor, in this case, was the more exigent and the more aggressive in political plans.[24]

More generally, the creditor governments found that by involving themselves so systematically in financial relations, they incurred costs that tended to mount greatly over time. These costs were both economic and political, reflecting the issues of efficiency and external relations that are raised whenever public officials consider intervening politically in private international finance (see chapter 3). Economic costs were manifested in the distortions of capital flows that resulted from governmental manipulation. Investors were often encouraged to make loans that were fundamentally unsound, leading to outcomes as calamitous as the fate of the Medici Bank's Milan branch centuries earlier; they were also frequently restrained from making investments that could have been truly productive. Political costs resulted from the addition of a foreign policy dimension to bondholder negotiations with sovereign borrowers. With creditor governments involved, financial disputes came to be taken up as national causes, exacerbating diplomatic frictions and adding to the accumulating atmosphere of tension and animosity. In the end, the creditors all got sucked deeper and deeper into the whirlpool and ultimately into the deepest whirlpool of all—World War I.

IV

From that whirlpool, only the United States emerged comparatively unscathed. When hostilities began in 1914, America was still a net debtor nation—indeed, in gross terms, the largest single debtor anywhere. By the time a peace treaty was concluded five years later at Versailles, America had become financier to the world, eclipsing every other capital-exporting nation. In the 1920s, New York rapidly displaced

London as the center of global finance, and American banking institutions came to dominate the market for international lending as completely as had British institutions in the nineteenth century. England and France declined notably as sources of new funds, and Germany—hobbled by its huge reparations burden—was transformed into one of the biggest borrowers ever.

As indicated earlier, American lending did not even begin until around the turn of the century and was concentrated almost exclusively in Canada and Latin America. (The first record of a public offering of foreign securities in the U.S. capital market dates from 1896.) But almost from the moment the guns of August started shooting in 1914, the United States found itself besieged with requests for funds from Europe and elsewhere. Over the course of the next five years more than $13.5 billion was lent abroad, including $3 billion of foreign issues publicly offered to private American investors (more than three times the total of all such issues in this country prior to 1914) and $10.5 billion of War Loans by the U.S. Treasury to allied European governments. In addition, more than $2 billion of foreign-held American securities were cashed in to help finance war expenditures. By the end of 1919, the United States had become a net creditor to the extent of about $14 billion, second only to Britain (which actually liquidated or lost about 15 percent of its foreign holdings during the war years). Even excluding intergovernmental debts, America was now a net creditor of nearly $4 billion.[25]

Moreover, that creditor position continued to grow through the following decade, particularly after 1924, when U.S. lending soared to ever greater heights. In absolute magnitude, the scale of foreign investment by Americans during the euphoric Roaring Twenties surpassed even the records set by Europeans in the previous century. In the twelve years from 1920 to 1931, no less than $11.5 billion of foreign bond issues were floated in the United States, primarily for private or official borrowers in Europe (40 percent), Canada (30 percent), and Latin America (20 percent). By comparison, international loans in London during this same period amounted to not much more than $6 billion, going mostly to British dominions and colonies; and other financial centers provided little or nothing in the way of new funds internationally. On the eve of the Great Depression, America's net creditor position was up to some $22 billion ($10.5 billion excluding war debts). England had clearly been relegated to second place and France to a distant third.[26]

In one respect, America's lending in the 1920s was strikingly different from foreign lending in the years leading up to World War I. Unlike the European powers earlier, the U.S. government now, more than ever, was reluctant to become systematically involved, either diplomatically or militarily. In this new era of self-conscious isolationism, Washington preferred to leave the allocation of international capital to the marketplace. There were exceptions, to be sure. In several instances, new bond issues were barred for countries that seemed disinclined to service their war debts to the U.S. Treasury. And then of course there was the whole knotty question of German reparations, which could hardly be avoided. Although the United States did not ratify the Treaty of Versailles and had waived all claims to reparations, Washington played a key role in the repeated reschedulings of Germany's overdue obligations, most notably through the Dawes Plan of 1924 and the Young Plan of 1930. But on the whole, policymakers were not eager to mix private finance and politics. In the words of one noted historian, "Financial developments were more closely related to the impact of the war, the evolution of political developments abroad, and the workings of the marketplace than to any official acts in Washington."[27] The great costs, economic and political, that had been incurred because of the new degree of politicization introduced in the nineteenth century were, it seemed, to be avoided if at all possible in the twentieth.

In other respects, however, World War I changed little in international finance. The elements of continuity were strong. For one, investment banking continued to account for the bulk of overseas lending, as it had earlier from Europe. Only a relatively small amount of foreign claims were added directly to the balance sheets of U.S. banks. Most were placed instead with the broader investing public in a business dominated by a handful of giant New York houses including such familiar names as J. P. Morgan, Kuhn Loeb, Brown Brothers, Bankers Trust, Guaranty Trust (later merged with Morgan to form Morgan Guaranty), National City Bank of New York (the forerunner of today's Citibank), and Chase National Bank (forerunner of today's Chase Manhattan). Risks were still borne in large part by individual savers rather than directly by financial intermediaries.

Likewise, in another element of continuity, sovereign loans or their equivalent continued to dominate overall lending totals, as they had earlier in Europe. Of all the foreign bonds floated in the United States in the 1920s, some two-thirds were accounted for by governments or governmental units (42 percent by national governments, 23 percent by states, provinces, departments, or municipalities), and an additional 15 percent by government-controlled corporations.[28] The American investor's enthusiasm for sovereign lending at this time was no less than that of his English and French counterparts in the nineteenth century, despite the known hazards of the slippery path.

Indeed, American investors soon fell prey to the same disaster myopia that had periodically characterized much of the previous era—high finance's own version of a "return to normalcy." As a later analyst pointedly concluded,

> Investors in foreign bonds had not suffered any losses for a long time; on the contrary, they had repeatedly made sizable profits. This pleasant state came to be regarded as normal; investors assumed that the world had entered a period of permanent, defaultless prosperity.[29]

In good part, this optimism was bred of World War I itself. Despite the chaos in both world politics and economics after the hostilities ended, all of the issues that had been publicly floated in the United States during the war were quickly repaid or refunded (except for two Russian loans totaling $75 million that, along with all other czarist debt, were repudiated by the new Soviet government). Investors were not entirely unjustified, therefore, in their complacency. The public's appetite

for the novelty of foreign securities had been whetted. Now
the stage was set for the spirited lending boom that followed:

> In the absence of any previous experience and traditions,
> the New York banking houses plunged with reckless en-
> thusiasm into international lending. They competed with
> each other and with the banking houses of other centres
> for every single loan transaction. It was very easy for any
> foreign Government, province, or municipality to raise
> large loans since lenders were cutting each other's throats
> for the privilege of satisfying the demand for capital. It
> was said at the time that the leading hotels in Germany
> had a very prosperous time because most of their rooms
> were taken by representatives of American financial
> houses who came to Germany to persuade some obscure
> municipality to accept a large loan. While Germany was
> the favourite hunting-ground, other countries also had a
> due share of this lending fever. Huge amounts were lent
> to some continental countries and to every country of
> Latin America. Loans were granted to provinces whose
> very existence was unknown until their names appeared
> on the prospectus. Every device of supreme salesmanship
> was made use of in order to place foreign bonds with an
> ignorant and indiscriminate investing public.[30]

Given such "reckless enthusiasm," so reminiscent of the
periodic frenzies of the nineteenth century, should anyone
have been surprised by the denouement? Little more than a
decade after the end of the Great War came the Great Crash—
the final element of continuity in this experience. Starting in
1931, one country after another suspended debt-service payments, first in Latin America, then in Europe and elsewhere.
Partly this was caused by the depression-induced collapse of
world trade and consequent decline in debtors' export prices,
which deprived countries of needed foreign-exchange earnings. And partly it was due to the abrupt cessation of new
lending out of the United States and other creditor nations,
following Black Thursday on the New York stock market,
which made it impossible for borrowers to refinance maturing

obligations. In a manner similar to that of international banks in the Incredible Quarter Century, lenders first promoted an inordinately high level of loans and then retrenched just when new funds were most needed:

> The volume of overseas lending in the 1920s was certainly too large. A smaller and more stable flow of foreign capital would have been better. Instead borrowing countries were allowed and even encouraged to live beyond their means, and the ready availability of foreign funds postponed the basic readjustments in the balances between debtors and creditors. With ample foreign funds available the economic systems of countries such as Argentina, Brazil and Australia became adjusted to a condition in which new borrowing furnished annually the rights to money abroad to pay for interest charges on old indebtedness. . . . The final mistake of the creditor nations was that, having allowed the debtor nations to run up large obligations, they suddenly turned their backs on their customers at the worst possible moment—like a man being hauled up a cliff by a rope which is slackened before he reaches the top and brings him crashing down.[31]

By the end of 1935, no fewer than fourteen Latin American nations and ten European states, plus Canada and China, were in arrears on interest and/or principal due on at least some of their outstanding obligations, representing in all nearly 40 percent of the value of foreign bonds listed in New York at the time.[32] In addition, following Germany's default in 1931 on its rescheduled reparations, payments on practically all of the Treasury's War Loans were suspended as well. Once again, investors had gambled—and lost.

Investor reactions were also reminiscent of those in the nineteenth century. Organizing themselves into the Foreign Bondholders Protective Council, investors sought to negotiate satisfactory settlements of their claims with delinquent foreign states. Foreshadowing a parallel move in more recent times (see chapter 2), they even created an Institute of International Finance to collect relevant factual information on the financial position of sovereign debtors.[33] Unfortunately, most such efforts went for nought. The disasters of the 1930s proved too overwhelming to permit many governments to honor even a fraction of their external obligations. Investor revulsion, therefore, was total too. Private foreign lending largely ceased for several decades—until the coming of a new generation of bankers in the Incredible Quarter Century.

V

Viewed in historical perspective, then, the Incredible Quarter Century hardly seems novel. Quite the opposite, in fact. The internationalization of banking is a common theme in financial experience, as is the tendency for financial markets at times to get carried away with themselves. Periodic loan frenzies are a veritable leitmotif of banking history. Moreover, there is nothing new about lenders becoming intimately involved with governments: high finance has often intersected with high politics. Today's problems, clearly, have antecedents in the past.

Yet there are also variations, and these matter too. Each historical epoch, including ours, has unique characteristics. We see ourselves in the past—but imperfectly, as through a glass darkly. The challenge is to know what lessons of history are applicable to our own times.

Our own times were supposed to avoid a recurrence of international banking problems. The world of the 1960s and 1970s was intended to be a different place from the 1920s or earlier periods reviewed in this chapter. At the national level, governments had responded to the disastrous interwar experience with reforms designed to strengthen both prudential supervision and monetary management. Central bank powers were reinforced and regulatory authority broadened in the hopes of reducing the recognized risks inherent in private banking activity. At the international level, the Bretton Woods regime and the International Monetary Fund had been created to help restore stability to global financial relations. Yet for all these precautions, history did manage to repeat itself— in its fashion—after all. The precautions proved not to be effective enough. Once again, therefore, we are faced with the need to define the public interest in international banking. What lessons does history teach for the contemporary era?

One lesson is obvious. High finance would benefit from more effective limits on its own excesses. Disaster myopia recurs repeatedly, as new generations of lenders have complacently discounted the risks encountered by their predecessors. Like audiences in a theater, bankers have time and again engaged in willing suspension of disbelief, deceiving themselves by one convenient assumption or another that there was really little to worry about. For the bankers of the Renaissance, it was the conviction that sovereign loans could be secured with collateral of various kinds. For bondholders of the nineteenth century and the 1920s, it was faith in their own bargaining leverage vis-à-vis foreign debtors. Time after time, investors have succumbed to the temptations of reckless enthusiasm. International banks in the 1970s were certainly no exception in that regard.

One way to limit such excesses would be through more prompt and timely regulation or moral suasion—systematic interventions by public officials to temper the drives that naturally result from the intensity of competition in the financial sector. Lenders' animal spirits must be kept firmly in check. As the episodes reviewed in this chapter demonstrate, bankers in the Incredible Quarter Century were by no means the first to get caught up in the momentum of a race to share in an attractive, expanding market. New York banking houses in the 1920s, London investors and French *rentiers* in the nineteenth century, even the branch managers of the Medici Bank all fell victim to the same irresistible impulse. To counter these forces born of competition, governments must be strict in their prudential supervision of banks. Indeed, that is precisely where the public interest in prudential supervision lies. I shall have more to say about this issue in the final chapter of this book.

Likewise, governments must be more strict in their monetary management of banks, to contain any tendency toward prolonged periods of excess liquidity in the international markets. Ever since the Medici Bank, foreign lending manias have been closely associated with an oversupply of capital. Investors have been driven to find outlets for surplus funds. This is precisely where the public interest in monetary management lies. I shall have more to say about this issue too in the final chapter.

A second lesson—in case anyone in this day and age needs reminding—is that cross-border lending is inherently dangerous, owing to the risk of a general foreign-exchange constraint in borrowing nations; and that lending to sovereign governments is potentially the most dangerous activity of all. Ever since the first Edwards of England, princes have at times proved to be exceedingly poor credit risks, often with tragic results for their financiers. Not all the difficulties of debtors have been of their own making, of course. As I indicated, borrowers frequently have been caught up by circumstances beyond their own control—war or political reversals, such as those suffered by the Hapsburgs in the seventeenth century; severe depression or adverse terms-of-trade shocks of the sort experienced by cotton-exporting American states in the 1830s and by Latin American primary producers a century later; or unexpectedly high oil prices and interest rates combined with global recession, as occurred in our own day. But even apart from such exogenous disasters, sovereigns have a troubling penchant for overcommitting themselves at times, owing to the exigencies of budget demands and balance-of-payments deficits. The Incredible Quarter Century was only the latest illustration of how governments cannot always be relied upon to exercise prudential self-restraint in their borrowing. As far back as the Bardi and Peruzzi, lenders have learned the hard way how difficult it may be, once engaged, to extract themselves from the embrace of sovereign debtors without courting disaster. The path is slippery indeed. Once again, the main preventative would appear to be firmer prudential supervision and monetary management.

The third lesson is that there are dangers, too, in systematic political interventions by creditor governments. To attempt to manipulate capital flows explicitly on foreign policy grounds is also to court disaster, as the continental Europeans, in particular, learned in the run-up to World War I. Issues of effectiveness and equity aside, economic and political costs could be considerable. Home governments have a legitimate interest in the overseas activities of their private financial institutions. Reasons of state, however, cannot be used to justify irresponsible exercise of authority. Here too, more prudent self-restraint would appear to be called for if undue politicization is to be avoided.

The fourth lesson is that once debt-service difficulties do arise, there is no realistic alternative to a negotiated settlement of claims. Negotiations may not always succeed, as the experience of the 1930s vividly reminds us. But without negotiations, there are only two other possibilities. One is to rely on the rational self-interest of debtors to honor their commitments so as to preserve their external creditworthiness. Unfortunately, as historical examples stretching from the Italian *banchi grossi* to our own century's Great Depression testify, pure economic rationality may not suffice when it comes to sovereign borrowers. For political or economic reasons, debt payments may simply be suspended indefinitely or even formally repudiated, with consequences that could be fatal to private lenders unless they are sheltered by an umbrella of public assistance. The other possibility, mimicking the nineteenth century, might be to rely on diplomatic or military initiatives by home governments. That route could have fatal consequences in foreign policy terms. In a postcolonial era, private finance and politics can make a highly volatile mixture, to be handled with extreme care. The room for unilateral political interventions on behalf of private creditors is far more constrained than it used to be.

Finally, a fifth lesson is that when negotiations on troubled sovereign debts are in fact undertaken, a little give and take on all sides would appear to maximize chances for success. Here the nineteenth-century experience is especially instructive. Debtors then helped to preserve their creditworthiness by agreeing at times to a degree of foreign participation in the management of their domestic affairs. Public finances were reorganized and economic policy conditions were imposed by consortia of foreign creditors, playing an IMF-type role. In return, some form of debt relief was typically conceded, investors realistically accepting partial losses rather than stubbornly insisting on terms no longer consonant with a borrower's altered capacity to pay. The keynote was flexibility: instead of risking total breakdown, which would have meant losses for all, settlements were sought that would allow a quick resumption of lending. This last lesson, in particular, is well worth recalling as we work our way through the global debt problems of the 1980s.

CHAPTER 5

An Arab Money Weapon?

At the outset of the Incredible Quarter Century, few bankers worried about the potential foreign policy repercussions of their activities. International banking had nothing to do with politics, they insisted. It had to do simply with the accepting of deposits, making of loans, and other commercial services. But that ignored one of the most fundamental features of the internationalization of banking after 1960—banks' growing involvement with governments. Anyone familiar with financial history might have predicted such a trend. Yet it seemed to come as a surprise to many Americans. Indeed, not until the 1970s was there any public debate in the United States about the growing interaction between high finance and high politics.

Ironically, when debate did start, after the first oil shock, concern was expressed much less with the loan side of the ledger than with the deposit side. From a foreign policy point of view, the risk of a debt crisis at the time seemed secondary. The primary challenge appeared to lie, rather, in the rising flood of investments in the United States by petrodollar-rich OPEC governments, led by the biggest oil exporter of them all, Saudi Arabia. Some Americans began to worry out loud that these investments might be used by the Saudis or other Arab states to threaten a potentially dangerous leverage over

119

U.S. foreign policy—as an instrument of linkage, in effect, to pressure Washington on Middle East political or military issues. As the Senate Foreign Relations Committee staff asked in 1977:

> In the event of another major outbreak of hostilities in the Middle East in which the U.S. and Saudi Arabia are likely to find themselves on opposite sides, can one be sure that they will continue to act in the best interest of the Western financial system? Saudi Arabia did not hesitate to use the oil weapon against the United States in the last Mid-East war, despite earlier warm U.S.-Saudi relations; there is no guarantee that next time they won't wield the money weapon, too.[1]

Was the purported Arab "money weapon" a real threat? The question is important not just for the sake of historical curiosity but, more generally, for what it can teach us about intrafinance foreign policy challenges of any kind arising from foreigners' net claims on the U.S. financial system (subset A in table 1.2). In fact, as we shall see, the threat posed after the first oil shock was never so great as it appeared to be to many Americans and is even less dangerous today. Public debate over the issue, quite heated for a time, subsided after the middle of the decade and (despite sporadic efforts in the Congress and elsewhere to revive concern after the second oil shock) eventually faded away more or less anticlimactically in the 1980s. Nonetheless, caveats are in order. Large concentrations of assets in the hands of foreign governments could pose a number of risks for the public interest, and officials must be alert to them. Foreign policy linkages may indeed be created, and capabilities in international diplomacy may indeed be affected.

I

I will begin with some numbers. Statistics, in this case at least, are by no means apolitical. For reasons that are as much diplomatic as technical (see below), available data on Arab investments in the United States still leave much to be desired. Deficiencies persist despite substantial formal improvements in collection and reporting by U.S. government agencies over the years, especially after two major pieces of legislation in the mid–1970s, the Foreign Investment Study Act of 1974 and its successor, the International Investment Survey Act of 1976. Three agencies are principally responsible for these data—the Departments of Treasury and Commerce and the Federal Reserve Board of Governors. The Treasury compiles the most comprehensive statistics, providing considerable detail on Middle Eastern portfolio investments here as well as summary figures for direct investment flows obtained from the Department of Commerce. Additional detail on direct investment is provided by the Commerce Department, while the Federal Reserve supplies information on banking relationships. Yet for all these numbers the picture remains fuzzy at best—and possibly misleading at worst—owing to significant gaps, incompatibilities, and aggregation in the data. Systematic analysis of Arab investments in the United States still requires a large measure of guesswork.

Consider, for instance, the Treasury data. Although these are the most comprehensive, they are nonetheless critically lacking in at least four key respects. First, capital flows and investment positions are reported merely for an eight-nation group labeled Middle East Oil Exporters (Bahrain, Iran, Iraq, Kuwait, Oman, Qatar, Saudi Arabia, and the United Arab Emirates). All other Arab countries are excluded, while one non-Arab country, Iran, is included. Since we have no way of knowing to what extent the financial activities of excluded Arab countries and Iran may be mutually offsetting, we really cannot tell how accurate these figures may or may not be in representing the overall level of investment in the United States by the Arab world as a whole. Of course, given the financial predominance of the gulf oil producers among Arab countries, the loss of precision is not crucial. But the qualification needs to be kept in mind.

Second, the Treasury refuses to disaggregate the data for the eight nations identified in the group, thus making it impossible to trace the behavior of any one country individually. In fact, this has been a bone of contention between the Treas-

ury and some members of Congress, who insist on the legis-
lature's prerogative of access to information in the executive
branch as well as the public's right to know. According to
Treasury officials, a breakdown of the statistics by country is
precluded by the terms of the 1976 International Investment
Survey Act as well as by several other pieces of legislation,
all pledging confidentiality of individual investors' accounts.
Since the principal investor in most of these countries tends
to be the government, disaggregation would be tantamount
to revealing the affairs of individual investors. As a result, we
are necessarily forced to look for clues elsewhere to gain insight into the investment practices of individual Arab
countries.

Third, the Treasury data report bank deposits in the
United States only, excluding deposits in foreign branches of
American banks. Since the latter can also be regarded as a
form of investment in the United States—as liabilities of
American financial institutions, they are certainly a U.S. financial interest—their exclusion may be regarded as a serious
omission.

Finally, the Treasury data fail to take into account investments made through and in the name of financial intermediaries—banks, brokers, and the like. The sensitivity of the
wealthy oil countries to possible disclosure of their foreign
investments is well known. For them, these are strictly confidential matters. Most are thought to take advantage of the
fact that portfolio acquisitions are mainly reported on the
basis of the holder of record, even where assets are held in
nominee or custody accounts, to conceal a substantial portion
of their investments by channeling them through fiduciaries
in Switzerland, the Caribbean, or elsewhere. The Treasury
itself admits to some downward bias in its figures because of
the difficulty of identifying ultimate beneficial ownership in
individual transactions.[2] How much downward bias is of
course difficult to say.

Why such deficiencies in the data are permitted to persist
is a matter of some interest and will be considered below. As
we shall see, reasons of state—not just technical difficulties—
are clearly involved. First, though, what do the numbers, for

all their fuzziness, have to say? Treasury statistics, showing
net flows of investments into the United States by the eight-
nation Middle East Oil Exporters group over the decade following the first oil shock, together with the group's cumulative investment position at the end of 1983, are reproduced
in table 5.1. As can be seen, there have in fact been two distinct
cycles in the movements of funds by these countries, sparked
by the two oil shocks—in each case, first a heavy capital inflow,
reflecting the rising tide of OPEC surplus revenues after oil
prices were raised; and then, eventually, some outflow again
as oil exporters found new ways to spend their excess petrodollars. Peaks were reached in 1977 and 1982. According to
the Treasury, almost all of the inflows have represented investments by official institutions rather than by private individuals or enterprises.[3]

Of the recorded total of $72 billion invested at the end of
1983, most was held in the form of liabilities of the U.S. government (61 percent), corporate stocks and bonds (19 percent),
and commercial-bank liabilities (9 percent). If to this we add
the recorded deposits of Middle East oil exporters in major
foreign branches of American banks, which according to the
Federal Reserve amounted to some $13.5 billion at the end
of 1983,[4] we come to a grand total of just over $85 billion. If
in addition we allow for unrecorded transactions, the figure
could easily top $100 billion or more.[5]

This is by no means an insignificant sum. Nonetheless,
the magnitude must be kept in perspective. Accumulated Arab
holdings account for less than a sixth of all foreign holdings
of U.S. government securities and for less than 3 percent of
total Treasury debt. Deposits in American banks here and
abroad amount to less than 2 percent of total U.S. banks
deposits, and investments in corporate stocks and bonds to
less than 1 percent of the total outstanding. One hundred
billion dollars is certainly a cool bundle of cash, but in an
economy as large as America's it is not an overwhelming
stake.

Within the total of Arab investments in the United States,
three countries clearly stand out, despite the Treasury's reluctance to disaggregate the data—Saudi Arabia, Kuwait, and

TABLE 5.1. Investments of Middle East Oil Exporters in the United States, 1974–83 (in millions of dollars)

| | Capital Flows | | | | | | | | | | Investment Position End Dec. 1983 |
	1974	1975	1976	1977	1978	1979	1980	1981	1982	1983	
U.S. government securities	3,176	4,368	4,857	4,676	−2,504	2,455	9,173	14,052	7,486	−6,537	39,944
Treasury bills & certificates	2,092	1,504	209	−733	−837	3,552	51	1,088	62	−725	6,344
Treasury bonds & notes	200	1,797	3,887	4,451	−1,785	−1,014	7,672	11,156	7,575	−5,419	27,939
Federal agency issues	884	1,067	761	958	118	−83	1,450	1,808	−151	−393	5,661
Corporate bonds	0	488	418	737	691	507	2,049	1,657	−601	−775	5,127
Corporate stocks	216	1,649	1,803	1,390	781	688	1,206	1,140	366	−807	8,608
Commercial bank liabilities	1,979	1,133	1,796	352	−605	−4,233	−897	−2,551	425	375	6,806

Demand deposits	—	90	77	603	55	1,314	−323	−1,263	−322	206	911
Time deposits[a]	—	−376	107	−42	406	68	30	−46	855	427	1,932
Other	—	1,419	1,612	−209	−1,066	2,851	−604	−1,243	−107	−258	3,963
Subtotal[b]	5,371	7,638	8,874	7,155	−1,637	7,883	11,531	14,298	7,676	−7,744	60,485
Nonbank liabilities[b]	432	500	227	167	43	−506	861	−1,053	−2,482	−1,324	4,348
U.S. government liabilities[c,d]	149	922	2,444	396	102	−1,117	592	406	305	−16	4,130
Direct investment[c]	77	6	−15	−13	100	16	212	2,666	708	−4	3,982
Total investment in the U.S.	6,029	9,066	11,530	7,705	−1,392	6,276	13,196	16,317	6,207	−9,088	72,945

Source: Treasury Department.

Note: Detail may not add to total due to rounding.

[a]Excludes negotiable time certificates of deposit, which are included in "Other" liabilities.

[b]Iran, Iraq, Kuwait, Qatar, Saudi Arabia, United Arab Emirates, Bahrain, and Oman.

[c]Excludes Bahrain and Oman.

[d]The position consists of cumulative flows from 1972.

to a lesser extent the United Arab Emirates. The cumulative payments surpluses of the other oil exporters in the region have, by comparison, been very small. These three states control more than 80 percent of all OPEC's net foreign assets.[6] Informed sources in financial circles generally agree that when speaking of Arab financial interests in this country, we are really talking mainly about this wealthy trio. And among the three, Saudi Arabia clearly stands out. Most estimates suggest that the Saudis alone account for anywhere from one-half to three-quarters of all Arab investment in the United States.[7]

Interestingly, remarkably few Arab investments to date have taken the form of direct investment in the American economy—only some $4 billion in all outstanding at the end of 1983, according to the Treasury data (table 5.1), amounting to less than 3 percent of total foreign direct investment here. And of this total, more than half was accounted for by a single transaction—Kuwait Petroleum Corporation's $2.5 billion takeover of Santa Fe International Corporation in December 1981. Of the remainder, as much as 40 percent has involved real estate acquisitions of various kinds, according to Commerce Department data reproduced in table 5.2. In this category too, as in the overall investment totals, Kuwait and Saudi Arabia dominate. The Commerce Department reports that of Arab direct investments outstanding in the United States at the end of 1980, all but some $35 million worth were accounted for by just these two countries.[8]

II

At the official policy level, Arab investments have always been welcome in the United States. From the moment the money began pouring in after 1973, policymakers in Washington stressed the numerous benefits that would accrue to the American economy. By bringing substantial amounts of capital into the country, it was said, these investments would: (1) augment the availability of funds needed by American enterprise for additional spending on new plant and equipment, thus fostering improvements of productivity, domestic growth, and

TABLE 5.2. Middle East Direct Investment Position in the United States, Year-end 1983[a] (in millions of dollars)

	All Industries	Petroleum	Manufacturing	Finance	Real Estate	Other
Middle East	4,435	4	81	421	597	3,332
Israel	450	0	95	280	*	75
Other	3,985	4	−14	141	597	3,257
World	135,313	18,458	47,803	19,499	13,946	35,607

Source: Department of Commerce, *Survey of Current Business*, October 1984.

*Less than $500,000

[a]*Investment position* is defined as book value of foreign direct investors' equity in, and net outstanding loans to, their U.S. affiliates.

the creation of new jobs; (2) keep interest rates lower than they would otherwise be; (3) help finance the budget deficits of the U.S. government by reducing the need for Treasury borrowing from the private sector; and (4) help support the U.S. balance of payments and strengthen the exchange rate of the dollar (which was anything but healthy at the time). Indeed, a positive attitude toward these inflows has been one of the most enduring themes of formal government policy over the last decade, surviving successive changes of control of the executive branch from the Republican party to the Democrats and back again. The following quotations demonstrate this posture:

> "To the degree we are successful in attracting additional capital we facilitate to that degree economic recovery" (Edwin Yeo, under secretary of the Treasury for monetary affairs, Ford administration, 1975).[9]
>
> "We are fully satisfied that the U.S. has benefitted from the placement of these funds in the U.S." (C. Fred Bergsten, assistant secretary of the Treasury for international affairs, Carter administration, 1979).[10]
>
> "It represents not a threat but an opportunity for the United States to strengthen our economic structure and revitalize our economy" (Marc E. Leland, assistant secretary of the Treasury for international affairs, Reagan administration, 1981).[11]

Outside the executive branch, however, attitudes from the start were more skeptical. However substantial such benefits might be, critics argued, it was also necessary to consider the costs. The inflow of Arab funds was but a partial return on an even greater outflow required to pay for higher-priced OPEC oil. Insofar as the two oil shocks contributed to our domestic recessions, inflation, high interest rates, and balance-of-payments difficulties, it was misleading to focus only on the credit side of the ledger. There were debit entries too.

Beyond that, critics continued, there was a risk of potential disruption of the U.S. economy as a result of the concentration of such large sums of money in the hands of such a small group of countries—countries, moreover, with whom our diplomatic relations were, to say the least, uncertain. Here was the Arab money weapon issue, which surfaced almost immediately after the first oil shock. Just as what goes up must come down, it was suggested, so money that is invested might later be disinvested. At any time, securities could be sold or bank deposits withdrawn on a massive scale, threatening potentially grave consequences for the dollar and for domestic financial institutions and markets. Might Saudi Arabia and its allies use such a threat to pressure the United States on Israel or other Middle East issues? The debate had begun.

That a question of this sort might be raised at all—for example, by representatives of the American Jewish community or other groups traditionally friendly toward Israel— was no surprise, of course. For some observers, mistrust of Arab intentions comes quite naturally. What was striking in this instance was how much more widespread the concern was, even among Americans not normally attuned closely to the nuances of the Arab-Israel dispute. At the time, the general public needed no reminding of who was responsible for the long lines at gasoline pumps. By their embargo on oil exports to the United States during the Yom Kippur War as well as by their long-standing economic boycott of Israel (which had always included the blacklisting of U.S. firms doing business with Israel), Arab governments had seemingly demonstrated a clear readiness to use whatever economic leverage they could, when it suited them, to pursue political or strategic interests. Moreover, everyone knew that Arab money was flooding into the country in unprecedented quantities. All people had to do was read their daily newspaper. Even the most conservative early projections of OPEC earnings suggested accumulations literally in the hundreds of billions of dollars; the Treasury's own forecast was for a minimum of $200–250 billion (inflation-adjusted) by 1980.[12] And best-selling novels were being published featuring hair-raising predictions of depression or worse as a result of Arab manipulation of their newfound wealth.[13] Who knew how many dollars might eventually be at the disposal of potentially hostile governments?

In retrospect, it is easy to see how much of an element of

alarmism, even hysteria, there was in these reactions. Dollar accumulations in fact never reached anything like the sums then being predicted; the threat of a money weapon hardly seems credible today, at a time when oil revenues are declining and Arab governments are obliged to be as prudent as possible with every dollar they own. I have already mentioned the need to keep the magnitude of these investments in perspective: the total at present is not an overwhelming stake when measured in relation to domestic U.S. financial aggregates. Quite the contrary, in fact. Overall, the amounts involved simply do not appear large enough to have a significant impact, in and of themselves, on our financial markets or domestic economy. As Governor Henry Wallich of the Federal Reserve Board argued in 1981, at the height of the second cycle of OPEC investment inflows,

> In principle, we would not expect OPEC investments to affect significantly the general level of dollar interest rates, which is determined primarily by financial and economic conditions in the U.S. economy. Moreover, the levels of U.S. monetary aggregates are the result of Federal Reserve policy decisions, and cannot be thrown off course by OPEC investments.[14]

Indeed, the threat of a money weapon was never all that credible even back in the mid–1970s, when the relative magnitude of Arab investments was considerably greater and oil revenues were still rapidly growing. Undoubtedly some degree of apprehension was justified, particularly when one considers the notoriously important role of psychology in financial markets. The possibility of serious disruption, or worse, could not be dismissed entirely out of hand. Even the most informed opinion at the time could not be sure what untoward ripple effects might ensue from a sudden liquidation of Arab assets. (That is true even today.) But it is also necessary to be realistic about such apprehensions—to avoid undue exaggeration of the hazards or probabilities involved. Good policy is served no better by panicky overreaction than it is by complacent disaster myopia. In fact, critics of the Arabs tended to underestimate considerably the capacity of the U.S. financial system to absorb an abrupt withdrawal of foreign claims as well as to overestimate substantially the chances that such a blow might actually fall. More careful analysis from the start might have moderated the most extreme perceptions of risk.

For example, given the daily rate of turnover in domestic capital markets—in excess of $10 billion a day, for example, in the market for U.S. government securities—even a massive liquidation of Arab holdings could most likely have been absorbed in relatively smooth fashion, with only temporary and limited adverse impacts. Certainly prices of some individual assets would have been eroded significantly; interest rates might have been elevated for a time; and the dollar could have been sharply depressed in exchange markets, with unpredictable consequences. But overall, there seems little reason to believe that instability would have been either pronounced or prolonged. Any psychological ripple effects could probably have been effectively contained owing to the great depth and resilience of U.S. financial markets and institutions.

Likewise, in our banking system even a sizable withdrawal of deposits would most likely have inflicted only relatively limited damage, not least because of the ability of the banks concerned to replace lost funds through the international interbank market. Suppose Arab depositors had in fact decided suddenly to transfer their dollars abroad, either redepositing them in other countries or selling them for other currencies. In the first instance, foreign banks would simply have become the new owners of the same deposits; and these in turn would have been available for lending back to American banks to help them maintain their liquidity. In this sense the system is closed: deposits do not disappear—they just change ownership. Second, American banks could have borrowed from the Federal Reserve, whose basic purpose is to be lender of last resort in the event of a liquidity crisis. True, such scenarios might well have resulted in some net increase of funding costs for the U.S. banks involved, perhaps impairing their profits and competitiveness, and could also have eroded public confidence in their soundness. But even so, there seems little reason to suppose that the viability of the U.S. banking system as a whole would have been seriously threatened. Even a severe blow from the Arabs could probably have been absorbed effectively.

How likely was it, then, that such a blow might ever fall? Here, too, critics tended to exaggerate potential dangers. In fact, the wealthy Arab countries have always been cautious and conservative investors, whose main concerns tend to be low risk, high liquidity, satisfactory yield, and anonymity. To date there has been little evidence of any "irrational" or irresponsible propensity on their part for rapid shifts of funds out of the country. Quite the contrary, they are well aware that this could result in substantial losses on all their remaining dollar assets. The Saudis, in particular, are reported to be "terribly suspicious" of any "churning" in their investment portfolio.[15] On the few occasions when they have tried actively to promote more diversification in their holdings, they have done so mainly by channeling new receipts into other currencies rather than by liquidating existing assets here. There has been no evidence at all of substantial movements of funds by the gulf countries motivated by purely political considerations.

In any event, even had they tried to shift their funds quickly, they could not have done so all at once. Their most liquid assets are their balances in U.S. banks, yet even of these only a small fraction could ever have been withdrawn immediately. Most are time deposits, not available on demand, and may be withdrawn only as they mature. And in practice their other portfolio holdings would probably have proved even less liquid, owing to the practical difficulties of organizing transactions on such a massive scale. Financial markets elsewhere have nowhere near the capacity of U.S. markets to absorb such large amounts of money in the short term.

Sober assessment thus suggests that the danger of.an abrupt liquidation of Arab assets was in reality rather farfetched. Not that we can ever truly be sure, of course. The example of Iran, to be discussed in detail in the next chapter, is instructive—a financially prudent government suddenly succeeded by fanatical revolutionaries prepared to make any sacrifice for their beliefs. Was it really so farfetched to imagine something similar happening in Saudi Arabia or Kuwait? In fact, it did not seem at all implausible at the time that, in the event of yet another Arab–Israeli conflict, one or both of these countries might be prepared to unsheath the money weapon for the sake of their Palestinian brethren. We simply did not know. On such matters, sincere people could sincerely disagree. Some apprehension, therefore, probably was justified—though not nearly so much as appeared to many Americans at the time.

III

Confronted with these apprehensions, as expressed by critics on Capitol Hill and elsewhere, officials of the executive branch have always tended to respond in generally soothing tones. Stated President Ford's assistant treasury secretary, Gerald L. Parsky, in formal congressional testimony in 1975, "I do not believe there is a threat that oil producers will use their investments to ... disrupt sectors of the U.S. economy."[16] His successor under President Carter, C. Fred Bergsten, a few years later said, "In the very unlikely event that all of the OPEC countries dumped their entire holdings of U.S. securities at one time ... the effects might be pronounced and undesirable—but they would clearly be manageable."[17] Such statements in public debate, however, must be read as political rhetoric rather than as serious analysis. If we really want to understand the assumptions underlying government policy, we must look at what officials did—or did not do—not at what they said. The facts are instructive.

One of the first things officials did, as Arab investments began growing after 1973, was to fudge the data. Here reasons of state began to intervene in the provision of information. Relevant statistics for individual oil-producing countries started disappearing from government publications in December 1974. Initially, the public explanation for lumping all the gulf states together under the label Middle East Oil Exporters was that as reporting coverage increased, data that previously had been reported separately were now subject to

aggregation. Only subsequently did officials shift to the
theme, mentioned above, that disaggregation was precluded
by pledges of confidentiality to individual investors. This
theme has been adhered to through three successive administrations, despite the fact that government publications do
report the investments of, for example, individual communist
countries, where surely the principal investor is the government. If the affairs of these individual investors can be disclosed, why not the affairs of individual gulf states?

The reason, apparently, is that promises have been made
to the gulf states—to Saudi Arabia, in particular—to keep
their holdings secret, going back to an agreement with the
Saudis negotiated by then Secretary of the Treasury William
E. Simon in early 1974. The existence of the agreement was
later confirmed by the former secretary in an interview with
two auditors from the General Accounting Office. According
to the two auditors,

> Mr. Simon discussed negotiations with the Saudis held
> in 1974 for the purchase of U.S. securities. The fear was
> that the Saudis would have bought securities from the
> United States when they felt like it. In order to bring more
> order to this purchasing system, and because the United
> States wanted the investment, the Saudis were asked to
> purchase large amounts of securities. A separate facility,
> or add-in, was set up to handle the sales. . . .
>
> In exchange for these security purchases, the United
> States assured the Saudis confidentiality in reporting
> data on them by region. According to Mr. Simon, "this
> regional reporting was the only way in which Saudi Ara-
> bia would agree to the deal for add-ons."[18]

The depth of the Treasury's commitment to the Saudis
was underscored in a February 1975 memo from the then
Treasury under secretary to the secretary of state: "The sine-
qua-non for the Saudis in this arrangement is confidentiality
and we have assured them that *we will do everything in our
power to comply with their desires*." [19] Apparently this pledge
now extends to all Saudi assets in this country, not just to
government securities, and to other wealthy gulf states as
well, all of whom had specifically requested the change of

reporting practices that was initiated in 1974.[20] These countries have always attached critical importance to the confidential placement of their assets and were well aware of the political sensitivity of their investments here. Since 1975 the Treasury and other agencies have successfully resisted all pressures, from Congress and elsewhere, to compel them to retreat from their promises.

Consider, for example, what happened in 1975 when the Multinational Corporations Subcommittee of the Senate Foreign Relations Committee, then headed by Frank Church of Idaho, began looking into the money weapon question. At the time, little information was publicly available on Arab deposits in banks in the United States, and nothing at all on deposits in U.S. bank branches abroad. Indeed, not even the Treasury or Federal Reserve knew exactly what the numbers were. So Senator Church tried to find out. In April 1975, a questionnaire was sent to some three dozen of the country's most internationally active banks asking for details on amounts, terms, and the like. Fuller disclosure on a bank-by-bank basis was essential, he argued, if we were to be able to gauge accurately how much of a threat of disruption there might actually be:

> There is something to worry about. . . . an important subject that we must look into, in my view, and that is the extent to which major banks in this country may have permitted deposits from these particular countries to grow so large that if the deposits are quickly withdrawn, it could cause the collapse of the banks and trigger very serious repercussions all through the economy. . . .
>
> In the OPEC countries we have countries that are clearly very volatile. . . . They are in basic disagreement with our policy toward Israel. Some of them have already imposed an embargo on us, and at any time they might decide to just pull this money out and we don't know how much there is. We don't know on what basis it has been deposited, how much of it is short-term.[21]

The questionnaire produced an interesting rift among the banks addressed, reflecting their differing degrees of commercial interest in the Middle East. Smaller banks, which by and large held very few Arab deposits, found no difficulty in complying with Senator Church's request. But the larger money-center institutions, where most of the deposits were concentrated (see below), registered strong objections. In an obviously coordinated maneuver, the big New York, Chicago, and California banks wrote similarly worded letters to the senator declining to answer any of his specific questions. "Much of the information you request would involve a breach of our obligation to keep confidential the affairs of particular clients," responded the chairman of Morgan Guaranty.[22] "We consider information of the type requested to be highly confidential," wrote a vice president of Chase Manhattan.[23] Bankers were especially worried about the possibility that their Arab depositors might be provoked by such disclosures into making massive withdrawals; and in this fear they were joined by officials of the executive branch. Indeed, the Treasury was warned explicitly by the finance minister of Kuwait that his country would pull all of its funds out of American banks if its position were revealed as demanded by the subcommittee.[24] Vigorous efforts were undertaken to water down Senator Church's request, particularly by the biggest banks, which made use of all the powers of persuasion at their disposal to get their point of view across. David Rockefeller, then chairman of Chase Manhattan, which was known to be a principal recipient of both Saudi and Kuwaiti deposits, traveled to Washington to lobby key subcommittee members.[25]

In the end, Senator Church and the subcommittee had to settle for a deal worked out through the Federal Reserve designed to preserve the confidentiality of individual bank involvements with individual governments. Under that deal, the Federal Reserve itself would undertake to collect the data—on a confidential basis, of course—and then provide it to the subcommittee in aggregated form, as in table 5.3.[26] No greater detail on individual banks has been supplied at any time since 1975, despite subsequent requests from the Multinationals Subcommittee as well as from others on Capitol Hill.[27] With the subsequent waning of public debate over the Arab money issue, the executive branch had little motive or need to compromise on its early promises to the gulf states. The battle was won with little more than a skirmish.

Why have the Treasury and other agencies been so adamant about their commitment to secrecy? Former Illinois Senator Charles Percy, then a member of the Multinationals Subcommittee who sided with bankers and the executive branch on the disclosure issue, perhaps summed it up best when he said, "We are dealing with dynamite right now."[28] At first, it appears, officials simply wanted to attract back some of the dollars that were suddenly flowing out of the country to pay for higher-priced oil imports—in effect, to get a piece of the petrodollar action. But very soon, as Arab investments continued to pile up, a second motive emerged—a perceived need to keep the money here. Policymakers began to worry about what a sizable and sudden withdrawal might do to the competitive position of American banks, the stability of domestic financial markets, or the exchange rate of the dollar. As Washington's reaction to revolutionary Iran's threat of withdrawal in 1979 demonstrated (see chapter 6), nerves clearly were uneasy on this score—despite the soothing political rhetoric.[29] Looking at what officials did, rather than at what they said, one can see that the danger of disruption was indeed taken seriously. They did not want to rock the boat. Again, in the words of former Senator Percy,

> We know the perilous ground we are on now, and I don't want to tread on that kind of ground for this possible tenuous pulling the plug down the line, if there is another war, if there is an embargo, if they act in unison and they withdraw all of their deposits.[30]

Fear of financial reversal, accordingly, became a basic element of U.S. policy vis-à-vis the wealthy gulf states. Monetary concerns were by no means the only—or even the most important—of Washington's motives for cultivating these nations' good will. In the middle 1970s, the maintenance of amicable relations with Arab governments, and in particular with Saudi Arabia, was deemed an overriding foreign policy objective for a variety of reasons, political as well as economic.

TABLE 5.3. Deposits of Middle East Oil Exporters in Domestic Offices and Foreign Branches of Large U.S. Banks, 1975–81 (in billions of dollars)

	December 1975			March 1979			March 1981		
	Six Largest Banks*	Second Largest Six Banks*	Next Nine Banks*	Six Largest Banks	Second Largest Six Banks	Next Nine Banks	Six Largest Banks	Second Largest Six Banks	Next Nine Banks
(1) Total deposits (consolidated)	197.5	76.3	49.9	273.8[a]	99.9[a]	68.4[a]	328.5	126.5	85.2
(2) Deposits of Middle East oil exporters[b]	11.3	2.2	1.1	19.4	2.1	0.8	19.8	3.0	1.2
Of which:									
Domestic offices	1.5	1.0	0.4	4.1	0.4	0.3	5.0	0.3	0.3
Foreign branches	9.8	1.2	0.7	15.3	1.7	0.5	14.8	2.7	0.9

| (3) Line (2) as per-cent of line (1) | 5.7 | 2.9 | 2.2 | 7.1 | 2.1 | 1.2 | 6.0 | 2.4 | 1.4 |

Source: Federal Reserve Board of Governors.

*Six largest banks
Bank of America
Chase Manhattan
Chemical Bank
Citibank
Manufacturers Hanover
Morgan Guaranty

Second largest
Bankers Trust
Continental Illinois
Crocker National Bank
First National Bank of Chicago
Security Pacific
Wells Fargo

Next nine
European American Bank & Trust
First National Bank of Boston
First National Bank of Dallas
First National Bank of Detroit
Irving Trust
Marine Midland
Mellon
Republic National Bank, Dallas
United California Bank

[a]Deposits as of December 1978.

[b]Includes Iran, Iraq, Kuwait, Oman, Qatar, Bahrain, Saudi Arabia, and the United Arab Emirates.

U.S. officials hoped to promote moderation on oil pricing and production decisions as well as to retain market access for American business in the Middle East. They also aspired to curb the worst manifestations of anti-Israel militancy in the Arab world, as a prelude to possible peace negotiations in the region. In this atmosphere, limitations on public disclosure of financial data seemed a small price to pay to avoid any abrupt liquidation of Arab assets. Toward this end, officials over the years have indeed done "everything in their power."

IV

Unfortunately, the price could yet turn out to be higher than expected, as disclosure was not the only dimension of policy that was in fact affected. In their concern not to rock the boat, U.S. officials were evidently also led to discount or ignore two other risks of Arab investments that, potentially at least, were even more threatening to American interests than the low-probability danger of financial disruption.

One was the risk that by generating excess liquidity in financial markets, the massive inflow of Arab funds might eventually jeopardize the safety and soundness of the U.S. banking system. Officials would have benefited from a greater sense of history. If the past had anything to teach us about such situations, it was that an oversupply of capital often leads to a lowering of standards on international lending; and that this, in turn, can ultimately have disastrous consequences for lenders (chapter 4). I have already emphasized in chapter 2 the role played by the rising tide of petrodollars during the 1970s in inducing U.S. institutions as well as others to get so deep into the business of making sovereign loans. OPEC's surplus dollar revenues represented a net increase of the world savings rate. Now awash in liquidity, bankers looked for customers where they could find them, including Eastern Europe and the Third World. The result was a buildup of debt exposure overseas that in more recent years has clearly posed challenges not only for our financial system but for our foreign policy as well. Officials might have recalled the fate of the Medici Bank five centuries earlier, when (in the words of the bank's historian) it too "succumbed to the temptation of seeking an outlet for surplus cash in making dangerous loans to princes."

Many of these challenges could have been avoided had the countries that started it all, namely, the oil exporters, been encouraged to undertake a larger share of the lending themselves. Let them recycle their petrodollars back to oil importers. They, however, were not eager to assume the responsibility. The nouveaux riches around the gulf understandably found it far more convenient to park surplus earnings in Western financial markets and let the banks lend the money onward—in effect, interposing the banks as a buffer between them and high-risk sovereign borrowers. They got the investment security and liquidity they craved; financial intermediaries got the risk (at a price, of course); and the American government, anxious to cultivate Arab good will, went along with the whole process. Some of the consequences of this policy of acquiescence will be considered in chapters 7 and 8.

The second risk was that the large concentration of assets in the hands of Arab governments might afford them undue control or influence over the U.S. economy or key segments of it. Questions about this threat, like questions about the danger of disruption, surfaced quickly on Capitol Hill and elsewhere after the first oil shock. And like the apprehensions being expressed about disruption, these fears tended for the most part to be met with generally soothing words from the executive branch. "OPEC countries each emphasize return on investment, not domination," said Gerald Parsky in 1975.[31] Insisted Fred Bergsten four years later, "[As regards] a concern that OPEC governments might gain undue influence in specific U.S. companies, or specific sectors of the economy . . . the laws and regulations which we now have on the books presumably cover all potential abuses."[32] In this case, however, no dissonance exists between political rhetoric and action. Just as it has on the lending issue, government policy on this matter has for more than a decade remained essentially benign.

For example, in 1975, under congressional prodding, President Gerald Ford established the Committee on Foreign Investment in the United States (CFIUS) to monitor investments here, both direct and portfolio, that might have adverse implications for U.S. national interests, particularly investments proposed by governments or government-controlled entities. Composed of representatives of the Departments of Treasury, State, Defense, and Commerce and the Executive Office of the President, CFIUS was charged with a responsibility to review prospective investments and, "as the need arises," to submit recommendations to the National Security Council.[33] Yet in the years since, under three administrations, the need seems never to have arisen. Not once has the committee ever raised a formal objection to any proposed acquisition—even one as potentially controversial as Kuwait Petroleum's 1981 takeover of Santa Fe International Corporation (see below). This could be, of course, because the very existence of the committee has sufficed to discourage most politically questionable investments; it might also be that informal signals by CFIUS in the context of preliminary discussions with prospective investors have served to render more formal action unnecessary. The evidence, however, suggests an explanation more consistent with other elements of the government's policy over the last decade, namely, a reluctance to offend Arab sensibilities. The House Committee on Government Operations seems to have been closer to the mark several years ago when it concluded that "in reality, CFIUS is a dormant entity . . . interested more in assuaging concerns than in determining harm to the economy."[34]

Of course, it is certainly possible to exaggerate the risk of undue Arab control or influence over the economy (just as it was possible to exaggerate the danger of disruption). On the face of it, this threat too has seemed limited. Less than one-fifth of Arab investment in the United States has been in corporate stocks and bonds, and these, according to reliable sources, have been distributed widely across a broad spectrum of industries and enterprises.[35] There has never been any evidence of concentration in key industrial sectors; and in many cases holdings are managed passively by third parties rather than by the Arab investors themselves. Likewise, as already indicated, direct investment from the Middle East has been remarkably small and, until Kuwait Petroleum's takeover of Santa Fe International in 1981, was confined in good part to real estate ventures—hotels, office buildings, shopping centers, and the like.[36] Furthermore, a substantial body of federal legislation and regulations exists that is intended to ensure against undue foreign influence in strategic or sensitive industries, by limiting new investments or prohibiting takeovers in such sectors as domestic communications, internal air transport, coastal and freshwater shipping, and nuclear and hydroelectric power generation; and by denying defense procurement contracts to foreign-controlled enterprises that cannot by special arrangement qualify for security clearance.[37]

However, in this case the risk might actually be greater than it appears. Consider, for example, the matter of Arab bank deposits (which of course means mainly Saudi Arabian and Kuwaiti deposits). While these may be a quite modest fraction of deposits in the U.S. banking system as a whole, they account for a much greater fraction of the deposits in those few banks where they are mainly lodged. I pointed out in chapter 2 that large international depositors prefer the safety of well established name institutions. This is especially true of the fiscally conservative Saudi and Kuwaiti governments, which have long channeled the bulk of their liquid funds to a small circle of giant money-center banks capable of absorbing deposits on such a scale. As indicated in table 5.3, Arab deposits in U.S. institutions are overwhelmingly concentrated in the six largest of America's banks—Bank of America, Chase Manhattan, Chemical, Citibank, Manufacturers Hanover, and Morgan Guaranty. In March 1981 (the latest date for which such figures are publicly available), these deposits amounted to some 6 percent of the $328.5 billion of total deposits then outstanding in these same six institutions.[38] Can there be any doubt that such a skewed deposit structure could conceivably constitute a source of leverage for Arab depositors? Is it not possible that such leverage might have led some of America's top bankers to revise their view of Middle East issues and, perhaps, even to use their influence in Washington on behalf of Arab interests? Some members of

Congress have been worried about this sort of possibility for some time, ever since Senator Church's first inquiries in 1975.[39]

Or consider again the matter of Arab direct investments here. There may be grounds for concern that existing laws and regulations are not as adequate as they might be to prevent undue foreign influence in sensitive industries. Although Arab direct investments outside of real estate to date have not been extensive, some have been strategic, including especially the takeover of Santa Fe International. As a diversified company engaged primarily in natural resources exploration and development, Santa Fe held a relatively small amount of proved oil and gas reserves in this country and in the North Sea as well as leases for mineral exploration on federal lands; and through its subsidiary C. F. Braun it possessed considerable expertise in petrochemical plant construction and refinery system engineering, particularly in the field of catalytic cracking. Although none of Braun's technologies were unique, they were sophisticated. In addition, Braun had been heavily engaged in three plutonium-producing and processing facilities owned by the Department of Energy and involving classified and sensitive information. Were there really no risks for this country when such a high-technology company was taken over by an enterprise wholly owned by a potentially unfriendly government? The absence of any express concern by CFIUS in the Santa Fe case suggests that the net of existing laws and regulations affecting foreign investments in the United States may, in fact, be rather more porous than is advisable; and while not many sensitive Arab acquisitions apparently have slipped through yet, there seems little reason, on the basis of past U.S. policy behavior, to think that more might not do so in the future.

V

We are faced, then, with an irony. Though the purported money weapon was in reality far less of a threat than it appeared to many Americans at the time, it nonetheless worked—in the sense of exercising practical leverage over

U.S. government policy. Officials did permit Arab holdings to act as a constraint on their behavior. Not only did they do "everything in their power" to comply with the gulf states' desires about disclosure. They also took care to avoid offending Arab sensibilities regarding either the responsibility for petrodollar recycling or the risk of undue investment control. Like nuclear arms, the money weapon did not have to be used to be effective.

But there were also limits. There is no evidence that the influence of Arab holdings ever extended beyond the immediate area of financial relations. So far as is publicly known, U.S. policies on Middle East political and military issues were never directly affected by apprehensions over monetary disruption; nor were any explicit attempts made by Arab governments to make use of an intrafinance challenge to achieve extrafinance objectives. Linkages remained confined to questions of investment policy only.

These observations suggest four conclusions. First, the inflow of Arab funds did have a significant impact on the general foreign policy environment (even if Middle East political and military issues did not become directly involved). Issues of salience in the finance area clearly were altered by the purported money weapon. The risk of a sizable or sudden withdrawal of Arab assets was definitely regarded as disadvantageous from a public-policy point of view.

Second, the issue rapidly became politicized because of widespread apprehensions on Capitol Hill and elsewhere. Government officials felt obliged to downplay the seriousness of any threat in public, even if in private their nerves were apparently rather uneasy on the question. And some of the most important banks concerned felt obliged to lobby vigorously on behalf of their Arab clients' penchant for privacy, becoming quite self-conscious political actors in the process.

Third, it would seem that the government overreacted somewhat. There was of course a whole variety of reasons, political as well as economic, for cultivating the good will of key Arab governments after 1973. But the threat of a money weapon as such was never as credible as officials in Washington apparently believed at the time, their rhetoric notwithstanding; and as a result they would seem to have given away more, on both recycling and investment control, than was strictly necessary in the circumstances to prevent any financial disruption. In any event, there hardly appears much need for nerves to be uneasy on this score today. At a time of growing economic stringency for the gulf states, we certainly have little reason to worry about rocking the boat now. A strong argument can be made, therefore, for taking another look at relevant government policies, particularly with respect to the issues of disclosure and screening of foreign investments.

Finally, most generally, the facts suggest a certain cautious optimism about intrafinance challenges to U.S. foreign policy of any kind arising from foreigners' net claims on the American financial system. If even the Arabs, with their massive concentration of assets during the 1970s, were unable to use their holdings here to achieve much effective leverage, apart from the concessions they received on disclosure and investment control, who could? In practice, the potential constraint on U.S. policy would not appear to be very large.

To be sure, risks remain. As the experience with Arab investments demonstrates, policy linkages may indeed be created in the immediate area of financial relations if not beyond it. These can hardly be ignored by public officials. But opportunities may be created as well, to exploit the claims of foreigners to achieve extrafinance objectives of our own. Like captured armaments in wartime, the money weapon may be turned around to point the other way. That is what happened in the case of Iran, to which I now turn.

CHAPTER 6

Freezing the Ayatollahs

The seizure of the American embassy in Tehran on November 4, 1979, together with several dozen American hostages, posed one of the most painful challenges to U.S. foreign policy in recent memory. Here was a great superpower—the Great Satan, according to Iran's fanatical Islamic revolutionaries—humbled and embarrassed by an unruly mob of "students." International law was blatantly violated, the niceties of diplomatic immunity ignored, and American lives put at risk. What could Washington do about it?

One thing Washington did, exactly ten days later, was to freeze all Iranian assets in the United States and in the foreign branches of American banks. The amount at the time was more than $11 billion. Motivations for the freeze, by far the largest such action in U.S. history, were only partly related to the hostage crisis as such. As we shall see, other concerns, including especially a fear of financial disruption in the United States, also figured prominently in Washington's calculations. But in the end the sanction proved to be one of the most influential elements in the negotiations leading to the hostages' release. The large concentration of Iranian assets turned out to be a weapon that could be effectively deployed by American officials to help achieve a key diplomatic objective. High finance was thus linked to high politics in a way

147

that proved quite advantageous for the U.S. government. Much can be learned from this experience about extrafinance challenges to American foreign policy at a time of net liabilities to foreigners (subset C in table 1.2).

I

Iranian assets had grown dramatically in the years prior to the 1979 freeze, starting with the first oil shock in 1973. Indeed, until the disruption of revolution and a war with Iraq at the end of the decade, Iran ranked as OPEC's second largest producer, with literally tens of billions of petrodollar earnings pouring into its coffers. Much of the money was quickly spent by the government of Shah Mohammed Riza Pahlevi on armaments and other imports or else was used to repay foreign debts that had been contracted before the bonanza began. But much also was set aside in Western financial markets, in the form of bank deposits or investments of various kinds. Not surprisingly, the United States and U.S. banks were most favored as outlets for surplus revenues by the then pro-American Iranian authorities. Close political ties between the two countries were paralleled by a preference for the dollar and dollar-based financial institutions.

Because of those close political ties, few Americans at the time worried about an Iranian money weapon, even as public debate was heating up over the potential for disruption by newly rich Arab governments. The shah, it was said reassuringly, was a solid and dependable ally of the United States. Unlike the other states ringing the gulf, Iran could be counted upon to behave sensibly and responsibly. True, the shah had been instrumental in pushing through the rise of oil prices that had so upset the world economy after 1973. But this could be construed simply as pursuit of legitimate economic interest—something Americans could empathize with, even as they made the painful adjustment to higher energy costs. Never had the shah gone beyond this, to embargo oil exports or manipulate financial holdings on openly political grounds. Experience gave much less justification for mistrusting Iranian intentions under the King of Kings than it did for mistrusting Arab intentions.

Experience, however, also gave few portents of the revolution of the ayatollahs. Who could have imagined that the all-powerful shah would turn out to have feet of clay, a latter-day Ozymandias? Backed by an army of 400,000, a large police force, and a fearsome secret police, his domestic position seemed impregnable. His government controlled the mass media and kept a tight rein on the press. There was only one sanctioned political party, and it was subservient to the monarchy. Yet in little more than a year, from the time public demonstrations first broke out in several provincial cities in early 1978, he was swept from the scene and driven ignominiously into exile. Even as late as the summer of 1978, it was still not clear whether the popular protest movement, coalescing around the charismatic figure of the Ayatollah Khomeini, represented anything more than a passing nuisance for the Pahlevi dynasty; only in December did the shah make his first genuine political concessions, putting out feelers to the opposition and appointing a new government committed to a transition to a constitutional monarchy. But it was a classic case of too little too late. On January 16, 1979, the shah left the country on a "vacation" of undetermined length. Two weeks later, Khomeini returned to Tehran in triumph.

Almost immediately diplomatic relations with the United States deteriorated. For Khomeini and his followers, America was the enemy—the Great Satan who had kept the shah on the Peacock Throne against the will of Allah and the people. Daily, demonstrators marched outside the U.S. embassy chanting anti-American slogans. Despite efforts at rapprochement by Washington, tensions steadily mounted, particularly after President Jimmy Carter's decision in October 1979 to admit the shah to the United States for medical treatment. The administration had been under pressure for months from influential friends of the deposed monarch, including former Secretary of State Henry Kissinger and Chase Manhattan Bank chairman David Rockefeller, to offer refuge to a former ally; President Carter finally relented, on humanitarian grounds, when it was learned that the shah was suffering from a case of lymphatic cancer requiring immediate treatment. In retaliation, the Ayatollah Khomeini, who all year long had been demanding the shah's extradition back to Iran to face trial, exhorted his followers to undertake even more forceful anti-American actions. Demonstrations in Tehran grew increasingly frenzied, and on November 4 the embassy was seized together with sixty-six hostages (later reduced to fifty-two). The freeze of Iranian assets followed ten days later.

II

The freeze quite literally transformed America's financial liabilities into a foreign policy asset. All through the debate in the 1970s over the purported Arab money weapon, what many Americans tended to overlook was the statutory authority of the president, in extremis, to stop any sudden or sizable withdrawal of funds in its tracks. Hostile governments might conceivably threaten to liquidate their claims on a massive scale. But under laws dating back to early in the century, the executive branch had all the powers necessary to preempt any such challenge by blocking deposits and preventing the sale of U.S. securities—in effect, to turn the money weapon around to point the other way. What appeared to many as a potential constraint on policymakers could in fact be an opportunity.

The first grant of such powers was in the Trading With the Enemy Act (TWEA), passed in 1917. Under that act, the president was authorized to regulate various domestic and international economic transactions for an indefinite period in time of war or (as amended in 1933) during peacetime national emergencies. Over time, the TWEA was used to freeze the assets of the People's Republic of China, Cuba, North Korea, Vietnam, and Cambodia. In 1977 the president's powers were updated and clarified in the International Emergency Economic Powers Act (IEEPA), enacted as an amendment to the TWEA. Under the IEEPA, the executive branch may control or prohibit credit transfers or transactions in foreign exchange or other property "to deal with any unusual and extraordinary threat . . . to the national security, foreign policy, or economy of the United States."[1] It was this act that was invoked against Iran in 1979.

Formally, the freeze took the form of an executive order (E.O. 12170) blocking all assets owned or controlled at the time by the government of Iran in the United States, including dollar-denominated assets in the custody of U.S. institutions or individuals overseas. Property of private Iranian nationals was excluded on the grounds that this would have unduly inconvenienced a large number of Iranians then living in the United States, many of them students or refugees and friendly to the American government. In any event, the overwhelming percentage of Iranian claims on the United States belonged to government-controlled entities such as the National Iranian Oil Company and the Bank Markazi, Iran's central bank. Overseas assets, by contrast, were included in the freeze order because it was known that the bulk of Iran's dollar deposits had in fact been booked in foreign branches of American banks (principally in London and Paris) rather than in domestic U.S. offices.

What was not known was how much all these assets added up to. In good part because of its own policies on collection and disclosure (see chapter 5), Washington simply had no idea what the numbers were. On November 14 an estimate of $6 billion was announced by the Treasury, later modified to "in excess of $8 billion." But it was not until a special census in April 1980, which mandated the filing of detailed reports by all U.S. individuals and institutions holding Iranian claims, that reasonably reliable information was in fact obtained— though, for bargaining reasons, little of this was publicly released until the hostage crisis was finally settled in January 1981.[2] At that time, as table 6.1 shows, the total was revealed to come to something over $11 billion, almost twice the amount originally estimated, and very close to the $12 billion first claimed by Iran when the freeze was imposed. This was a considerable sum, one large enough to inflict real pain on the Iranians.

III

Inflicting pain, however, was not the principal reason for the freeze, at least not at the outset. Initially, Washington's motives were much more defensive than aggressive in nature—

TABLE 6.1. Iranian Assets Subject to U.S. Freeze, as of
January 1981 (in millions of dollars)

At Federal Reserve Bank of New York		
Deposits and securities	$ 1,418	
Gold (1,633 million ounces, valued		
at $576/oz.)	940	
		$ 2,358
At overseas offices of U.S. banks		
(deposits and securities)		5,579
At domestic branches of U.S. banks		
(deposits, exclusive of accrued		
interest)		2,050
Other assets held in the U.S. or over-		
seas by U.S. individuals	1,000–	2,100
Total		$10,987–12,087

Source: Robert Carswell and Richard J. Davis, "Crafting the Financial Settlement," in *American Hostages in Iran: The Conduct of a Crisis*, ed. Warren
Christopher et al. (New Haven: Yale University Press, 1985), p. 205.

mainly, to reduce any risk of more pain or embarrassment to
ourselves that might have resulted from an abrupt withdrawal of Iranian funds. Only later was the question of Tehran's assets directly tied, in a calculated diplomatic strategy,
to the release of American hostages. What ultimately turned
out to be an artful and effective instrument of foreign policy
linkage started out largely as a tactical, reactive measure to
fend off a perceived danger of financial disruption, taken literally in the middle of the night.

The trigger was a statement by the then acting foreign
and finance minister of Iran, Abolhassan Bani-Sadr, at a press
conference in Tehran on November 13, threatening to pull all
of his country's claims out of the United States and U.S. financial institutions. America, he said, was waging economic
war on Iran. On November 8, four days after the hostage
seizure, Washington had halted the supply of all spare parts
for Iranian military equipment previously purchased from the
United States. On the tenth, the Carter administration ordered the deportation of Iranian students residing illegally in

this country. And on the twelfth, a ban on oil imports from Iran was announced. In reprisal, Bani-Sadr asserted, Teheran would use its U.S. financial holdings, which he estimated at about $12 billion, to launch an attack against the dollar. News of his announcement reached Washington at four o'clock in the morning of the fourteenth.

Reaction was swift. Two of the Treasury officials most closely involved in these events, Robert Carswell, then deputy secretary, and Assistant Secretary Richard J. Davis, described the chain of events in a contribution to a recent comprehensive study of the hostage crisis sponsored by the Council on Foreign Relations:

> Upon being notified by the Treasury watch offices, Treasury Secretary [G. William] Miller conferred by telephone with Secretary of State [Cyrus] Vance and the President, and the decision was made to implement the freeze immediately. Calls went out, and by 7 A.M. the responsible Treasury officials . . . were already at work. Key congressional leaders were consulted by telephone, at 8:10 A.M. the President signed the required executive order, and by 10 A.M. the first regulations implementing the freeze were filed at the Federal Register.[3]

The reason for this remarkable speed is not hard to understand. Washington had a real fear of financial disruption. Two dangers, in particular, were stressed in early administration statements. One was the risk that an attack on the dollar might actually be successful—that an abrupt liquidation of Iranian assets could trigger an even more widespread run on U.S. currency. At the time, the dollar was still convalescing in the exchange markets, following two years of grave weakness; just the previous month, for the second time in a year, officials had been obliged to mount a major rescue effort to fend off adverse speculation. The last thing they wanted at this stage was another substantial sell-off. In the words of Anthony Solomon, then under secretary of the Treasury, "Our central concern that morning was the dollar."[4] This theme came up repeatedly in subsequent explanations by Washington policymakers.

The other danger was that an attack on the dollar might be accompanied by a repudiation of Iranian debts in the United States. Officials were determined to avert any threat to the safety or competitive position of U.S. financial institutions. All through the 1970s, even when the gusher of petrodollar earnings was at its height, the shah had been eager to take advantage of his country's solid credit rating to help finance some of his ambitious development projects and arms buildup. And lenders all over the world, including all of the biggest U.S. banks, had been more than happy to oblige. Said one American banker, "When Iran indicated that it wanted to borrow, everyone wanted to be getting in. No one thought that the Shah was a real risk."[5] But now the King of Kings was gone, and advisers to the Ayatollah Khomeini, questioning the legality of some of these loans, particularly to enterprises associated with the shah's family, were known to have argued against honoring what they called the shah's debts. Creditors now had reason to wonder if they would ever get their money back.

Iran's loans were more than covered by its external assets, of course. As of November 1979, Tehran owed only about $2 billion to U.S. banks and perhaps $1 billion more to U.S. nonbank claimants (exporters, contractors, etc.)—far less than the sums then held by Iran in the United States and U.S. institutions. But precipitate withdrawal would have effectively meant the loss of security for all these claims: U.S. creditors would have become, in Treasury Secretary Miller's words, "a second hostage" to Iran.[6] Another motive for the freeze, therefore, was to ensure the availability of collateral funds to satisfy legitimate claims on the Iranians. The need to protect the interests of U.S. claimants was stressed in particular by President Carter in his initial report to Congress on the freeze order, as required under the IEEPA.[7]

Subsequently, the freeze was supplemented by a variety of additional economic sanctions against Iran. Some were worked out multilaterally with U.S. allies in Europe and Japan. These included, in December 1979, bans on premiums for Iranian oil, on military sales, and on new credit extensions o Iran. And some were imposed unilaterally, including most prominently prohibitions for American citizens on all non-oil trade, travel, or service contracts in Iran declared in April 1980. In reality, however the value of these additional sanctions was little more than symbolic. Their substantive impact was greatly limited for two reasons. On the one hand, U.S. allies were reluctant to jeopardize seriously their access to Iranian oil by associating themselves too closely with Washington on the hostage issue; in fact, they did not wish to have any of December's multilateral measures publicly disclosed. And on the other hand, American economic relations with Iran were already at a low ebb following the actions of the previous November. In practical terms, clearly, the asset freeze was the sanction with the most immediate bite.

Did U.S. claimants ask for the freeze? According to commentators of a somewhat sensationalist bent, a number of well-known American bankers, including especially David Rockefeller of Chase Manhattan, played a key role in persuading the Treasury to forestall an Iranian withdrawal.[8] Chase Manhattan was among the biggest holders of Iranian paper, with loans totaling some $350 million on its books; and the Iranians are known to have begun running down their deposits at Chase as early as September, in good part out of pique over Rockefeller's role in lobbying for the deposed shah's admission to the United States. It is tempting to infer a connection between Chase Manhattan's financial interests and the freeze order. But in fact there is no evidence at all that bankers participated in any way in the Treasury's decision. The charge is explicitly denied by Carswell and Davis;[9] and on this point they are fully backed by the House Banking Committee, which in 1981 conducted a comprehensive review of the whole freeze episode. The committee "found no evidence of requests from any U.S. financial institutions or any other sources for an assets freeze."[10] Banks neither had any control over the timing of the sanction nor even received advance notice of its implementation. In fact, most banks were initially quite critical of the action, for reasons to be discussed below.

More recently, some of the officials involved at the time have sought to play down the element of apprehension in their swift reaction to Bani-Sadr's threatened attack on the dollar. No one panicked, they say; the limits of the financial dangers were well understood. The freeze was a measured political decision to respond to the incessant provocations of an unfriendly government. As Carswell and Davis have written,

> While the Bani-Sadr announcement provided the final impetus for ordering the freeze, it was not its primary cause. The decision was based on a political judgment that the United States could not be continually passive in the face of repeated hostile acts by another country (taking hostages, attacking our financial institutions) without responding with some form of action.... The freeze was ... not predicated on a belief that financial calamity would flow from the withdrawal of these deposits. In fact, most of the bank deposits were time deposits that could have been withdrawn only over many months and thus could not be used effectively in an attack on the dollar or on U.S. financial institutions.[11]

Indeed, we are now told, all that talk about the dollar and U.S. financial institutions was really just a smokescreen—propaganda designed for the consumption of other governments, particularly the oil-rich Arab states, who might worry that if the money weapon could be turned on the Iranians, it could be turned on them too. To pacify countries like Saudi Arabia and Kuwait, that had their own sizable dollar investments, it was necessary to minimize the political nature of the freeze. The administration did not want them to think that their assets in U.S. banking offices here or abroad might also at some stage be blocked for political reasons. The sanction had to be presented in strictly financial terms, as a unique riposte to a highly unusual set of circumstances. Hence the claim of Treasury Secretary Miller, at a White House press briefing on the morning of November 14, that the freeze was "purely in response to the Iranian announcement that it was going to withdraw its deposits from U.S. banks, and not because of the take-over of the U.S. embassy in Tehran."[12] According to former Deputy Secretary Carswell, "There was less than candor here."[13] In fact, Secretary Miller's purpose was

supposedly "to minimize any sense that the U.S. dollar and
U.S. financial institutions were unreliable or insecure. . . . Relying on [this] rationale might create fewer problems with
Saudi Arabia and other major investors who themselves had
sensitive political relationships with the United States."[14]

These remarks smack a bit of revisionist history. Undoubtedly, officials did feel a need to calm Arab nerves. But
that only confirms how uneasy Washington's own nerves were
about the larger potential for financial disruption. Robert Carswell was obviously correct when he wrote in 1981 that there
was always a "surrealistic quality" to Bani-Sadr's threat:
with the sums then immediately available to Tehran, the risk
from Iran alone "was not significant."[15] The point, however,
is precisely that the risk was not from Iran alone. Rather, as
was well understood at the time, a possibility existed that
psychological ripple effects could be generated through the
markets that might really have endangered the dollar or U.S.
institutions (especially with the dollar then still in conva-
lescence). Some element of apprehension was present. As Carswell himself admits, "In the political heat of the moment the
naive Iranian rhetoric was blandly accepted. . . . Faced with a
unique situation in which psychological elements played a
large part, it was not difficult to conclude that the President
had to do something."[16] In an interview, Carswell conceded
to me that a principal issue for him and his colleagues at the
time was indeed that the money would "run away," with
potentially severe repercussions here at home.[17]

Further evidence of Washington's unease can be found in
what was going on behind the scenes, even before the seizure
of hostages and Bani-Sadr's threat. In fact, contingency planning for a withdrawal of Iranian funds had begun months
earlier, almost from the moment the revolutionaries took
power in Tehran. Once it was certain that the shah was gone
for good, misgivings about Iran's intentions no longer seemed
quite so out of place. Publicly, of course, consistent with their
standard rhetoric on OPEC investments, U.S. officials continued to discount any serious danger from the Iranians. But
privately questions soon were being raised within the executive branch; and at the Treasury, draft freeze regulations

actually were prepared as early as February 1979 (later to
provide the basis for the order that was so quickly implemented in November)—all despite the fact that financial relations with Tehran never deteriorated in anything like the
manner that diplomatic relations did.[18] Indeed, throughout
the year, despite the known doubts of some of the Ayatollah
Khomeini's advisers, the new Islamic government went out
of its way to project a sober image on investment matters,
for example, by staying meticulously up to date on all of Iran's
debts to foreign banks. One can only surmise that even then
U.S. officials were more nervous than they wished to let on.
According to Carswell and Davis, "The work undertaken during this period . . . constituted only routine staff work and such
an action was not seriously considered at that time at the
policy level."[19] But their claim was directly challenged by the
House Banking Committee in its 1981 review:

> While there was no apparent justification on the basis of
> Iran's economic posture for anything more than close
> monitoring of economic developments in Iran (a moni-
> toring which disclosed no unusual happenings), there was
> *much more than routine contingency planning* in the De-
> partment of Treasury during this period with regard to
> a freeze. Nine months before the provocation of the No-
> vember hostage seizure, and without any serious threat
> of economic warfare directed against the U.S. by Iran,
> the Treasury Department had laid the legal groundwork
> for a freeze on Iran's assets. . . .
>
> Thus there is no apparent reason why the consideration
> of the freeze under those circumstances in February 1979
> progressed as far as it did, except out of . . . excessive con-
> cern for the consequences of Iran's instability.[20]

A reasonable conclusion, therefore, would seem to be that
fear of financial disruption was in fact a major influence on the
administration's thinking on the morning of November 14,
complemented by an impulse to "do something" in the face
of all these "repeated hostile acts." The limits of the dangers
may have been well understood. Nonetheless, some kind of
decisive action seemed called for. The Iranians simply could

not be allowed to get away with another one, to declare their intention to walk away with all that money and possibly endanger America's currency and financial institutions in the process. Again to quote former Deputy Secretary Carswell, "The United States could not afford to be seen as a paper tiger."[21] In the rush of events, deliberate use of the freeze as a bargaining device to help free the hostages does not appear to have been actively discussed. Officials were too busy reacting to the immediate threat at this stage to think much in terms of an explicit linkage strategy for negotiating purposes. That came later.

IV

In fact, it was not until late the following summer that the first serious negotiations began between the U.S. government and Iran directly linking the asset freeze to the hostage question. Until then, administration officials persistently resisted being drawn into any kind of bargaining process that would connect the two issues formally. Anxious though they were to get the hostages home safely, they did not want to appear willing to pay ransom for American lives. Washington's line was simple—first, the hostages must be released; and then all other differences would be resolved, including the freeze. Ironically, it was the Iranians who ultimately ensured the development of an explicit linkage strategy by the United States, for practical diplomatic purposes, by repeatedly insisting that there could be no hostage release without a simultaneous return of Tehran's blocked assets and a settlement of mutual claims. Although at first the Ayatollah Khomeini's government was unwilling to sit down and talk with the Great Satan at all, by the time the Iranians finally did relax their intransigence, in September 1980, the fate of the hostages and the outlook for the asset freeze had become inextricably linked.

In the meantime, Washington found itself preoccupied with negotiations with its own banks. The strategic interaction between the U.S. government and Iran was considerably complicated by the actions and influences of private financial institutions, whose interpretation of their commercial inter-

ests in this affair did not always coincide with the public
interest as interpreted by the administration. Solutions had
to be found for a number of sensitive issues. For government
officials, the challenge was the classic one described in chapter 3—how to balance the legitimate interests of both the
banking community and U.S. foreign policy. In the delicate
words of Carswell and Davis,

> The freeze interrupted a wide array of ongoing transac-
> tions and relationships. . . . This required the government,
> in administering the freeze, to make a variety of judg-
> ments affecting the rights of various parties. Treasury
> policy was, to the extent possible, to protect legitimate
> U.S. commercial interests but to avoid actions that might
> adversely affect the hostages or reduce the future flexi-
> bility that might be needed to resolve the crisis.[22]

For example, one of the first issues to arise involved so-
called setoffs that were being sought by banks with loans then
outstanding to Iran. Setoffs are a traditional banking device
by which the debts of shaky borrowers are safeguarded by,
in effect, attaching their deposits. Several banks with large
Iranian holdings were understandably eager to use them in
this way; and in the first hours after the freeze was announced,
numerous telephone calls were made to the Treasury requesting the necessary authorization. Indeed, at Citibank all of
Iran's deposits were immediately set off despite the fact that
this was supposed to be prohibited under the original order.
One day later, however, on November 15, the prohibition was
lifted, and other major holders of Iranian deposits moved
quickly to imitate Citibank's initiative.[23]
  Interestingly, though, setoffs were permitted only for deposits at foreign branches of U.S. banks, and not for those at
domestic offices. The explanation for such an action says
much about the difficult balancing act then being demanded
of policymakers. On the one hand, there was the question of
what to do about the claims of banks lacking Iranian deposits
and of nonbank claimants. On the other hand, there was the
question of foreign reactions to the extraterritorial reach of
the freeze order as promulgated on the fourteenth. By block-

ing assets in U.S. institutions abroad as well as at home, Washington had challenged traditional rules of national sovereignty. The administration knew that the Iranians would do everything possible to recover their blocked overseas assets, precipitating a huge legal wrangle, and it was not at all sure that it could convince foreign courts of its right of jurisdiction over Euro-dollar deposits in London, Paris, and elsewhere. So officials resorted to a truly Solomon-like solution, aptly described by Karin Lissakers:

> From the start...U.S. government lawyers had serious doubts that the freeze order would stand up in British and West European courts. If pushed to judgment, the United States was very likely to lose the extraterritoriality issue. Therefore, Treasury told the banks they could offset Iran's overseas deposits against loans due the banks, thus pre-empting any court ruling that might allow Iran to regain control of its money. Treasury, however, did not allow offsets against Iranian deposits in the United States because it wanted that pool of resources to remain as security for banks with no Iranian deposits and for nonbank claimants against Iran.[24]

The solution also had the convenient advantage of more closely aligning the interests of America's internationally active banks with U.S. diplomatic objectives. Other things being equal, banks could normally have been expected to oppose any extension of U.S. legal jurisdiction to banking transactions outside the United States; indeed, one of the greatest attractions of the Eurocurrency market had always been precisely its comparative regulatory freedom. But with setoffs of their overseas deposits permitted against outstanding loans, banks now had an incentive to defend the freeze in foreign courts against Iran's attempts to get its money back. The government's lawyers now had allies.

A second issue involved the possibility, owing to Iran's inability to use its blocked funds to meet current debt-service obligations, that some of its loans might be declared in default. Through the operation of so-called cross-default clauses that are standard in international syndicated credits, a formal declaration of default on any one loan can cause all loans to be accelerated—that is, called for immediate payment. Administration officials would not have minded such a scenario at all and even privately discussed the merits of promoting such a step.[25] Financial pressures on Iran would have been immeasurably increased, as any bank anywhere in the world holding Iranian paper would then have had an arguable right to seize any deposits it could to set off against its claims—in effect, extending America's freeze to virtually all of Iran's foreign assets. But most banks, in this country and elsewhere, were adamantly opposed to the precedent of such a blatant use of private credits for political purposes; and in the end, policymakers decided not to press lenders on the issue. In only one major case, concerning a $500 million syndicated loan that had been arranged under the leadership of Chase Manhattan in 1977, was default actually declared, on November 19, and this failed to ignite a chain reaction.

A third issue involved disclosure—the same question that had bedeviled the bank–government relationship ever since OPEC assets started piling up after the first oil shock. At the time of the Church subcommittee inquiry in 1975, executive branch officials had backed the banks in their opposition to prying questions about their holdings. But now, with a freeze on, these same officials needed to be able to monitor compliance with their order—and that required precisely the sort of information that the banks had always been reluctant to divulge. As indicated above, Washington simply had no idea what the numbers were; and although banks were initially requested to submit weekly reports, they were less than wholly cooperative. Again, in the delicate words of Carswell and Davis, "These reports proved only partially satisfactory, since . . . some banks reported on the basis of undisclosed legal theories that produced some underreporting."[26] Ultimately, the Treasury was forced to undertake the special census in April 1980 as well as a follow-up survey in December. But at no time, right up to the moment the hostages were finally released, were fully reliable figures ever available to policymakers. The House Banking Committee, in its later review, was particularly critical of the Treasury for its data-gathering methods throughout the course of the freeze.[27]

V

Still other issues, involving everything from standby letters of credit to foreign nondollar accounts, had to be dealt with after the freeze was imposed, all adding to the complexity of the government's foreign policy challenge.[28] Unfortunately, matters did not get any simpler once the Iranians finally showed some willingness to talk directly to Washington about the hostage question. As early as April 1980, Tehran had initiated confidential contacts with some representatives of American banks looking toward an "economic solution" of their differences. By the time government-to-government talks got under way in September, the discussions between the Iranians and the banks were already rather well advanced; and thereafter negotiations with Iran actually were conducted on two parallel tracks—one private, one official—that ultimately converged only at the very end of the whole process. The bad news, from the government's point of view, was how much more complicated this made the task confronting policymakers, who in effect now had to bargain simultaneously with both the Iranians and the banks. The good news was that despite all the complications the process worked, leading in the end to the release of all fifty-two hostages on January 20, 1981.

The colorful story of the two parallel tracks of negotiations has been well told by some of the principal actors involved—from the U.S. government side by Carswell and Davis; and from the banks' side by John E. Hoffman, who as a partner of the New York law firm Shearman and Sterling represented Citibank in these matters.[29] All emphasize that from the very beginning, once the freeze was promulgated, regular contact was maintained between administration officials and bank representatives, partly to stay abreast of the many legal battles touched off by the sanction, both at home and abroad, and partly to explore various possible solutions to the financial side of the crisis. Hence by the time Tehran put out its first confidential feelers to the banks in late April (via the West German counsel for the Iranian government), channels of communication were already well established between bank representatives and relevant U.S. policymakers. Mindful of the Logan Act, which prohibits negotiations by private American citizens with a foreign government on issues directly affecting U.S. government policy, the banks first sought official clearance for any discussions with the Iranians. Permission was quickly granted on three conditions—first, that the banks keep officials fully informed of all developments; second, that no deal be cut without explicit government approval; and third, consistent with the administration's line up to that point, that there be no settlement of any kind without prior release of the hostages. Thereafter, following every meeting between representatives of the banks and the Iranian government (which were always secret and were held in a variety of locations), one of the bank representatives would personally brief appropriate figures in Washington. Normally this meant John Hoffman for the banks and Robert Carswell for the U. S. government.[30]

By contrast, bank representatives were told nothing about the confidential government-to-government talks that got haltingly under way in September, following signals from Tehran indicating Iran's readiness to reach a settlement. In part, this was because of traditional strictures on sharing classified information with private citizens; and in part, Carswell told me in an interview, because of an insistence on secrecy by the government of Algeria, which through these events played a crucial behind-the-scenes role as an intermediary between Washington and Tehran.[31] Indeed, the banks' representatives were not even aware that these talks were going on until they were publicly mentioned by the Iranians in November. Yet this does not seem to have created much problem of inconsistency between the two tracks. "Through my constant communication with Washington on the progress of the bank discussions," Hoffman writes, "it was possible for Carswell to keep that process on a course consistent with other U.S. government plans and activities."[32] In other words, the channels of communication established in this case were sufficient to ensure a fairly accurate reading of official policy priorities regarding the safe return of the hostages and the timing of any related financial measures.

What got the government-to-government talks finally started was a key speech by the Ayatollah Khomeini on September 12 formally outlining, for the first time, his conditions for the hostages' release. These were: (1) release of Iran's frozen assets; (2) return of all property "illegally" taken by the shah and his family; (3) cancellation of all sanctions and financial claims against Iran; and (4) a pledge not to interfere in Iran's internal affairs. Subsequently the pace of events picked up sharply after ratification of the Ayatollah's four conditions by the Iranian parliament in early November, and reached a veritable crescendo in the last two weeks before the impending inauguration of President-elect Ronald Reagan in January. As the two tracks of negotiations gradually merged, administration officials spent as much time bargaining with the banks as they did with the Iranians.

Representative was the intense bargaining with banks over what rate of interest to pay on frozen Iranian deposits. Since most were either demand deposits, on which customarily no interest is paid, or expired time deposits, banks fortunate enough to be holding them had the use of Iran's money, in effect, at no cost. The potential windfall was considerable, given the large amount of assets affected. By the time of the final settlement, as much as $800 million had come to be involved. The Iranians were understandably insistent that back interest be credited to their accounts; and in this they were joined by banks lacking such deposits as well as by foreign banks, who loudly protested the competitive advantage that would otherwise be enjoyed by deposit-holding institutions. The latter, on the other hand, at first opposed any interest accrual at all; and even after Washington made clear, on equity grounds, that interest would indeed be required, they bargained vigorously for the lowest possible rate. Ultimately an effective rate of approximately 14 percent was agreed upon, though not without a good deal of arm-twisting by Treasury officials.[33]

Nonetheless, despite the distractions of such bargaining, the administration was able to negotiate successfully with the Iranians for the hostages' release, even to the point of persuading Tehran to retreat from some of the Ayatollah Khomeini's celebrated four conditions. At the end, little more was heard about returning the property of the shah and his family. Instead, these claims, along with all other mutual claims were to be made subject to a formal settlement procedure before a duly constituted international arbitration tribunal. Nor were all of Iran's frozen assets simply released to Tehran. Some $5.1 billion was instead allocated to the settlement of debts owed to U.S. and other foreign banks; and an additional $1 billion was set aside in an escrow account to secure payments of any future arbitral awards to nonbank claimants on Iran.[34] Once the hostages were freed, on the other hand, the United States had no difficulty at all in agreeing to cancel its other economic sanctions and to renew pledges of noninterference in Iranian affairs. Such concessions hurt little and were but a small price to pay for ending a most painful affair.

VI

As matters turned out, therefore, the linking of the asset freeze to the hostage question clearly worked to America's advantage. Though not in and of itself decisive, the sanction did provide important extra leverage to Washington in its negotiations with Tehran. Says former Deputy Secretary Carswell, "The blocked assets proved a key bargaining chip in obtaining the hostage release."[35] Echoes John Hoffman, "[The financial settlement] was essential in freeing the hostages."[36] In this instance, at least, a net liability position in private finance offered a helpful instrument to U.S. public officials in responding to an extrafinance challenge to foreign policy. But what about other instances? Is the result generalizable? How easy would it be for Washington to make use of similar asset freezes—or threats of asset freezes—to help realize yet other policy preferences elsewhere?

In fact, the result is not easily generalizable. We need to recall the four issues that are raised whenever public officials

consider intervening politically in private finance—the four
e's: effectiveness, efficiency, equity, and external relations (see
chapter 3). There is no question about the first e: the blocking
of Iran's assets was indeed effective. The specific circumstances that helped to make it possible, however, are not all that
likely to be repeated frequently; and besides, there were actual or potential costs to the action, in terms of the remaining
three e's, that must be kept firmly in mind. An asset freeze
may be a powerful weapon of foreign policy, but like most
other armaments it should be handled with extreme care. Use,
if resorted to at all, must be cautious and selective.

Several special circumstances helped in the Iranian case.
First was the fact that the freeze was linked to an objective—
freedom for the hostages—that was clearly defined and essentially modest in terms of Tehran's perception of its own
interests at the time. The Iranians were not being asked to
reverse their revolution or invite back the shah. No truly fundamental policy changes were demanded. Simply, we wanted
our people back. As a recent comprehensive study by two
American scholars demonstrates, the success rate of economic
sanctions undertaken over the years by various governments
has tended to vary greatly, depending among other things on
the types of goals being pursued.[37] In instances in which quite
extensive policy changes have been sought in target countries,
the historical evidence suggests that economic sanctions are
rarely effective. Conversely, the more circumscribed the objective, as in the Iran episode, the greater the probability of
success. One reason Washington ultimately got what it
wanted was that, in the larger scheme of things, what it
wanted was not all that much.

Second, in this instance Washington spoke with one clear
voice. Although before November 14 there had been some
disagreement within the government, particularly among
Treasury staffers, over the advisability of the contingency
planning that was started early in 1979, once the freeze was
imposed no significant differences of view ever surfaced
among the bureaucratic actors involved, including most importantly key figures in the Departments of Treasury, State,
and (because of all the litigation precipitated by the freeze)

Justice. All officials had the same overriding priority—to get the hostages back safely. No mixed signals were sent, either to the private sector or to the Iranians.

Third, the economic distress inside Iran made access to its assets of critical importance to Tehran. The Iranian revolution was an extraordinarily tumultuous affair. An economy that many had thought destined for greatness was now having trouble even feeding its own people. And a further note of urgency was added by the invasion from neighboring Iraq on September 22, 1980, which severely damaged a good part of Iran's oil-exporting capacity. Money was needed to pay for everything from rifles to rice. More than most, the Iranians were susceptible to economic pressure.

Finally, there was the state of domestic politics in Iran. Most students of the Iranian revolution agree that the taking of the hostages had more to do with the ferocious struggles then going on among rival political factions in Tehran than it did with hostility for the Great Satan as such. In fact, the hostages were an instrument employed by the most radical of the Ayatollah Khomeini's supporters, banded together in the Islamic Republic Party (IRP), to mobilize public opinion against domestic "enemies of the revolution" (including, ironically, Abolhassan Bani-Sadr, who by then had been elected president under Iran's new constitution). The persistence of these internecine struggles explains why Tehran delayed for so long in indicating any interest in talking to Washington about the hostages. Conversely, once most of the IRP's internal enemies had been eliminated or neutralized, the value of the fifty-two Americans was correspondingly diminished, and some kind of settlement could now be contemplated. As Iran's chief negotiator said, "The hostages are like a fruit from which all the juice has been squeezed out."[38] Tehran was now ready to spit out the pits.

Circumstances like these are not apt to occur very often. And even where they may all come together again, the cost side of the calculus must still be considered. The Iranian freeze raised serious questions for efficiency, equity, and external relations, as U.S. officials themselves understood and anticipated. (Indeed, these questions had been at the heart of the earlier disagreement within the government over the advisability of contingency planning for such an action.) Happily, as matters turned out, actual costs in the specific case were kept reasonably low. However, that might not always be possible in other instances elsewhere.

When the freeze was announced, for instance, many observers thought that the costs, in economic terms at least, would not be low at all. Considerable concern was expressed, particularly by banks, over what the action might mean for the free functioning of international financial markets. Some recalled what happened in the nineteenth century once governments started to allow high politics to intrude on high finance (chapter 4). Might not global efficiency be impaired in our own day as well by Washington's politicization of banking relationships? In reality, little harm seems to have come from the incident, owing primarily to its limited application and duration. The blocking was restricted to just one country, was linked to a specific issue, and was terminated quickly once the hostages were released. On the other hand, who can guarantee that the same limits would always be observed elsewhere? If such limits are not maintained, efficiency losses might be rather greater by comparison. The risk is serious and must always be counted among the tradeoffs relevant to policymakers.

The same point applies as well to the equity questions raised by the Iranian incident. One question concerned the relationship between American and foreign banks. Might the competitive position of U.S. institutions have been impaired relative to other nationalities? At the time, the freeze was widely regarded as a precedent. The U.S. government had demonstrated not only its ability but its willingness, when provoked, to block an abrupt withdrawal of foreign dollar holdings, including even those in overseas branches of American banks. No country could now regard itself as exempt. American bankers were initially critical of the freeze because they feared it might lead to a significant diversification out of the dollar and U.S. financial institutions by foreign governments anxious to limit their future vulnerability. Especially troubling was the potential reaction of wealthy Arab governments, whose massive holdings in the United States, as we know, had already been the subject of considerable political controversy.

For its part, Washington publicly denied that there was any precedent here. There was no danger that the government would develop an addiction to asset freezes. In the words of Robert Carswell, "The United States took the view that the situation was unique because Iran had been recognized as a unique transgressor, beyond the pale of acceptable international conduct; no respectable nation need worry."[39] Privately, though, officials shared bankers' fears about a possible reallocation of Arab or other portfolios. Said one about the freeze, "We acted knowing it would have adverse side-effects, but there was little else we could do."[40] In effect, unease about financial disruption was not eliminated but only displaced by the administration's decision.

Fortunately, from the American banks' point of view, the unease proved unnecessary. In fact, little permanent diversification out of the dollar or U.S. institutions appears to have been caused by the Iranian episode. To be sure, there was some temporary movement of Arab deposits out of American banks in 1980 and 1981 (see chapter 5, table 5.1). But this was more than offset by a simultaneous rise in recorded holdings of U.S. government securities and corporate stocks and bonds, suggesting that the explanation probably lay more in a shift of investment strategy at a time of widening maturity gaps in interest rates—a shift from lower-yield, short-term accounts toward higher-yielding, longer-term assets—than in any apprehension about possible future sanctions. And in any event, in 1982 and 1983, the growth of bank deposits resumed, despite some overall decline of Arab dollar holdings (reflecting the decline of their oil revenues). The Saudi Arabians, in particular, reject allegations that their investment decisions have been affected by the Iranian freeze.[41] They as much as anyone recognize that, as indicated in chapter 5, there are real limits on the extent to which holdings as large as theirs can be pulled out of this country's currency and institutions and placed elsewhere. In the last resort, the United States still offers the widest range of opportunities for investments on such a massive scale.

However, this does not mean that there is no reason at all for concern. For that to be so, the United States would need to enjoy a monopoly of investment opportunities—which we patently do not. Over the longer term, therefore, should Washington be seen as developing an addiction to asset freezes after all—denials about precedents notwithstanding—significant diversification into other countries' institutions and currencies could yet occur, and that could indeed be costly for the competitiveness of American banks. One can go to the well only so often. That tradeoff too must be faced by policymakers.

Moreover, they must bear in mind the incentive that the Iranian experience created for foreign governments to disguise more of their investments here by channeling them through financial intermediaries in Switzerland, the Caribbean, or elsewhere. Though such behavior does not deprive U.S. institutions of financial resources, it does increase their funding costs (as foreign intermediaries add an extra margin of interest) and can cut them off from direct contact with important overseas customers. Former Deputy Secretary Carswell suggests that deception of this kind has indeed been on the rise since Iran's assets were blocked and could become more prevalent in the event of similar actions elsewhere.[42] That is apparently what he had in mind when he wrote in 1981 that "the lawyers and the bankers have learned the lesson of what the United States can do....A future blocking will be evaluated by a more knowledgeable and critical audience."[43] Ultimately, the competitive disadvantages for American banks could be considerable.

A second equity question raised by the asset freeze concerned relationships among American banks. Might the competitive position of some U.S. institutions have been impaired relative to others? Quite clearly, interests in the banking sector were by no means identical in this affair. Chase Manhattan, for example, knowing that it had little commercial future in Iran so long as the shah's enemies remained in power, did not hesitate to use its position as lead manager of Tehran's $500 million 1977 loan to initiate the default declared five days after the freeze order (see above), despite the reluctance of some of its syndicate partners who still had hopes of doing business with the Iranians. Such hopes also help to explain why Chase's maneuver failed to ignite a chain reaction elsewhere. This divergence among private interests posed a tricky problem for policymakers who, as indicated earlier, had their own interest in promoting a scenario of accelerating defaults. In the end, as I described, Washington decided not to press lenders on the issue.

Another example was the serious divergence of interest that developed between those banks holding Iranian deposits (mainly the big money-center institutions) and those without. Not only could the former enjoy the use of Iran's money at no cost; they could also set off deposits in their foreign branches against outstanding loans, something the latter obviously could not do. This too posed tricky problems for policymakers. On the cost issue, as indicated above, they eventually chose to eliminate any competitive advantage by requiring interest to be paid at a reasonable rate. On the setoff issue, by contrast, they chose to procrastinate for as long as possible, despite requests for rulings from various banks that wanted deposits to be shared. In the words of Carswell and Davis, "The Treasury stayed above the tangle and declined to rule ... in the hope that the situation would somehow get resolved."[44] Fortunately for the Treasury, the situation ultimately did get resolved when Iran agreed, as part of the final settlement, to pay off all of its debts owed to banks, including banks lacking deposits.

But this in turn highlighted a third question of equity raised by the freeze: the differential treatment of banks and nonbank claimants. Bank debts, in the end, were settled in full. Nonbank claims, by contrast, were deferred indefinitely to the jurisdiction of an international arbitration tribunal. Few aspects of the experience brought more criticism to the government. Concluded the House Banking Committee, "The U.S. Government appeared to be less concerned with resolving the problems of nonbank claimants than those of the banks."[45] Nonbank claimants themselves, more bluntly, simply charged that the settlement was unfair. Former Carter administration officials are probably correct, however, in suggesting that some disparity was inevitable, given the different starting points of the two classes of creditors. Under the circumstances, they appear to have done the best they could to protect the rights of nonbank claimants. As Warren Christopher, who as deputy secretary of state was the highest ranking State Department official involved in the negotiations, has written,

> The main reason why the banks came out better was that they began better. For one thing they held the money—the Iranian deposits—and in any dispute the party that starts out with the cash has a built-in advantage. In addition, their claims were for "liquidated," or readily discernible, amounts. In a straight loan arrangement, the amount due ordinarily is understood by both parties, and there is no real room for dispute.
>
> In contrast, when property is expropriated, when a contract is breached, or when a personal injury is inflicted, the amount of the damage usually is a major element of the dispute. In those circumstances, no one in the government could responsibly assign a value to each of the nonbank claims pending against Iran and then add up the total. To resolve these nonbank claims, the settlement included a procedure for settling or arbitrating claims against Iran.... In providing that avenue, the settlement probably did as much as it was possible to do to protect the interests of the nonbank claimants, whose claims were of indeterminate amounts and thus qualitatively different from the bank claims.[46]

Finally, tradeoffs must be faced in the area of external relations. Here too the Iranian episode raised serious questions, particularly concerning the extraterritorial reach of the freeze. As indicated earlier, Washington's decision to block deposits in the foreign branches, and not just in the domestic offices, of American banks challenged traditional rules of national sovereignty. Governments in Europe, where most of the deposits were held, were understandably irritated, if not offended, by this usurpation of their financial authority; and it took considerable diplomatic effort on the part of the U.S. government to gain their reluctant acquiescence. In this instance at least, deep rifts with our allies were happily contained, mainly by stressing the extraordinary nature of the hostage crisis.[47] Diplomatic costs turned out to be relatively low. But could that always be assured in the event of similar asset freezes under less extraordinary circumstances elsewhere?

VII

The bottom line of all this, to reiterate one of the conclusions of chapter 5, is that large concentrations of assets in the United States under the control of other governments do matter from a foreign policy point of view. In this instance, the presence of Iranian investments not only altered the issues of salience to U.S. government officials caught up in the throes of the hostage crisis. More important it offered them a new and powerful policy option to help secure the hostages' release. Once the crisis broke, there was eventually no way to avoid a linkage strategy incorporating American banking relations with Iran. The weapon was too convenient not to use.

As indicated, though, it is not a weapon to be used lightly. Indeed, given the Iranian experience together with the previous discussion of Arab holdings in chapter 5, it is clear that what we have here is a weapon that may be pointed in either direction, depending on the circumstances. Potentially hostile governments could conceivably seek to constrain U.S. foreign policy in some way by threatening an abrupt liquidation of funds; we, in turn, might again resort to the authority of the IEEPA to preempt any such challenge or to pursue foreign policy goals of our own. The two experiences described in this chapter and in chapter 5 also make clear that neither side has unlimited room for maneuver, owing to the considerable costs that might also be engendered. In effect, therefore, Washington and wealthy foreign governments are held as hostages to one another through private banking relations—we, to the finite risk of a sudden or sizable asset withdrawal; they, to the possibility of yet another freeze. The question, in concluding this chapter, is what the Iranian experience can teach us about how to maximize opportunities for U.S. foreign policy in the context of this complex set of strategic interactions.

In fact, the Iranian experience teaches us much. First, it underscores the importance of having the best possible information. After the freeze was imposed, much time was lost simply getting the numbers straight. In effect, the government found itself hoisted on the petard of its own questionable collection and disclosure policies. I shall have more to say on this topic in part III.

Second, the experience underscores the importance of the government getting its act together. At first mostly a tactical, reactive measure to fend off a perceived danger of financial disruption as well as to avoid appearing yet again as a paper tiger, the freeze became an effective instrument of foreign policy only after the administration began to think seriously in terms of an explicit linkage strategy for negotiating purposes. Moreover, it helped a great deal that there was no discernible difference in the policy priorities of the principal bureaucratic actors involved once the freeze was imposed. Being able to speak with one voice, the government could define its objectives clearly, take account more easily of potential costs and necessary policy tradeoffs, and, consequently, bargain more successfully with both the Iranians and our own banks.

Finally, concerning the banks, the experience underscores again the importance of clarifying the evolving relationship between the financial sector and public-policymakers. Bankers and administration officials alike were aware of the possibility of a collision of interests as each pursued negotiations with the Iranians on a separate track. In Warren Christopher's words (which echo the central theme of this book), "The government had as its principal aim the release of the hostages under circumstances that would protect the national honor. The banks had a distinct primary interest, which was to assure that Iran's outstanding debts to them would be repaid. Those aims were not necessarily in conflict.... Nevertheless, it remained possible throughout the negotiations that one set of discussions could interfere with the other."[48] Collision was avoided partly because of the efficiency of the channels of communication that were established over the course of the crisis, partly because of the willingness of American bankers to compromise their own concerns and priorities in a situation of national emergency, and partly because of the skill displayed by administration officials in balancing the legitimate interests of both the banking community and U.S. foreign policy. In the end, private as well as public interests appear to have been well served, though as Robert Carswell acknowledges, "The margin of success was very thin."[49] In part III, we shall consider what improvements in the bank–Government relationship might be possible to ensure a broader margin of success in any similar situations in the future.

CHAPTER 7

Solidarity Suppressed

The Iranian experience dramatically confirmed the extent to which high finance and high politics had been brought gradually, but irresistibly, closer together by the internationalization of banking in the Incredible Quarter Century. Yet by the time the hostages were released, public attention in the United States was already beginning to shift from the deposit side of the ledger to the loan side. Worries about a purported Arab or Iranian money weapon cooled off as a result of the asset freeze. Concern started heating up about the danger of a debt crisis instead. Increasingly, the primary challenge to U.S. foreign policy appeared to lie not in the foreign liabilities of U.S. banks but, rather, in their claims—particularly those on shaky sovereign borrowers. Might not U.S. national interests be threatened by the growing exposure of American financial institutions to the risks of lending to "recreant foreign governments"?

In fact, warnings started early, though few listened. By 1976, some popular commentators were beginning to sound the alarm, suggesting that a crisis was coming.[1] Likewise, in 1977 the Senate Foreign Relations Committee staff cautioned, "There is every reason ... for the U.S. Government to be concerned about the present debt buildup, not only because of the large exposure of American banks, but also for its broader foreign policy implications."[2] But these were isolated voices, easily dismissed by bankers and others as unjustifiably gloomy and Cassandraish, not to say sensationalist. In the midst of the lending euphoria of the 1970s, few Americans were troubled by the occasional difficulties of an Argentina or Zaire, an Indonesia or Peru. Such problems, it seemed, were sui generis and could each be managed individually through established and evolving debt-rescheduling techniques. No adverse implications for U.S. foreign policy were perceived. Not even the near-bankruptcy of Turkey in 1978–79 did much to shake the general air of complacency.

But then came a problem that could not be ignored, and from a most unexpected quarter—Poland. As early as 1979, the Polish economy had stopped growing. By the summer of 1980, even as the Solidarity trade union movement was being born out of the travail of widespread industrial strikes, it was clear that Warsaw was nearing the brink of default. With some $26 billion of debt outstanding, this was no small matter: the stakes were far higher than they had ever been before, not only for banks but for the U.S. government too. And this became even more painfully obvious once the government of General Wojciech Jaruzelski moved to suppress Solidarity on December 13, 1981, by declaring martial law and jailing the movement's leaders. As we shall see, Washington's efforts during the following months to pressure the Polish authorities into reversing their political course were plainly compromised by the high level of Western bank exposure in the country. In effect, an unwelcome foreign policy linkage had been created. For the first time since the start of the Incredible Quarter Century, international debt now appeared to impose a real constraint on U.S. diplomacy. A good deal of insight can be gained from this episode about extrafinance challenges to American foreign policy at a time of net claims on foreigners (subset D in table 1.2).

I

Poland's massive debt accumulation had its origins in the détente in East–West relations that was pushed by the U.S.

and Soviet governments in the early 1970s. As indicated in chapter 3, strengthening of economic ties across the Iron Curtain was quite clearly to include encouragement of loans from American and other Western banks. Lending to the Soviet Union and its six East European allies (Bulgaria, Czechoslovakia, East Germany, Hungary, Poland, and Romania), in the form of both official credits and private bank advances, expanded rapidly throughout the 1970s. (So did lending to Yugoslavia, which although a Communist country is not a Soviet ally.) In none of these nations was there more lending than to Poland, which by 1977 had gained the dubious honor of having the largest foreign debt in the entire Soviet bloc.

Not that Western banks needed a great deal of encouragement. Washington did not have to twist any arms to promote an increase of private lending in the East European region (including Yugoslavia) during the go-go years of the 1970s. No directives were issued or threats made. Mainly it was a matter of altered signals: the effect of détente was to switch the traffic light from red or amber to green. As in the matter of petrodollar recycling (see chapter 2), the banks themselves—not government officials—chose to put the accelerator to the floor and, for a long time, to keep it there. In fact, there were several reasons for bank enthusiasm for lending in Eastern Europe at the time.

First, of course, was the flood of liquidity in Western financial markets, especially after the first oil shock, which resulted from the preference of OPEC's nouveaux riches to park their surplus earnings in safe and convenient forms. Banks, as I have said, were forced to look for customers wherever they could find them. Moreover, at a time of intense competition for international league standing, the East European region appeared to offer particularly attractive opportunities for new asset growth. All of these nations had good records in the postwar period for low debt, punctual repayments, and sound debt management. In addition, their central planning systems seemed to most bankers to guarantee uninterrupted debt service. In a command economy, presumably, the governmental authorities could always act to cut imports or promote exports as needed to assure availability of the requisite foreign exchange. Finally, should any troubles arise, many hopefully assumed, the East Europeans would ultimately be backed by the substantial gold and foreign-exchange reserves of the USSR—the so-called Soviet umbrella. All in all, lending in the bloc appeared to be a good bet, and despite doubts expressed by some (particularly about the purported Soviet umbrella), most bankers were happy to lend.

Conversely the East Europeans, for their part, were happy to borrow. Their domestic growth rates had been faltering for some years, owing to a variety of increasingly evident inadequacies in their mechanisms for formulating and implementing economic policy. The planning methods of the 1950s, which depended foremost on centralized resource allocation, physical targeting, and administered pricing, had proved economically counterproductive in the 1960s; and except in Hungary (and nonaligned Yugoslavia), market-oriented reforms had been either resisted by conservative party bureaucracies or reversed by forceful Soviet action (as in Czechoslovakia in 1968). By the end of the sixties existing regimes recognized the need to shift emphasis toward a more technology-intensive scheme of development if greater efficiency and improved performance were to be achieved without risking any new "Prague springs." The necessary technology could be obtained only in the capitalist West. Export prospects to the West, however, were not favorable, owing especially to the poor quality of the region's manufactured output. Western credits, therefore, seemed to offer a convenient means of financing sought-after capital-goods imports while sustaining domestic consumption levels. In effect, savings of the outside world would be used to underwrite investment objectives at home. Debts would be serviced out of the proceeds of enhanced production in the future.

The result of this congenial convergence of interests was a rapid expansion of borrowing, especially in the first few years after the Nixon-Brezhnev summit of 1972. From 1970 to 1981, as table 7.1 shows, the net hard-currency debt of the Soviet Union and its East European allies (gross debt less deposits in Western banks) multiplied nearly tenfold, from $7 billion to $66 billion, before declining in 1982–84. (Yugo-

TABLE 7.1. Net Hard-Currency Debt of the Soviet Union, Eastern Europe, and Yugoslavia, 1970–84[a] (in billions of dollars)

	1970	1975	1980	1981	1982	1983	1984
Soviet Union	1.0	7.8	8.7	10.8	9.7	10.4	7.5
Eastern Europe							
Bulgaria	0.7	2.1	2.5	2.1	1.7	1.3	0.7
Czechoslovakia	0.6	1.2	3.4	3.4	3.3	2.8	1.9
East Germany	1.4	4.8	11.2	11.0	10.7	9.0	7.7
Hungary	0.6	2.3	5.8	6.2	5.2	5.0	4.4
Poland	1.1	7.7	22.0	23.2	25.9	25.5	25.0
Romania	1.6	3.1	9.3	9.7	8.1	6.7	3.8
Soviet bloc	7.0	29.0	62.9	66.4	64.6	60.7	51.0
Yugoslavia	1.9	5.7	16.8	18.0	15.2	15.6	14.4

Source: Wharton Econometrics, *Centrally Planned Economies Outlook* (March 1983 and April 1985).

[a]*Net hard-currency debt* is defined as gross hard-currency debt to Western banks, Western governments, and international financial organizations minus deposits in Western banks.

slavia's debt also multiplied tenfold during the same period, from $1.9 billion to $18 billion, before leveling off.) Soviet bloc gross debt reached an estimated $88 billion, as some of the borrowed funds were used to build up skimpy foreign-exchange reserves. By far the fastest rate of growth of debt in the region was Poland's. From not much more than $1 billion in 1970 (the result of loans contracted mostly in the late 1960s to finance grain purchases), net Polish liabilities to Western banks and governments soared to $23 billion by the time martial law was declared in late 1981—$26 billion on a gross basis (table 7.2). In little more than a decade the country contrived to become one of the world's biggest sovereign debtors as well as one of the shakiest.

II

The story began innocently enough. In late 1970, Edward Gierek replaced Wladyslaw Gomulka as first secretary of the Polish United Workers Party and quickly embarked on an

TABLE 7.2. Poland's Gross Hard-Currency Debt and Debt-Service Ratio, 1972–81 (in billions of dollars and percentages)

	1972	1973	1974	1975	1976	1977	1978	1979	1980	1981
Gross debt	1.6	2.8	4.6	8.0	11.5	14.0	17.8	21.1	25.0	26.0
Debt service (as a percentage of exports)	15	19	23	30	42	59	79	92	108	173

Source: Treasury and State Department Fact Sheet on Polish Debt, in *The Polish Economy*, Hearings before the Subcommittee on European Affairs, Senate Committee on Foreign Relations, January 1982, p. 12.

ambitious and comprehensive program of industrial modern-
ization. Gomulka's fall, after fourteen years in power, was a
direct result of the failure of his economic policies; the final
straw was a proposed rise of domestic food prices, which
caused rioting in a number of Polish cities. The Gierek government's intended solution was, in effect, a "dash for
growth" designed to placate all of the country's important
social groups—rapid expansion of both agricultural and industrial investment, increased consumer-goods production,
and higher wages, all to be supported by loans and technology
from the West. In the words of one New York banker, "This
was populism pure and simple, a strategy to gain political
support by giving everyone what he wanted."[3] But opportun-
istic though this may have been it was not an unreasonable
policy, given the willingness of Western creditors to lend.
After all, why risk popular discontent at home if the necessary
ingredients for economic development could be imported so
easily from abroad?

At first, Gierek's populist strategy was remarkably successful. Indeed, until mid-decade Poland enjoyed the highest
growth rate in the Soviet bloc, with living standards rising
substantially. In the absence of basic reforms, however, these
gains could not be sustained for long; by 1976, economic performance was once again beginning to flag. Investment projects
were falling behind schedule, bottlenecks developed, and
wages started to outrun the availability of consumer goods.
In response, like Gomulka before him, Gierek felt impelled to
call for an increase of food prices, to bring prices in line with
real production costs as well as to ease the heavy burden of
subsidies on the state budget. But as before, the reaction was
rioting in the streets; and while, because of the riots, the price
hikes were swiftly rescinded—within twenty-four hours in
fact—by then, the damage was done. Worker resentment
steadily mounted, and soon the economy went into a tailspin.
Growth dropped to 5 percent in 1977, half the rate recorded
earlier in the decade, and to just 3 percent in 1978. By 1979,
national output was actually declining in absolute amount.

Falling output meant insufficient exports to repay foreign
debts that were coming due. Yet the Gierek regime felt unable

either to squeeze workers further, for fear of adding to popular discontent, or to challenge entrenched bureaucratic resistance to reforms of the domestic planning system. Instead, apart from some tinkering with ad hoc administrative measures and direct controls, even greater reliance was placed on the expedient of Western credits. Borrowing was accelerated, both to pay for essential imports and to refinance outstanding loans. As a result, hard-currency debt increased by 50 percent between 1975 and 1977, and then doubled in the next three years, with debt-service payments soon eating up virtually all of the country's meager export revenues (table 7.2). "It was a completely irresponsible borrowing policy," commented a prominent Polish figure recently.[4] But for the government at the time it simply seemed the easiest, if not the only, way out of an increasingly desperate situation. The tough decisions needed to come to grips with the economy's underlying structural faults could be conveniently postponed in the hope that something—anything—might eventually come along to turn things around.

Unfortunately, nothing came along. Instead, matters only got worse as world interest rates began to take off in 1979, exacerbating the country's debt-service difficulties, and as export prospects were further depressed by renewed recession in the West. By 1980 it was clear to all that the situation was unsustainable: something had to be done. And so, for the third time in a decade, an increase of food prices was proposed. Some adverse reaction was expected, of course, which Warsaw hoped to ameliorate by making the price hikes selective rather than across-the-board. But no one anticipated the veritable tidal wave of strikes that broke out across the country, most spectacularly at the Lenin Shipyard in Gdansk. Ultimately, the Gierek regime had no choice but to negotiate a "social compact" with striking workers, guaranteeing their right to establish free and independent trade unions. On August 31, 1981, the day the agreement was signed, the Solidarity movement was formally born.

But not even that brought the economy out of its tailspin. As important as Solidarity was to workers' political rights, its economic impact in the short term was bound to be negative so long as the authorities continued to resist its growing demands. Chaos reigned as Solidarity and the government wrangled over everything from wages and work conditions to the removal of corrupt public officials and the people's right to vote. Not even the dismissal of Edward Gierek in September and the full assumption of power by General Jaruzelski the following February stemmed the ebbing tide. National output, which had fallen by 2.5 percent in 1979 and some 6 percent in 1980, dropped at an annual rate in excess of 12 percent in 1981, and the debt-service ratio skyrocketed to an incredible 173 percent. By the start of 1981 it was an open secret that Poland could no longer meet its scheduled obligations, and much of the year was spent working out reschedulings of its current debt with Western creditors, even as domestic tensions continued to mount and Soviet troops massed on the country's frontiers. This was the setting in which martial law was declared on December 13, posing a challenge not only to Western banks but also to the foreign policy of the United States.

III

For Western banks, Poland was the biggest scare yet. True, it was not the first time since the start of the Incredible Quarter Century that sovereign debt had become a problem. As indicated, a number of countries had already experienced occasional difficulties in debt service. But never before had the stakes been so high. After Zaire got in trouble in 1975, Walter Wriston could say of Citibank's $40 million exposure, "If we lost our total unguaranteed portion in Zaire, that would be a third of what we wrote off on the Penn Central. That's not a very exciting number."[5] Zaire's whole bank debt at the time added up to less than $1 billion. Similarly, no more than $2 billion was owed to bank creditors when Peru had a payments crisis in 1976; and no more than $3 billion when Turkey neared bankruptcy in 1978–79.[6] In Poland, on the other hand, the exposure was far greater. Of the country's gross debt of $26 billion outstanding in 1981, almost two-thirds—some $16 billion—represented obligations to banks. To say the least, this was a rather more exciting number. As one observer later commented, "In the case of Poland, the banks were for the first time clearly prisoners of their own commitment."[7]

Not that they had become prisoners involuntarily: quite the opposite, in fact. Banks had vigorously pursued their lending in Poland despite a paucity of hard data on the country's financial and economic circumstances. Like most other East European governments, Warsaw refused to provide even basic balance-of-payments statistics; information on such matters as foreign-exchange reserves and short-term debt was treated as a state secret. Yet financing continued freely until late in the game, even after Poland's economic managers had plainly lost control of the situation.[8] In the early 1970s, new loans could be justified by the size of the Polish economy, by the early success of Gierek's populist strategy, and above all by the country's large coal deposits (among the richest in the world), which in an age of energy scarcity appeared to make Poland an especially good credit risk. But later in the decade, once the economy started into its precipitous decline, the accelerated pace of lending was far less justifiable. If Poland's aggressive borrowing policy was irresponsible, so too, it may be said in retrospect, were the loan practices of many banks. At the very least, this can be regarded as a prime example of disaster myopia.

Banks in Western Europe and Japan, which accounted for almost all of the new lending in the latter part of the decade, were the most nearsighted of all. After the food riots of 1976, American banks—showing an uncommon caution—virtually ceased to provide new credits to Poland, evidently hoping to pressure Warsaw to get its financial house in order. The idea, according to one New York banker, was "to take a wait and see attitude rather than 'pull out' loans which would have made economic adjustment much more difficult."[9] Between 1976 and 1980 net claims of U.S. institutions rose by no more than $250 million, to a level near $3 billion, at a time when bank claims in the aggregate were swelling from $6 billion to $16 billion. The West Europeans and Japanese were more than happy to fill the gap left by the Americans.

There were several reasons for this. First was the inten-

sifying competition in international financial markets. These
were the years when the ascendancy of U.S. institutions in
the business was being challenged seriously for the first time:
West European and Japanese banks were eager to establish
themselves anywhere and everywhere they could. And second
was the closeness of these banks to commercial exporters in
their own countries, who were then aspiring to increase sales
in Poland. From the middle of the decade onward, in an effort
to sustain essential imports, the authorities in Warsaw began
to insist that Western suppliers arrange the necessary financing themselves, forcing them to approach their customary
banks back home for export credits for the Poles. West European banks, in particular, found it difficult to turn down
such requests. Since they are frequently shareholders in the
very corporations that are also their clients, they stood to
profit in two ways, from the lending itself and also from the
exports that would be promoted. Japanese banks, closely tied
to major domestic industrial groups, were faced with an essentially similar temptation. Despite signs of a gathering
storm in Poland, few of these institutions were willing to fore-
go the attractive pecuniary gains that could be had in the
short term.

Finally, Western governments, especially in Western Europe, had their own reasons for not wanting to see any disruption in the flow of financing to Poland. Partly this was crass
commercialism—a desire, shared with the banks, to promote
profitable export sales. And partly, in a manner reminiscent
of the politicization of lending in the nineteenth century, it
was diplomatic calculation—a desire to cultivate centrifugal
forces within the Soviet bloc, by continuing to underwrite a
relatively open and moderate Communist regime. For both
reasons, bank behavior was subjected to considerable government influence, particularly in West Germany.[10] New flows
of funds were deliberately and openly encouraged by guarantees of private credits as well as by direct lending on official
account. Even Washington got into the act, substantially augmenting the amount of private financing available for Polish
grain purchases under arrangements with the Commodity
Credit Corporation (CCC) of the Department of Agriculture.

Washington's initiatives reflected both the pressure of farm interests in Congress and reasons of state. In all, nearly half of the total of $16 billion owed to Western banks in 1981 was covered by formal guarantees of one kind or another from the lenders' home governments. Unguaranteed bank exposure amounted only to about $9 billion in all.

Official intervention became most forceful in 1980, when even the West European and Japanese banks were beginning to look askance at what was going on inside Poland. In early 1979 a syndicated loan of $550 million had been organized for the Poles, albeit somewhat reluctantly. But when Warsaw came back for yet more funds a year later, to repay maturing debts as well as to keep up needed imports, bankers balked. Lending no longer seemed such a good bet. Not only was it obvious by now that the Polish authorities, despite their central planning system, could no longer guarantee uninterrupted debt service; it was also apparent (confirming the earlier doubts of some bankers) that no Soviet umbrella existed, despite the USSR's deep political interest in Poland. Although some Soviet loans had been made earlier, the Russians were now making it quite clear that they no longer wished to put up much money of their own to help pay for Warsaw's mistakes (particularly if Moscow's aid was, in effect, to be used simply to service interest obligations to capitalist banking institutions). Ultimately, new private credits could be arranged only after vigorous prodding from key Western governments. In West Germany, a consortium of leading banks agreed to a refinancing package totaling 1.2 billion deutsche marks ($675 million) only after direct pleas from the highest level of the government in Bonn, including Chancellor Helmut Schmidt himself.[11] Likewise, on the U.S. side, officials found it necessary to lobby with unusual frankness to help persuade a reluctant syndicate of lenders, led by the Bank of America and four other major U.S. banks, that it was in their own interest to provide $325 million in fresh money. Said William Schaufele, who was then America's ambassador in Poland, "We told the banks they wouldn't get their money out if they didn't continue to lend."[12] Both loans were finalized over the summer of 1980. Neither was as large as the Poles had hoped for; the terms were also considerably tougher. Yet Warsaw would not have done even this well had it not been for the prompting from Bonn and Washington.

But the aid came too late. On March 5, 1981, Warsaw formally notified its creditors that loans then falling due would have to be rescheduled. Payments of interest had already dried up; and on March 26, a formal moratorium was announced on all amortization of principal. The banks then had no choice but to agree to negotiations, which continued for most of the year until an accord was reached in the first week of December—the first major comprehensive rescheduling of the Incredible Quarter Century. Some $2.3 billion of debt due in 1981 to 501 Western banks (95 percent of the total amount of principal due in the final three quarters of the year) was to be stretched out over an eight-year period, on condition that the Poles repay $500 million in interest obligations that had been temporarily waived earlier in the year. Even before the declaration of martial law a week later, it was obvious to creditors that Poland was going to be a problem for years to come. Default suddenly seemed a distinct possibility.

IV

For the U.S. government, that possibility was an unwelcome complication at a most inopportune time. With the rise of Solidarity in 1980, Poland had become the touchstone of American foreign policy in Eastern Europe. Here suddenly seemed a real chance to promote political liberalization in the Soviet bloc. Opportunity turned to constraint, however, after Solidarity was suppressed in December 1981. During the following months, the risk of default on Warsaw's shaky bank debt added considerably to the difficulties experienced by the United States in trying to exercise leverage over the course of events inside Poland. Washington found its strategic interaction with the Polish authorities to be inescapably linked to a strategic interaction with its own financial institutions. Once again, officials had to find some way to balance the legitimate interests of both the banking community and U.S. foreign policy.

The irony was that Washington had encouraged the growth of bank debt in the first place, not only at the start of the era of détente but even as late as the German and U.S. refinancing loans of 1980. High finance and high politics had already been effectively linked in American policy. The only change now was in the policy objective, which, after martial law, shifted dramatically from reward to punishment of the governing regime in Poland.

In fact, during the year and a third of Solidarity's brief lifetime, U.S. officials maintained an essentially benevolent posture toward Warsaw's debt problems, even after Ronald Reagan assumed the presidency in January 1981. Under both the Carter and Reagan administrations, Washington's fundamental strategy was consistent and clear: Do everything possible to avoid destabilizing the situation inside Poland; do nothing to jeopardize the infant labor movement's achievements. Naturally, no massive new official credits could be contemplated—certainly not before the Polish authorities managed to get a better grip on their own economic affairs. But a number of smaller actions might be taken to help ease Warsaw's desperate financial plight, so long as the liberalization process within the country was not diluted or reversed. In effect, economic assistance would be traded in exchange for continued tolerance of Solidarity by the Polish government.

Washington's strategy was especially evident after Poland's moratorium on debt service was announced in March 1981. Even before negotiations with the country's bank creditors got under way, an agreement was rapidly worked out with the governments of fifteen Western nations (later sixteen) to postpone for four years $2.3 billion of debt payments due official creditors in 1981. At the urging of West European governments and with the Reagan administration's blessing, the terms of the agreement, which was signed in April, were made unusually liberal. For example, fully 90 percent of the principal and interest falling due from May 1981 to December 1981 was rescheduled, in contrast to the 80 percent that had previously been the norm in official restructurings. The United States made no secret of the fact that it was still trying to underwrite a relatively open and moderate Communist regime. As I was later told by a former State Department official who was closely involved in the rescheduling, "The purpose was to ease their foreign payments problems in lieu of official aid. In essence, this was political relief." [13]

Likewise, in the spring of 1981 the CCC raised the interest rate guarantee for private export credits to Poland (for grain purchases) from 8 percent to 12 percent—an exceptional provision for the Poles, not generalized to any other country. In the summer, some $55 million of agricultural credits were made available to the Polish state-farm system to purchase surplus U.S. corn for its brooder chicken industry. And even as late as early December, plans were going forward for $100 million of new CCC credits that would, for the first time ever for any country, have fully guaranteed all interest payments in addition to principal. According to John D. Scanlon, a State Department expert on East European affairs (later to be named U.S. ambassador to Poland), presidential authorization for the credits was provisionally granted on December 11, just two days before Warsaw's declaration of martial law on the thirteenth.[14]

With the suppression of Solidarity, however, Washington's attitude quickly hardened. Western government talks with the Jaruzelski regime about a possible rescheduling of Poland's 1982 debt to official creditors were immediately suspended at the Reagan administration's behest, and numerous other economic sanctions were levied by the United States against both Poland and the Soviet Union, including most importantly the termination of all subsidized food shipments and most U.S. government-guaranteed bank credits to Poland (including the mooted new CCC credits), restrictions on Polish fishing rights in American waters and landing rights at American airports, suspension of talks with the Soviet Union on a new long-term grain agreement (due to have begun in February 1982), and an embargo on materials for Russia's natural gas pipeline from Siberia to Western Europe (the so-called Yamal pipeline). In subsequent months, Washington also made known that it would oppose Polish membership in the International Monetary Fund, effectively blocking an application that had been submitted in November 1981 (reflecting Warsaw's dogged search for new sources of finance). The aims of the U.S. sanctions were clear—to persuade Poland and its patron the Soviet Union to end martial law, free all political prisoners, and restore Solidarity to its previous domestic status. Pressure would be sustained, administration officials insisted, until these goals were achieved. In the words of then Assistant Secretary of State Robert Hormats:

> In these circumstances, our continuing objective is to apply sustained pressure on both Poland and the Soviet Union to have martial law lifted, the prisoners released, and the dialog [*sic*] between the government, the church and Solidarity begun in earnest in a free atmosphere. In short, our goal is the restoration of the process of reform and renewal in Poland.[15]

Unfortunately, the impact of the sanctions was substantially blunted by the continuing problem of Poland's debt. For 1982 alone, the country was estimated to owe private and official creditors a total of $10.4 billion in principal and interest—yet Warsaw was not even up to date on the interest due for its rescheduled 1981 bank debt.[16] Plainly, additional relief would be required if default was to be avoided; and Washington had no desire to precipitate a possible Western banking crisis. Policymakers were thus faced with an acute dilemma. How could pressure be sustained without jeopardizing financial stability?

It was recognized, of course, that the direct exposure of Western banks was not overly large (certainly not as compared with the exposure that had been built up in Latin America or the Far East). Of the $16 billion of outstanding bank claims on Poland, almost half, as indicated above, was guaranteed by creditor governments. Of the $3 billion owed to American banks, $1.6 billion was guaranteed by the CCC; and the remainder was so thinly spread among some sixty U.S. institutions that for most American banks guarantee-adjusted exposure amounted to less than 5 percent of capital.[17] Nevertheless, the fear of financial disruption was genuine. Who knew what might happen if a major debtor like Poland were compelled to default?

The biggest question was, Could a default be contained? Many U.S. officials were concerned about the possibility of a domino effect—a scramble by banks to reduce their exposure elsewhere in Eastern Europe, which might have led to a chain reaction of defaults throughout the region and perhaps in other areas of the world as well, endangering the entire Western banking structure. The threat of a regional contagion seemed real. Banks had their commercial interests to protect, after all.

Washington's apprehensions were by no means unfounded, as the events of subsequent months amply demonstrated. Contagion did indeed occur. Already in 1981, following the eruption of Poland's debt crisis, the flow of new bank financing to other Soviet bloc countries as well as to Yugoslavia had gradually started drying up. In 1982, with U.S.–Soviet relations back in the deep freeze and Eastern Europe's hard-currency exports severely curtailed by Western recession, the retreat from the region turned into a wholesale flight—a classic case of enthusiasm in international lending tranformed into investor revulsion, or "overkill," to use the phrase of one contemporary journalist.[18] As Western banks sharply reduced their interbank lines in Eastern Europe and declined to roll over many maturing short-term loans, two more of the area's countries, Romania and Yugoslavia, were forced to join the Poles in the rescheduling queue; and most others found it necessary to institute dramatic austerity measures in order to cope with the scarcity of credit. In 1982–84, regional hard-currency debt actually declined by a total of some \$19 billion (table 7.1) before bank lending finally began to show some cautious signs of revival. The dominos did come close to falling.

In trying to contain the threat, U.S. officials used both words and money. Efforts were made to communicate to the banks Washington's own interpretation of the interests involved in Eastern Europe. As early as the last year of the Carter administration, American bankers had begun requesting informal briefings from the State Department on the political situation in Poland. Once Warsaw's debt crisis erupted in 1981, policymakers used the opportunity of these periodic sessions to outline U.S. goals for the region as a whole, stressing in particular Washington's desire to avoid any undue destabilization of financially strapped governments. Banks were not told precisely what officials would like to see them do, at least not so far as can be determined. As John Scanlon told me, "All we could do was give political judgments. We told the banks that they had to make their decisions on banking principles."[19] Nonetheless, the message was clear, and banks do seem to have factored it into their calculus of prospective risks and returns in the region. My conversations with bankers suggest that, at a minimum, the government's signals helped to prevent the retreat from Eastern Europe from turning into a disorderly rout. Little new lending resulted, but at least the rate of reduction of existing exposure was moderated somewhat. The banks, in turn, kept officials informed on the status of rescheduling negotiations as well as their assessments of economic developments. Though never formalized, and always "correct," this ad hoc arrangement apparently functioned effectively enough to ensure adequate comprehension of Washington's policy priorities in the region at the time.

Only once did the State Department feel the need to go beyond this informal channel of communication—in April 1982, when banks were called in specifically to talk about the deteriorating financial situation in nonaligned Yugoslavia.[20] In this one instance policymakers did say what they would like to see the banks do, warning explicitly against an excessive credit squeeze that might drive the Yugoslavs into the arms of the Soviet Union. Convened by Lawrence Eagleburger, a former ambassador to Yugoslavia who was then under secretary of state for political affairs, the meeting was welcomed by bankers concerned over the panicky reactions of some of their fellow creditors, but was roundly criticized by the Treasury Department—though more for reasons of bureaucratic politics than on foreign policy grounds. In the words of John Scanlon, who was then deputy assistant secretary of state for European affairs,

Eagleburger was brilliant, because he made the bankers realize that Yugoslavia, politically, was of interest to the United States. That was his basic message. Some of the bankers were delighted that he said it. Marc Leland [assistant secretary of the Treasury for international affairs] was upset, though this was mainly a jurisdictional dispute: he felt that Larry was going off the reservation. Eagleburger never received one word of criticism from the banks.[21]

As for Poland itself, U.S. officials made it clear that they would not oppose continued bank contacts with the Polish authorities despite the suspension of talks with Warsaw by official creditors. When the Jaruzelski regime, in March 1982, finally came up with the last of the $500 million of back interest that had been promised to Western banks in return for their 1981 rescheduling, negotiations began for a similar rescheduling of payments due in 1982. Thereafter, the banks remained in almost constant consultation with the Poles, as successive rescheduling agreements were signed in November 1982 (for 1982 debt), November 1983 (for 1983 debt), and May 1984 (for debt due in 1984–87). Sanctions notwithstanding, Washington plainly preferred debt relief to default.

Indeed, Washington's concern was such that despite its tough rhetoric about martial law it decided to put some of its own money where its mouth was, with no strings attached, when Warsaw failed to meet payments due on part of Poland's $1.6 billion of CCC-guaranteed credits, beginning in January 1982. CCC guarantees are of course a legal obligation of the U.S. government: whenever guaranteed credits are not paid on time, Washington must make good to claimants, effectively taking over some of the borrower's debt service itself (and then transferring the overdue claims to its own books). Ordinarily in such an instance creditor banks are required to file a formal notification of default in order to qualify for CCC reimbursement. In this case, by contrast, for the first time ever, the statutory requirement was circumvented by an emergency waiver quietly adopted by the Reagan administration to avoid triggering "cross-default" clauses in other

Polish bank loans—in essence, a unilateral concession to the Poles. Washington let Warsaw off the hook unconditionally, without extracting any price at all: no formal default, no attempt to attach Polish assets, not even a public announcement. Some of America's biggest banks benefited from this decision, which was taken after a number of meetings between policymakers and leading bankers. In January alone, $71 million was paid out to such institutions as Citibank, Chase Manhattan, Morgan Guaranty, and Bank of America. By the end of the year, the total had come to $344 million—all at a time when the administration's objective was still supposedly to maintain "sustained pressure" on the Poles to reverse their repressive measures. Nothing could have more vividly demonstrated the dilemma facing U.S. officials. The balance appeared to tip in favor of banking interests, imposing a real constraint on American foreign policy.

V

Indeed, from a foreign policy point of view, the CCC decision was undoubtedly the turning point of the whole affair: before it, Washington's sanctions policy could be taken seriously; afterward, the position of the Reagan administration appeared to be fatally compromised.

The decision seems to have reflected two distinct fears on the part of administration officials. First was the fear of financial disruption—an "inchoate" fear, admits John Scanlon,[22] but nonetheless widely shared in Washington at the time. And second was a fear of political disruption in the Western alliance, reflecting Western Europe's far more extensive economic and strategic interests in Poland (as well as in other Soviet bloc nations). For West European governments, stability in the East was regarded as vital to continental security. In addition, profitable export markets were at stake; and loan exposure was of course substantially greater—in Poland, for instance, amounting to about three-quarters of Warsaw's total hard-currency debt. U.S. relations with its European allies had already been soured by Reagan administration efforts to block final agreement on the Yamal pipe-

line (as well as by earlier differences over how to react to the
Soviet invasion of Afghanistan). Given that West European
banks and governments had so many more links to protect—
and, in particular, a much greater investment position in Poland—there was a considerable risk that they might now respond favorably to some kind of a Polish overture to negotiate
a separate deal on debt. American bankers were worried about
this prospect; a confidential working document prepared by
one large U.S. bank warned,

> There is every reason to believe that European banks and
> governments would cooperate with the Poles. . . . There is
> [therefore] not only a significant probability that such a
> default action would fail, but it would also impose mas-
> sive costs on the alliance.[23]

The decision did not go unopposed within the administration. Defense Department officials in particular, led by
Fred C. Iklé, under secretary for policy, and Assistant Secretary Richard N. Perle, argued vigorously for maintaining the
hardest possible line toward the Poles, up to and including a
formal declaration of default.[24] The banking system would
survive, they said; and our allies, ultimately, would have no
choice but to go along, despite the greater exposure of countries like West Germany. The key issue, in their opinion, was
punishment: Poland as well as the Soviet Union must be made
to pay a real price for their suppression of Solidarity, in the
form of a total cutoff of financial relations. The sanctions must
really hurt.

The prevailing view within the administration, however,
reflecting a de facto coalition of the Treasury and State Departments, ruled out default under almost any conceivable
circumstance. In this view, the issue was not punishment but
persuasion—to retain instruments of leverage over the Poles
by keeping the sanctions flexible and, above all, reversible. By
keeping Poland's debt on the books, officials reasoned, Washington could actually hope to reinforce its pressure on the
Jaruzelski regime—"keep Poland's feet to the fire," to quote
a leaked State Department memorandum. With new lending
at a standstill, Warsaw's interest payments represented a net

transfer of financial resources to the West. An action as decisive as a formal default—however satisfying it might be to the emotions—would, on the other hand, have relieved the Poles of that burden and left no room for rewarding them for any possible future concessions to U.S. policy. Precious foreign exchange would no longer have to be found to meet debt-service obligations to Western banks. Instead, the martial law regime would have been freed to consolidate its authority with even greater force and harshness. According to one administration official, "Keeping the pressure on this way is the real hard line."[25] The view was summarized by then Assistant Treasury Secretary Marc Leland as follows:

> What should we do about the debt? Our feeling is that we should try to collect it. The more pressure we can thereby put on the East Europeans, particularly on the Soviet Union, to come up with the funds to help Poland, the better....
>
> To maintain maximum leverage...they should be held to the normal commercial concept that they owe us this money, so they should come up with it....
>
> In this way we hope to maintain the maximum amount of pressure on them to try to roll back the actions of December 13th and to enter into an internal political dialog [sic].[26]

The proof of the pudding, however, is in the eating. In reality, this "real hard line" proved scarcely effective at all and may even have been counterproductive in Washington's attempt to exercise leverage over the Poles. For once having signaled the depth of its apprehensions about default, the administration actually made itself more vulnerable to the threat of financial disruption; and the Jaruzelski regime was not above making veiled hints about such a possibility as a form of policy leverage of its own.[27] Washington's constraint, in effect, became Warsaw's opportunity. Poland could hold Western bank assets as a sort of hostage (not unlike what had been done to Iranian assets just a couple of years earlier), and perhaps even a wedge could be driven between the U.S. government and its West European allies. Despite their desperate economic straits, the Poles found themselves handed some additional room for manuever by the CCC decision.

At a minimum, the credibility of the administration's commitment to sanctions was strained by the action. The key question at the time was why the CCC guarantees were paid off unconditionally. Observers were entitled to ask: Why was no quid pro quo demanded of the Poles—for instance, by attaching some of their foreign assets as collateral for eventual repayment? Officials who were involved now argue that few such assets were available: a few airplanes and fishing boats plus some meager hard-currency reserves. Poland was no Iran.[28] But that misses the symbolic value of the lost opportunity. Psychologically, the impact of Washington's sanctions dissipated as a result of the appearance of vacillation by policymakers. What was left was an impression—right or wrong—that the administration, simply put, was more concerned about a Western banking crisis than it was about the future of Solidarity. Public perceptions at the time were accurately and colorfully summarized by right-wing columnist William Safire:

> The secret regulation giving the junta extraordinarily lenient treatment makes a mockery of pretensions of pressure.
>
> In an eyeball-to-eyeball confrontation, the Reagan Administration has just blinked. Poland's rulers can afford to dismiss the Reagan rhetoric because they have seen the U.S. is ready to do regulatory nip-ups to save them from default.[29]

In the end, of course, as we know, few of the administration's stated goals were achieved. Poland neither "came up with the money" nor "rolled back" the actions of December 13. Martial law, to be sure, was formally lifted after two years; but many of its key features remain, now incorporated into Polish civil law. And while most political prisoners were released in 1984, Solidarity is still an outlawed organization, replaced by tame, government-sponsored trade unions. In short, the process of "reform and renewal" was not restored. Yet one by one most of the U.S. sanctions imposed so dramatically in 1981 were either eased or eliminated. In July 1983 a new long-term grain agreement with the Soviet Union was announced. In November 1983 the most stringent sanctions directed against the Yamal pipeline were lifted, and restrictions on Polish fishing and landing rights were relaxed. The following month Washington joined other Western governments in reopening the suspended talks with Poland on rescheduling some of its debt to official creditors. And in December 1984, opposition to Polish membership in the IMF was finally dropped.

Admittedly, apprehensions about default were by no means the only—or even the most important—reason for such seemingly conciliatory behavior. The new Soviet grain agreement, for example, was best understood in terms of President Reagan's 1980 campaign promises to American farmers. Similarly, the easing of sanctions against the Yamal pipeline was most evidently motivated by a desire to improve roiled relations with our West European allies. Even the reopening of debt negotiations was a response, at least in part, to growing discontent on the part of other Western governments, who viewed Washington's continued refusal to talk as essentially self-defeating. From the time discussions were first cut off, following declaration of martial law, Warsaw had suspended all payments of interest as well as principal on its official debt, although interest payments to banks were maintained (albeit with delays). As a result, our allies began to argue, the Poles were actually able to save precious foreign exchange, in effect, at the expense of Western taxpayers. The situation, said a British official (with characteristic understatement), was "slightly absurd."[30] Initially, other creditor governments had needed no persuasion to go along with the suspension of negotiations; they were in full accord with Washington's impulse to isolate Poland politically. But as the situation dragged on, eventually they started to lobby the Reagan administration vigorously for agreement to an early resumption of talks.

The easing of sanctions might have occurred even without apprehensions about default. As the previous chapter demonstrated, the use of economic sanctions in pursuit of foreign

policy goals is a tricky business even in the best of circumstances. In the Iranian case, Washington's asset freeze ultimately proved successful in part because it was linked to an
objective—release of the hostages—that was essentially modest in scope. In Poland, by contrast, major policy changes were
being sought. Historical evidence suggests that, in such instances, sanctions have only rarely been effective.[31] Washington, in other words, was fighting an uphill battle from the
start. Even had there been no Western bank exposure in Poland, the Reagan administration would undoubtedly have experienced difficulties in trying to prevent the suppression of
Solidarity.

Poland's debt, therefore, cannot be blamed per se for the
evident failure of the administration's policies. Washington's
leverage in the situation was limited at best. But debt can be
blamed for adding to the administration's difficulties by undermining the effectiveness and credibility of its other policy
initiatives. The effort to avoid Polish default worked at cross-
purposes with other policy interests. I would not go so far as
to argue, as has one commentator, that the default issue thus
"allowed the tyranny of the debtor to replace the tyranny of
police-state Communism as the key to Western calculations."[32] But I would contend that it helped undercut whatever influence the U.S. government might otherwise have had
in its confrontation with Warsaw. The negative effect of the
linkage may have been marginal, but it was not trivial. Foreign policy capabilities were indeed diminished.

VI

Thus the early warnings of the likes of the Senate Foreign
Relations Committee staff turned out to be correct after all.
U.S. national interests were indeed put at risk by the growing
volume of claims on a "recreant foreign government." Sovereign lending by banks did have diplomatic consequences.
As in the Iranian case, private financial relationships inescapably altered the issues of salience for public officials at a
time of a serious extrafinance challenge to foreign policy. An
explicit linkage strategy could not be avoided. But unlike the

Iranian case, in this instance options for government policy were constrained rather than enhanced once the political crisis broke. Concern about the possibility of a default on some or all of Warsaw's foreign debt significantly weakened Washington's bargaining leverage as it sought to pressure the Polish authorities to reverse their suppression of Solidarity.

The difference, clearly, lay in the contrasting net balance-sheet positions of banks. Where Iran's large concentration of assets had offered an attractive new weapon to help officials realize their stated policy preferences, Poland's debt overhang effectively sapped U.S. diplomatic influence. The difference, moreover, appears systematic: the sort of difficulties encountered with the Poles could easily be replicated when dealing with possible challenges from other debtor states as well. The question is how to minimize such potentially adverse policy linkages in the future. What can we learn from the Polish experience?

In some respects, the implications of the Polish and Iranian experiences are the same. First, as in the Iranian case, we see the importance of having the best possible information. Lending to Poland in the 1970s might have been a good deal more prudent had better data been available on financial and economic conditions in the country; Washington would then have had less debt to worry about in the 1980s. Second, we see the importance of the government getting its act together. Given the inherent conflict between their concern for a Western banking crisis and their concern for Solidarity, policymakers would have had a public relations problem even in the best of circumstances. But the credibility of their commitment to sanctions was further strained by known divisions within the administration's ranks, between Defense Department hardliners on the one hand and the Treasury and State Departments on the other. Mixed signals inevitably sowed doubts about the government's resolve. And third, we see the importance of maintaining efficient channels of communication between the public and private sectors, to ease any potential for collision between commercial and political interests. Financial contagion in Eastern Europe might have been far worse had officials been less successful in conveying their policy priorities to the banks.

However, in one crucial respect the Polish experience contrasts quite sharply with that in Iran—namely, in the role played by the public sector in encouraging private lending to the Poles in the years prior to the declaration of martial law in December 1981. Washington and other Western governments obviously overdid it, particularly after the mid–1970s, in relying on banks to help underwrite alliance objectives in Poland. This, in turn, served to highlight all of the questions that are implicit in politically motivated interventions in private international finance (the four e's) and exacerbated the tradeoffs among policy objectives that officials ultimately had to face. As in the nineteenth century the costs of intervention, in economic and political terms, turned out to be considerable: bankers found themselves with a lot of dubious paper on their hands, jeopardizing financial stability; and Western governments found themselves with differing investment positions to protect, threatening diplomatic frictions as well. Likewise, serious equity issues were raised for banks that had been explicitly persuaded (for example, in 1980) to accept a higher degree of exposure in Poland than they might otherwise have preferred; these issues were only imperfectly resolved by the Reagan administration's unconditional decision to make good on maturing CCC guarantees after January 1982. Washington's sanctions policy undoubtedly could have been more effective had there been greater sensitivity to these questions in earlier years. I will consider in part III how it might be possible to promote more such anticipatory thinking in similar situations in the future.

CHAPTER 8

Latin Debt Storm

After Poland came Latin America, where a debt crisis erupted in the summer of 1982. If the stakes had been serious in Poland, in Latin America they were potentially catastrophic. Now the entire world financial structure appeared to be in jeopardy. This was a truly *global* crisis. Mexico alone, where the storm began, had a debt nearly three times Warsaw's; for the region as a whole, external obligations topped $300 billion. These were really exciting numbers, and they posed an unprecedented challenge to the foreign policy of the United States. High finance and high politics were now undeniably—and perilously—joined. As *The Economist* commented soon after Mexico's troubles started,

> How to resolve these difficulties is one of the biggest foreign policy questions facing Washington, for behind Mexico there stretches a line of other burrodollar [*sic*] debtors. Brazil, Argentina, and Venezuela between them owe $140 billion. The United States dare not risk the political consequences of calling default on any of them. ... Those in the Reagan administration who have calmly contemplated pulling the plug on Poland's debt, which is only a third of Mexico's, have to recognize that the problem facing them in Latin America is far bigger.[1]

Bigger—but not necessarily more constraining. Fears of financial disruption were evident in Washington, of course, just as they had been earlier during the Polish crisis. Yet as we shall see, at the outset at least, American foreign policy capabilities were actually enhanced rather than diminished by the difficulties of debtors in the region. In fact, the Latin American experience has much to teach us about intrafinance challenges to foreign policy arising from the net liabilities of foreigners (subset B in table 1.2). Initially, genuine opportunities were created to further U.S. government objectives, even if eventually, as the crisis wore on (and continues to wear on) these gains turned out to be essentially transitory. New policy linkages were indeed generated, but they were anything but simple.

I

The roots of the Latin American debt crisis go far back, at least to the late 1960s, when several governments in the region (along with a number of other Third World nations) made a deliberate decision to finance accelerated investment domestically with borrowing from public and private institutions abroad—"indebted industrialization," in the phrase of one observer.[2] Like the East Europeans after the start of détente, they hoped to use savings of the outside world to underwrite investment objectives at home; also like the East Europeans, they intended to service their debts out of the proceeds of enhanced production in the future. Superimposed on this was the first oil shock, which spurred further borrowing to pay for higher-priced oil imports; and then the trend after 1976 toward negative real interest rates in global financial markets, which whetted appetites even further. By the time of the second oil shock, at the end of the decade, many Latin governments had seemingly become addicted to foreign finance, and debt was piling up at a dizzying pace. By 1982, as can be seen in table 8.1, total debt in the region had swollen to some $315 billion—a fourfold increase in just seven years.

The bulk of the debt was concentrated in a handful of the region's largest countries—Brazil and Mexico, which between

TABLE 8.1. Latin American Foreign Debt, 1975–82[a] (in billions of dollars)

	1975	1976	1977	1978	1979	1980	1981	1982
Latin America	75.4	98.2	116.2	152.0	184.2	229.1	279.7	314.4
Of which:								
Argentina	6.0	7.1	8.2	12.2	19.7	27.1	32.3	36.7
Brazil[b]	23.3	28.8	35.1	46.6	51.5	64.6	74.1	83.2
Chile	4.9	4.7	5.2	6.7	8.5	11.1	15.5	17.2
Colombia	3.6	3.6	3.9	4.5	5.9	7.3	8.2	10.3
Mexico	16.9	21.8	27.1	33.6	40.8	52.7	75.5	82.4
Peru	4.1	5.5	6.2	7.1	7.1	8.8	8.8	10.4
Venezuela	5.7	8.7	12.3	16.3	23.7	27.5	29.3	31.8
Others[c]	10.9	18.0	18.2	25.1	27.0	30.0	36.0	42.4

Source: Inter-American Development Bank, *External Debt and Economic Development in Latin America: Background and Prospects* (Washington, January 1984).

[a]Includes disbursed external public and private debt from all sources; includes short-term as well as medium- and long-term debt.

[b]Short-term debt not included in the figures for 1975–79.

[c]Includes Bahamas, Barbados, Bolivia, Costa Rica, Dominican Republic, Ecuador, El Salvador, Guatemala, Guyana, Haiti, Honduras, Jamaica, Nicaragua, Panama, Paraguay, Suriname, Trinidad and Tobago, and Uruguay.

them accounted for half the total; plus Argentina, Chile, Colombia, Peru, and Venezuela, which together accounted for another third. These seven were all among the top twenty borrowers of the Incredible Quarter Century (see chapter 2). In most respects, they were a heterogenous bunch. Some were oil importers, others oil exporters. Some aimed for export-led growth, while others focused on development for their home markets. And some were interventionist while others practiced varying degrees of laissez-faire. But they all shared a distinct taste for foreign borrowing, particularly from commercial banks. Of their total debt outstanding in 1982, some 80 percent was owed to private creditors, up from 70 percent in 1975.

Banks, for their part, were happy to accommodate the Latins (as they were other Third World borrowers), for all the reasons enumerated in chapter 2. The Incredible Quarter Century now was in full swing. Newly rich OPEC countries were parking their surplus earnings in Western financial markets, and banks were eagerly searching for new outlets for excess liquidity. Forgotten or ignored was the long history of lending frenzies in the Americas—the sorry cycles of boom and bust that had characterized financial relations with the Latin republics almost from the moment of their birth (chapter 4). In the 1930s, Britain's Royal Institute of International Affairs had warned, "The history of investment in South America throughout the last century has been one of confidence followed by disillusionment, of borrowing cycles followed by widespread defaults."[3] But in the 1970s, who remembered—or even cared? Rates of return in the region looked good, debt performance since the Great Depression had been prudent, and any residual risks, presumably, could be limited through diversification or by shortening the maturities of new credits. In Latin America, as in Eastern Europe, lending appeared a good bet. Almost two-thirds of all bank loans to developing countries in the decade went to nations of the Western Hemisphere.

Enthusiasm was most marked among U.S. banks, for whom the Latin region had long held a special commercial attraction. American bankers may have shown a commend-

TABLE 8.2. U.S. Bank Exposure in Latin America, June 1982[a] (in billions of dollars)

	All U.S. banks	Nine largest U.S. banks[b]
Latin America	82.5	49.1
Of which:		
Argentina	8.8	5.6
Brazil	20.5	12.3
Chile	6.1	3.3
Colombia	3.0	2.1
Mexico	25.2	13.6
Peru	2.3	1.3
Venezuela	10.7	7.1
Others	5.9	3.8

Source: Federal Financial Institutions Examination Council, "Country Exposure Lending Survey" (Statistical Release No. E.16), December 6, 1982.

[a]Includes total amounts owed U.S. banks after adjustments for guarantees and indirect borrowing.

[b]Bank of America, Bankers Trust, Chase Manhattan, Chemical, Citibank, Continental Illinois, First National Bank of Chicago, Manufacturers Hanover, and Morgan Guaranty.

able caution in Poland, but Latin America was our backyard, a place where U.S. trade and investment interests were considerable and widespread. Moreover, American financial predominance south of the border had been widely acknowledged since at least the Roosevelt Corollary early in the century. The share of U.S. banks in loans to Latin America has always tended to be larger than their share of bank lending worldwide. In the 1970s, therefore, the American banking community took the lead in promoting capital flows, particularly in the form of syndicated credits, to its hemispheric neighbors. By mid–1982, this had resulted in an accumulation of U.S. bank claims totaling some $82.5 billion (table 8.2), equal to one quarter of all U.S. bank claims overseas. Nearly two-thirds was accounted for by just the nine largest American banks, whose Latin exposure amounted to more than twice their total capital. The exposure of European and Japanese banks, by comparison, while also sizable, was far smaller in relative terms (that is, in relation either to their other international claims or to their own capital). The U.S. banks stood to lose the most should something go wrong and history repeat itself.

For a time, of course, little did go wrong. Throughout Latin America, as in other major capital-importing areas, high growth rates were achieved in both domestic income and foreign exports, seemingly justifying the rapid accumulation of debt. As impressive as the loan numbers were in absolute magnitude, they did not appear far out of line in relative terms, when compared to the expansion of borrowers' export revenues. Debt-service capacity, as we saw in chapter 2, showed little erosion on average up to the end of the 1970s. Although occasional problems did arise—in Chile during the Allende period, for instance, and in Argentina and Peru in 1976—none was perceived by lenders as serious enough to shake their underlying confidence.

Financing continued to flow, therefore, despite growing apprehensions outside the banking community about the provision of so much credit "without strings." Might not governments use their easy access to the markets, some observers began to ask, to evade hard policy choices? Cautioned Arthur Burns, then chairman of the Federal Reserve Board of Governors, in 1977, "Countries ... find it more attractive to borrow than to adjust their monetary and fiscal policies; and if they can do this without having lenders write restrictive covenants into loan agreements, so much the better."[4] Echoed the International Monetary Fund, "Access to private sources of balance-of-payments finance may ... in some cases permit countries to postpone the adoption of adequate domestic stabilization measures."[5] Bankers, though, demurred, arguing that in principle variations of market terms alone (interest-rate spreads, maturities, etc.) ought to suffice to exercise effective discipline on borrowers. Governments would not willingly jeopardize their creditworthiness, bankers said, by choosing inappropriate economic policies.

In practice, however, that is precisely what many governments did—just as sovereign borrowers have so often done through the ages (chapter 4). One study of ten borrowing countries in the 1970s found no evidence of such a market discipline at work: none seems to have been deflected from its chosen policy course by a mere hardening of terms on new loans.[6] Quite the contrary, in fact. Lulled by their high growth rates, more and more Latin governments in time succumbed to the temptation of overcommitting themselves, growing dependent on foreign financing as an alternative to painful policy adjustments at home. Under pressure from the twin exigencies of internal budget demands and external payments deficits, economic management grew increasingly lax in a number of countries. Over the course of the decade fiscal deficits soared, credit often was allowed to expand too rapidly to contain inflationary forces, private savings rates declined, and most exchange rates became significantly overvalued. Moreover, in some of the more notable cases, an increasing portion of borrowed funds was wastefully diverted from productive investment projects to support current consumption, military expenditures, or even accelerating capital flight.[7] Time began to run out for effective domestic stabilization.

And then came the triple whammy of shocks of the end of the decade—the second round of oil-price increases, which worsened many debtors' terms of trade; the renewal of global recession, which depressed their export prospects; and the escalation of world interest rates, which added to their debt-service burdens. For Latin America as a whole, the effects of this unprecedented combination of events were devastating. Average debt-service rose from 38 percent of export revenues in 1980 to 59 percent by 1982; for the seven major Latin borrowers, from 42 percent to 65 percent.[8] Even without these external shocks, many countries in the region would by then undoubtedly have faced severe difficulties in trying to get their economies back under control. With the shocks, it was evident that something was indeed going wrong. Would history repeat itself after all?

Certainly it seemed so to the banks. Suddenly, after years of keeping the accelerator to the floor, they started to apply the brakes to new borrowing in the region. As early as 1979, in a classic example of the herd effect in international banking, maturities began to be trimmed significantly, as lenders sought to cut back on their credit lines to key debtors. Pre-

viously, short-term advances had accounted for no more than
about one-eighth of Latin America's overall debt. By 1980–
81, that share had doubled to almost one-quarter.[9] And then,
in the latter half of 1981, financing at any maturity started
to fall off, partly in reaction to the region's own growing difficulties and partly as a reflex to Poland's debt problems at the
time. Clearly, a storm was brewing in Latin America.

The first threatening clouds appeared in the spring of
1982 during the Falkland Islands (Malvinas) conflict between
Britain and Argentina. Hostilities broke out on March 25 when
Argentine commandos invaded and, within a week, seized the
British-held islands in the south Atlantic. In retaliation, following the example of the Carter administration's riposte to
the 1979 seizure of American hostages in Tehran, the government of British Prime Minister Margaret Thatcher froze all
Argentine assets held in banks in Britain, amounting at the
time to about $1 billion. This action, in turn, caused Argentina
to fall behind in some of its debt-service payments and raised
fears around the world of a general moratorium on Argenti-
nian loans. And this, in turn, discouraged new lending to other
Latin countries that were known to be sympathetic to the
Argentinians.[10] Bankers remained cautious even after the
fighting was ended by Britain's successful counterinvasion of
the islands in May.

Really rough weather, however, did not set in until the
summer, when political and economic uncertainties in Mexico
sparked a major capital flight from that country. The Mexican
economy had been weakening for some time under the impact
of sagging prices for oil (Mexico's principal export) and high
interest rates as well as an overly ambitious—and highly inflationary—domestic growth policy. Although in February
1982 the overvalued peso had been devalued by almost 50
percent, much of the measure's impact was lost because of
an upcoming presidential election scheduled for July, which
made the government reluctant to institute the politically
painful adjustments (for example, budgetary cutbacks, wage
restraints) that would have been needed to make a devaluation effective. When an austerity program finally was announced on August 1, following Miguel de la Madrid's

convincing victory at the polls, panic ensued as fears of a new
devaluation erupted. With Mexicans rushing to convert all
available cash balances into dollars, official foreign-exchange
reserves were quickly exhausted, and Finance Minister Jesus
Silva Herzog was forced to announce, on August 12, that his
government could no longer meet its external debt-service
obligations. Suddenly, one of the Third World's two largest
debtors seemed on the edge of default. The tempest had
broken.

II

For the U.S. government, Mexico's announcement represented a truly world-class foreign policy challenge. The debt
of this one country alone exceeded the entire sum of loans
that had been at risk earlier in East Europe. Should the Mexican storm spread to other major Latin borrowers, such as
Brazil or Argentina, there was no telling what might happen
to the structure of international finance—or to the whole
world economy, for that matter. A chain reaction of defaults
in the region, threatening global economic collapse, seemed
a real possibility. Could this intrafinance threat be averted?

Certainly Washington was determined to try. On broad
foreign policy grounds, Latin America had always been regarded as a region vital to U.S. national interests; and no
Latin nation was deemed of more strategic importance than
Mexico. From the moment the Mexicans made their difficulties known, therefore, U.S. officials assumed that America's
own security, not just Mexico's, was at stake—that the United
States too was threatened by serious economic or political
instability south of the border. High finance, now, had clearly
become high politics. No one doubted that the storm could
spread to other Latin nations as well. Washington simply
could not ignore the potential for disorder in its own backyard
that might have been sparked by spreading financial default.

More narrowly, policymakers were of course also worried
about the direct risks to American banks, particularly our
large money-center institutions, owing to their extraordinarily high loan exposure in Latin America. As indicated above,

U.S. banks stood to lose most should history repeat itself in the region. In Mexico alone at the end of 1982 exposure in relation to capital exceeded 40 percent in nine of the country's twelve largest banks; taking the region's five biggest borrowers together (Argentina, Brazil, Chile, Mexico, and Venezuela), the exposure of these same dozen banks ranged from a low of 82.7 percent of capital (Security Pacific) to a high of 262.8 percent (Manufacturers Hanover), with most falling in a range of 140–180 percent.[11] Plainly, the solvency of these key institutions was threatened, making the whole U.S. banking system vulnerable. If Poland in 1981 had provoked fears of financial disruption, Latin America in 1982 triggered absolute nightmares.

Finally, there was also concern about U.S. trade interests in Latin America. By 1982, the region had surpassed all but West Europe as a market for U.S. goods; Mexico, on its own, was now America's third largest customer. As soon as the Mexican storm broke, it was evident that commerce and real estate markets throughout the American Southwest would be seriously damaged.[12] U.S. government officials were well aware that many exports, and hence jobs, would be jeopardized if something were not done for Mexico and other troubled debtors. Washington's motives were neatly summarized by Federal Reserve Chairman Paul Volcker:

> The effort to manage the international debt problem goes beyond vague and generalized concerns about political and economic stability of borrowing countries.... The effort encompasses also the protection of our own financial stability and the markets for what we produce best.[13]

Motives and determination were one thing, however—capacity to act, quite another. In fact, the Reagan administration was manifestly unprepared for a threat of this magnitude. Despite the Polish scare just a year earlier, policymakers had steadfastly discounted signs of an impending storm in Latin America and had developed no firm game plan for dealing with one. The result may actually have been to add to the sense of urgency, even panic, in many quarters when the tempest finally broke. According to a New York

lawyer who works closely with some of the major international banks, "This whole debt crisis business could have been
avoided if the Treasury had been doing its job."[14] Some in-
dications hint even that Mexico's dramatic announcement on
August 12 was deliberately designed, above all, to push Washington into action. Says a former Reagan administration official, "Silva had to create an international crisis on debt . . .
to get the attention of the Treasury. He had to hit them over
the head to let them know something was the matter."[15]

To their credit, though, once they were "hit over the
head," administration officials together with the Federal Reserve did move quickly to get the crisis under control, and
within months a more or less coherent policy program began
to crystalize out of their initially hurried, ad hoc efforts. Labeled a formal "strategy" by government spokesmen, it was
really rather less than that—not much more than a glossary
of the essential elements of one, in fact. Still, it was better
than having no game plan at all, and it demonstrated that
policymakers were committed to translating their motives
and determination into practical action. According to then
Treasury Secretary Donald Regan, who first outlined it in
testimony before the House Banking Committee in December
1982, the strategy had five main parts:

> First, the crux of any lasting effort to remedy the debt
> problems of less-developed countries must be orderly, but
> effective, domestic adjustment efforts by each country
> concerned. . . .
>
> The second key element is readiness to provide official
> financing on a transitional basis where that is needed to
> permit orderly adjustment to take place. The interna-
> tional institution best able to provide official support
> within the context of domestic economic adjustment is
> the International Monetary Fund. . . .
>
> A third key element is commercial bank financing. . . .
> a necessary component of the overall financing package
> required to support orderly economic adjustment. . . .
>
> A fourth element is the official will and capacity to act
> in potential emergencies. . . .

The fifth key element is a set of economic policies in the major industrialized countries that will produce economic growth and a counter to the risks of inward-looking protectionism.[16]

Informally, the administration's strategy could best be understood as a mixture of short-term crisis management (the fourth element) and longer-term stabilization (the other four). The immediate problem was to avert the imminent threat of default—a relatively straightforward task of quick emergency assistance at the government-to-government level. Beyond that, the problem was to lessen the risk of any recurrence of financial crisis in the future—a far more demanding objective achievable, if at all, only over a rather more distant time horizon and requiring the involvement not only of governments (the first and last elements of the strategy) but also of the relevant transnational actors, namely private banks (the third element) and the IMF (the second). Washington's challenge was complex: to negotiate its way through both problems at least cost to America's own economic and political interests. How successful was it?

III

On the first problem, Washington was quite successful. Default was indeed averted. In fact, no sooner had Silva Herzog made his announcement than the U.S. government rushed to the rescue like the cavalry of old (although this time on behalf of the Mexicans). August 12 was a Thursday. On Friday, the finance minister flew to Washington to begin discussions with key administration and Federal Reserve officials; and by Sunday night, the fifteenth, terms had been agreed on some $2 billion of emergency assistance for the Mexicans—half in the form of a food credit from the Agriculture Department's Commodity Credit Corporation (CCC), and half as advance payment for oil purchases by the Department of Energy for the U.S. Strategic Petroleum Reserve. In addition, the Treasury Department's Exchange Stabilization Fund (ESF) and the Federal Reserve together contributed about half of a $1.85

billion "bridging" loan provided by a number of Western central banks through the Bank for International Settlements (BIS). And Washington also backed a proposed $3.9 billion credit from the International Monetary Fund, to be negotiated as urgently as possible. By September the Mexican situation seemed, for the moment at least, in hand.

Unfortunately, by then other situations were getting out of hand. Despite the administration's efforts the storm kept spreading, and soon other Latin debtors were finding themselves deep in trouble too. Argentina, for example, never did recover from its defeat by the British in the spring. The Falkland Islands conflict, conservatively estimated to have cost the Argentinians $2 billion, had drained available financial resources and severely disrupted both the domestic economy and foreign trade relations. By the end of the summer, Argentina's balance of payments was in serious deficit, and hard currency reserves were nearing rock bottom. Likewise, in Brazil runaway inflation, high world interest rates, and a sharp terms-of-trade deterioration were wreaking havoc with that country's capacity to service its huge external debt. After Mexico, consequently, still more rescue packages had to be organized. In the fall, some $1.23 billion was made available to Brazil by the ESF. In December and January, bridging loans were arranged through the BIS, with substantial U.S. participation, for both the Brazilians and Argentinians. And new IMF credits were backed for these countries too as well as for other shaky Latin debtors. Only then could administration officials begin to breathe easier.

IV

But just a little easier. The more demanding challenge was yet to come—the problem of lessening the risk of any recurrence of financial crisis. Here evaluation of Washington's performance must be rather less upbeat. Achievement of longer-term stabilization would, by definition, require years of patient and determined effort. In this phase of the drama, there could be no obvious climax or denouement. The story continues still, and for the Reagan administration success for this part of its original strategy proved to be frustratingly elusive.

The requirements were daunting. Lessening the risk of future financial crisis demanded serious adjustment efforts by debtor governments (the first element of the administration's strategy); in a word, austerity. Could the Latins be persuaded to accept the pain and political risks involved in genuine reform of their past economic policies? But it was also going to demand the cooperation of commercial banks to help support sound adjustment programs (the third element of the strategy); in a word, financing. Could private lenders be persuaded to increase, or at a minimum to maintain, their credit exposure in the region? For U.S. officials, once more, this meant engagement in two separate, but linked, strategic interactions—one with Latin governments and one with America's own financial institutions. Yet again, some way had to be found to balance the legitimate interests of both the banking community and U.S. foreign policy.

This was not going to be easy. Banks at the time simply did not share the same goals as policymakers. Not only did they not regard it as being in their interest to increase exposure in the region significantly. More to the point, in another classic case of market enthusiasm suddenly transformed into revulsion, many lenders were eager to reduce their investments as quickly as possible: just as in Eastern Europe, a broad, regional contagion was sparked by the troubles of a single major debtor. The cautious retreat that bankers had begun in the spring of 1982 during the Falkland Islands conflict turned into a veritable stampede after the Mexican storm broke. As late as June, the Bank of America had been able to organize a $2.5 billion syndicated credit for the government of Mexico, albeit with some difficulty. After August, however, new private lending dried up throughout nearly all of Latin America, with banks cutting back even on routine short-term trade credits in most countries. In the United States the retreat was led by smaller local and regional banks, which had relatively few direct customer relationships in the region to protect.[17] But not even the major money-center institutions were much inclined to "throw good money after bad." In 1980 and 1981, total bank claims in Latin America had risen by some $30 billion a year. In the eighteen months from June 1982 to December 1983, by contrast, they increased by no more than $9 billion in all; and since that was actually less than the total of so-called involuntary lending arranged in connection with parallel IMF credits (more on that below), these numbers mean that there was absolutely no spontaneous new lending in the region at all.[18]

The results, for the region, were appalling. Suddenly cut off from accustomed financing and, as I indicated above, already reeling from both external shocks and internal policy mistakes, many Latin nations were pushed to the edge of default. The flight of private creditors was directly responsible for the spreading of the Mexican storm throughout the region and served to exacerbate an already grave economic plight. In the words of one careful analysis, "What could have been a serious but manageable recession...turned into a major development crisis unprecedented since the early 1930s."[19] No important borrower was able to maintain debt service without some difficulty. Most countries fell into arrears, and all had to enter into protracted and difficult negotiations with private and public creditors to reschedule maturing loans, being obliged in return to promise often Draconian domestic austerity measures. "Undoubtedly," commented Pedro-Pablo Kuczynski, a former Peruvian government minister, in late 1983, "the interruption of significant new lending by commercial banks has been the major stimulus for such measures."[20] Undoubtedly as well, the prospective costs of these measures in foregone income and lost growth threatened to be extraordinarily high.

Still, it could have been worse. Washington did its best to rein in the worst excesses of the bankers' stampede, using, as in Eastern Europe, both words and money to try to persuade lenders to avoid regional overkill. At the verbal level, all available private and public channels of communication were put to work to communicate the government's own priorities for Latin America. Despite already high exposure levels, banks were constantly exhorted by Treasury and Federal Reserve officials, in the name of the public interest, to resume lending—or at least not to contract existing lines of credit. Paul Volcker became the point man. Typical was a well publicized speech he made in November 1983, in which he laid great stress on easing the difficulties of major Latin borrowers. "In such cases," Volcker said, "new credits should not be subject to supervisory criticism."[21] Translated, this meant that considerations of banking prudence, for the moment at least, would not be allowed to prevail over the objective of keeping key debtors afloat. On the contrary, banks were reportedly threatened with closer scrutiny of their books by Federal Reserve examiners if they did not go along with fresh loans for countries like Mexico or Brazil.[22] Likewise, banks were urged to be more accommodating toward Argentina, in late 1983, after that country's first free presidential election in a decade. According to the *New York Times*,

> The bankers ... said that they were already coming under pressure from the United States ... to aid the country's new democracy after nearly eight years of military rule. Many are resigned to making some concessions.
>
> "We don't want to look like the bad guys," one American banker said.[23]

Officials also urged the banks to consider possible limits on the heavy interest-service burdens then weighing down hard-pressed debtors. In another well-publicized speech in early 1984, Chairman Volcker suggested that "one of the things certainly worth looking at is what arrangements could be made so that one particular important threat to their financial stability, the continued rise in interest rates, could be dealt with."[24] What he had in mind, he made clear, was some kind of a cap on interest payments, with any excess of market rates over the cap being added to loan principal ("capitalization"). A specific proposal for a cap tied to real interest rates was floated by the Federal Reserve Bank of New York at a meeting of central bankers in May.[25] Similarly, in the summer of 1984, Volcker publicly appealed to bankers to offer debtors more favorable terms, including longer maturities as well as lower spreads, when renegotiating loans. It was time, he said, to move to a "new phase in financing" in which additional concessions could now be made to countries like Mexico and Brazil that had demonstrated a genuine commitment to firmer economic management.[26] Officials representing the Federal Reserve chief were even reported to be phoning key bankers around the country in an effort to get his point across.[27]

Moreover, just as in Eastern Europe, Washington evidently hoped to encourage the banks by putting some of its own money where its mouth was, continuing the precedent set by the several emergency rescue packages organized earlier. One example was the U.S. contribution to a substantial increase of IMF funding, finally approved by Congress in the fall of 1983 (see below). Another was the decision of the Export-Import Bank in the summer of 1983 to extend new loan guarantees up to $1.5 billion to Brazil and $500 million to Mexico—the largest such package ever proposed by the bank. William Draper, the bank's president, made no secret of official intentions to prompt further private lending in these and other Latin countries. "We expect the proposed financing will strengthen the Mexican and Brazilian recovery," he said, "by acting as a catalyst for continuing support by the international financial community."[28] The initiative was unusual in that, unlike most guarantee proposals, these guarantees were not tied to any specific projects. Clearly, the government wanted to send a signal.

For all such efforts, though, the government's influence on bank behavior amounted to not much more than a holding operation. Conversations with bankers indicate that, as in Eastern Europe, the main result was to prevent the retreat from Latin America from turning into a rout. Panicky nerves were soothed: the rate of reduction of existing exposure was undoubtedly moderated somewhat. But little enthusiasm for renewed lending or significantly higher exposure appears to have been kindled by the interventions of U.S. officials. In 1984 aggregate bank claims in the region rose by no more than $3.5 billion—once again, far less than the $10 billion total of involuntary lending arranged in connection with parallel IMF credits.[29] Once again, therefore, there was absolutely no spontaneous new lending in the region at all. Nor was a cap of any kind ever seriously entertained by the banking community. Starting in the latter part of 1984 there was, to be sure, some easing of terms in debt negotiations, with multiyear reschedulings worked out for both Mexico and Venezuela in September and another then under consideration for Brazil.[30] But this had less to do with the exhortations of public officials than it did with the banks' own evolving strategy at the time for bargaining with troublesome debtors, particularly Argentina. Bankers, quite frankly, were seeking to avert formation of a common front on financial issues among the region's principal governments—the dreaded "debtors cartel."

In May 1984, the presidents of four of Latin America's largest debtors—Argentina, Brazil, Colombia, and Mexico—meeting in Buenos Aires, had issued a joint statement warning that they "cannot indefinitely" accept the "hazards" of the then current approaches to their debt problems. Expressing concern over the effects of "successive interest rate increases [and] prospects of new hikes," they called for better terms from the banks—lower spreads, longer maturities and grace periods, and smaller renegotiation fees when debts were rescheduled.[31] And these pleas were repeated at a broader gathering of eleven Latin governments held at Cartagena, Colombia, in June—the first of a series of meetings of what came to be known as the Cartagena Group.[32] To bankers, these initiatives looked ominously like the first tentative steps toward a new degree of militancy and collective action among debtors in the region. "This could lead anywhere," said one.[33] And their fears seemed confirmed by the newly elected government in Argentina, which at the time seemed particularly determined to resist creditor demands for a rigorous domestic austerity program. In response, bankers quietly moved to isolate the Argentinians by offering concessions to other big Latin nations like Mexico and Brazil that were still prepared to play by the prevailing rules—in effect, a strategy of "divide and rule," which surfaced at the International Monetary Conference, an annual bankers' meeting, held in Philadelphia shortly after the Buenos Aires joint statement in May.[34] Carrots (multiyear reschedulings, liberalized terms) would be

dangled as rewards for good behavior; the stick of tough bargaining would be reserved for recalcitrants like Argentina.
Such a strategy may have coincided with Paul Volcker's appeals for a "new phase of financing," but it does not appear
to have been caused by them.

In fact, to some extent the government's efforts may have
been compromised by contradictions in the signals it was
sending. On the one hand were the likes of Paul Volcker and
William Draper, as indicated, repeatedly urging the banks to
increase their lending and ease terms. But on the other hand
were officials charged with the prudential supervision of
banks—at the Office of the Comptroller of the Currency, the
Federal Deposit Insurance Corporation, and even (despite the
chairman's public posture) at the Federal Reserve—who were
expressing growing concern about the already exceptionally
high level of bank exposure in Latin America and were advising greater caution instead. In fact, the three regulatory
agencies had been trying for years, largely without success,
to get a handle on the overseas operations of U.S. banks (see
below, chapter 11). Now they seemed more determined than
ever. In April 1983, for instance, a joint memorandum was
issued outlining a five-point program of enhanced supervisory
initatives in international lending. Included in the program
were new rules tightening disclosure requirements and country-risk examination procedures, despite the dampening effect that these measures might have on the willingness of
banks to take on additional overseas exposure.[35] And in June
new minimum capital-asset ratios were adopted for the nation's largest money-center institutions, even though this too
could be expected to discourage some amount of new foreign
lending.[36] Regulators felt that they had no choice but to take
steps of this sort, given their mandated responsibilities to
preserve the safety and soundness of the U.S. banking system.

Furthermore, the signals coming from Capitol Hill were
anything but conducive to additional risk-taking abroad. During the 1983 debate over Washington's contribution to the
proposed IMF funding increase, (again, see below), the banks
came in for a great deal of blunt criticism for their role in
helping to create the debt problem in the first place. "Let's

face it," Iowa Congressman Jim Leach told bankers at hearings before the House Banking Committee, "you've screwed up."[37] For months, the IMF legislation was held up by concerns that fund credits might simply be used, in effect, to bail out imprudent lenders. And finally, when the legislation eventually was passed in November 1983, Congress insisted on tying in supervisory reforms in four areas of international banking, explicitly for the purpose of discouraging any recurrence of imprudent lending in the future—improved disclosure of lending data, strengthened capital-adequacy standards, mandatory increases of loan–loss reserves, and ceilings on renegotiation fees in debt reschedulings.[38] Is it any wonder that the banks now preferred to maintain a relatively low profile in Latin America?

Yet for all the limitations of the government's efforts, the adverse impact on U.S. foreign policy interests appears to have been remarkably mild, at least at the outset. Given Washington's motives and determination to avert financial calamity, it was not surprising that Latin debtors might at first gain a degree of leverage to extract official concessions from the *norteamericanos*. What was striking was how much good will and influence were initially generated for the United States in return, and therefore how much easier it became to realize U.S. foreign policy preferences south of the border despite the retreat of the banks. So far as we know, no formal quids pro quo were built into the initial rescue packages organized for the region's major debtors in 1982. Nonetheless, soon after, officials in the Reagan administration reported a marked shift toward a more accommodating spirit on the part of key governments on various international issues.[39] Washington was now in a position to say, when looking for cooperation, that "we were there when you needed us, now we need you." In Brazil, the administration's efforts to help out financially were reported to have given the U.S. "more leverage . . . than it has enjoyed in more than a decade."[40] Suddenly the Brazilians were willing to talk about problems that had been roiling relations with the United States for years, including most importantly nuclear policy and military cooperation. Likewise, in Mexico, diplomats noted a significant toning down of Mexican criticisms of U.S. policy in Central America. Of course, other events at the time also affected the overall diplomatic environment (for example, a softening of the Reagan administration's approach to certain hemispheric problems in the summer and fall, the succession of Miguel de la Madrid to the Mexican presidency in December). Still, given the Latins' understandable preoccupation with their debt crisis, it is difficult not to credit at least some of their change of attitude to America's financial concessions. In the short run, Washington's investment in these countries' economic stability seemed to yield significant foreign policy dividends.

But only in the short run. As the crisis wore on, it was bound to become increasingly politicized as a result of growing domestic resistance to prolonged austerity measures. Indeed, outbreaks of rioting and street demonstrations as well as election results suggested a steadily declining tolerance for belt-tightening in the region. More and more, the question began to be asked why the burden of "stabilization" should fall entirely on the shoulders of the debtors. What was at first perceived as generosity on Washington's part came in time to be viewed more as miserliness and insensitivity. U.S. concessions, it was noted, had been strictly financial and, for the most part, strictly short-term. (Most of the loans included in the emergency packages for Argentina, Brazil, and Mexico, for example, had to be repaid within one year.) No trade concessions had been forthcoming—indeed, barriers to key imports from Latin America, such as textiles and steel, were on the rise, despite the lip service paid to fighting protectionism in the fifth element of the Reagan administration's strategy—while at the same time persistently high U.S. interest rates, universally blamed on President Reagan's huge budget deficits, were adding to current debt-service burdens. Washington's emphasis on "adjustment" (not accidentally listed first among the five elements of the administration's strategy) translated, in the Latin mind, into nothing more than retarded development, increased unemployment, and declining living standards. The risk was that this changing mood could eventually push impatient Latin governments toward alienation and confrontation with the United States or lead to their replacement by regimes far less friendly to U.S. economic and security interests. It might even threaten the recent renaissance of democracy in the region.

Already by 1984, the straws were in the wind. At their May meeting in Buenos Aires, the presidents of Argentina, Brazil, Colombia, and Mexico had coupled their call for better terms from the banks with a warning that "Their peoples' yearning for development, the progress of democracy in their region and the economic security of their continent are seriously jeopardized."[41] Said one Latin official, "The debt issue is now firmly placed on a political level and is no longer just one for the banks."[42] This point was underscored at the subsequent, broader gatherings of the Cartagena Group by the participation not only of finance ministers, who had previously exercised sole responsibility for handling their countries' debt problems, but of foreign ministers as well. With an increasing sense of urgency, the Cartagena Group pleaded with the United States and other creditor countries as well as with the banks to accept a greater share of the burden of adjustment, lest regional governments be forced by popular pressures into a reordering of their domestic and foreign priorities. And yet more pressure was added in 1985 when Fidel Castro—America's public enemy number one in Latin America—began to speak out militantly on the issue, urging states in the region to cancel or repudiate all their debt obligations. What better evidence could there be that, by then, the crisis had become highly politicized? Although publicly disassociating themselves from the Cuban leader, many Latin officials privately were delighted by Castro's involvement. Said one, "He is improving our bargaining position.... He is saying things we don't dare say."[43]

A little more than three years after the crisis started, therefore—and despite scattered signs of recovery in some key debtor nations—Washington's initial foreign policy dividends in the region seemed to be on the verge of evaporating without some additional investment of financial or trade concessions. Longer-term stabilization had not been achieved. Fresh initiatives, it now appeared, would soon be needed if America was to protect its economic and security interests in the hem-

isphere. At first reluctant, the Reagan administration gradually came around to accepting that its original 1982 strategy
had not in fact lived up to aspirations; and finally, at the
annual IMF–World Bank meeting in Seoul, Korea, in October
1985, Treasury Secretary James Baker (who had succeeded
Donald Regan the previous January) formally proposed a Program for Sustained Growth that was intended, in his diplomatically chosen words, to "begin the process of *strengthening*
our international debt strategy."[44] Key to Baker's program
was to be additional long-term lending from the World Bank
and regional development banks as well as from the private
banking community to help support more growth-oriented
policies in debtor nations as an alternative to the prolonged
austerity measures of previous years. "There must," he said,
"be greater emphasis on both market-oriented economic policies to foster growth and adequate financing to support it."
Between them, the multilateral institutions and commercial
banks were urged to come up with some $29 billion over three
years for fifteen hard-pressed debtor nations in Latin America
and elsewhere. Whether the new Baker Plan was any more
likely to succeed than the older strategy it was intended to
"strengthen" was not immediately clear. (I shall have more
to say about that in chapter 11.) What was clear, however,
was that the United States had, in effect, conceded that the
risk of recurrence of financial crisis was still not effectively
contained. The intrafinance challenge to America's foreign
policy remained as threatening as ever.

V

The United States had one other card to play in attempting
to cope with the challenge to its interests after 1982—the
International Monetary Fund (the second element of the Reagan administration's original strategy). Once the Latin storm
broke, in fact, the government's attitude toward the IMF
changed dramatically and quite swiftly. Initially cool to any
significant or rapid enlargement of fund resources, the Reagan
administration soon became one of its strongest champions,
owing at least in part to an altered perception of how the

objectives of American diplomacy might be served by a strong IMF. In effect, the fund was to be used as an instrument of a linkage strategy to help achieve U.S. policy preferences. Yet here too, it must be noted, as the financial crisis wore on, Washington's short-run gains came to be significantly eroded. Reliance on the intermediation of the fund could not prevent an increasing politicization of the debt problem.

During its first year and a half, the administration actively sought to discourage any early increase of fund quotas (which determine a member-country's borrowing privileges). The Seventh General Review of Quotas had just been completed in November 1980, raising quotas by half, from approximately 40 billion Special Drawing Rights (the SDR, which is the IMF's own unit of account, then being worth about $1.05) to SDR 59.6 billion; and another review was not formally required before 1983. Yet already it was becoming clear that the IMF's usable resources would soon be running low. Mostly as a result of the second oil shock and subsequent recession in the industrial world, deficits of non-OPEC developing countries grew enormously, from $41 billion in 1978 to $89 billion in 1980 and $108 billion in 1981. Total borrowing from the fund rose quickly, from under SDR 1 billion in 1978 (new loan commitments less repayments) to SDR 6.5 billion in 1980 and SDR 12 billion in 1981.[45] As early as the spring of 1981, the fund's managing director, Jacques de Larosière, was warning of an impending threat to the fund's own financial position. Without a new quota increase, he insisted, the fund itself would need to borrow as much as SDR 6–7 billion annually to meet all of its prospective commitments.[46]

Nonetheless, the Reagan administration remained adamant. To a large extent, its opposition was rooted in a critical view of IMF lending practices as they had developed during the presidency of Ronald Reagan's predecessor, Jimmy Carter, particularly after the second oil shock. In early 1979, the fund's executive board had issued a revised set of guidelines on conditionality (the policy conditions attached to IMF loans) that put new emphasis on the presumed "structural" nature of many members' balance-of-payments difficulties.

The normal period for a fund lending arrangement had traditionally been one year. But with the revised guidelines, arrangements would now be extended for up to three years if considered necessary, confirming a trend toward longer adjustment periods and easier conditions that had already been evident in programs financed through such innovations as the Extended Fund Facility, introduced in 1974, and the Supplementary Financing Facility, established in 1977.[47] To the Reagan administration, this all smacked of development lending in disguise—totally inconsistent with the fund's intended role as a limited revolving fund for strictly short-term balance-of-payments assistance. Administration spokesmen were especially critical of large low-conditionality loans like the SDR 5 billion credit arranged for India in late 1981,[48] and were not at all eager to facilitate more such loans in the future. At most, they said, the government might be prepared to contemplate a quota increase of perhaps 25 percent, and even for that they were in no particular hurry.

But then came the Mexican storm—and with it, the dramatic shift in U.S. policy. Suddenly the government was in a hurry. Not only did it pronounce itself in favor of an accelerated increase of quotas (and a more sizable one at that); now it wanted to go even further. At the fund's annual meeting in Toronto in September 1982 then Treasury Secretary Regan suggested "establishment of an additional permanent borrowing arrangement, which would be available to the IMF on a contingency basis for use in extraordinary circumstances."[49] And during the following months the secretary pushed hard for formal consideration of such a proposal, surprising observers who had become accustomed to the administration's previous recalcitrance on the size and timing of any new IMF funding. Said a private banker, "Maybe there's a problem out there that we don't know about."[50]

With Washington no longer dragging its heels, it did not take long to work out the details. In February 1983, the IMF announced agreement on an increase of quotas from approximately SDR 61 billion to SDR 90 billion—a rise of 47.5 percent. Furthermore, the fund's General Arrangements to Borrow (GAB), a special supplementary funding facility dating back to 1962, was to be tripled from approximately SDR 6.4 billion to SDR 17 billion, and for the first time made available to finance loans to developing countries as well as industrial nations—thus converting the GAB into precisely the sort of emergency fund that Secretary Regan had earlier suggested.[51] The U.S. share of these increases, which at prevailing exchange rates came to a total of some $8.5 billion ($5.8 billion for a quota increase, $2.7 billion for the GAB expansion), was, as indicated, finally approved by Congress, after protracted lobbying by the administration, in November. The following month, the enlargement of fund resources was put formally into effect.

A policy shift of this magnitude demands some explanation. At one level the explanation was simple: there really was a problem out there—a threat of a chain reaction of defaults in Latin America and elsewhere that, by risking a global banking crisis, might well have plunged the whole world into the abyss of another Great Depression. The Reagan administration did not want to go down in history alongside the Hoover administration. It had to do something—and the IMF was there. It seemed only natural to make use of an instrumentality that was already available.

At a deeper level, however, the explanation was more complex. Use of the IMF, some administration officials began to believe, might actually serve U.S. policy interests more effectively than attempts to deal with debt problems on a direct bilateral basis. "A convenient conduit for U.S. influence" is the way it was described to me by one key policymaker, then Assistant Treasury Secretary Marc Leland.[52] Any effort by Washington itself to impose unpopular policy conditions on troubled debtors would undoubtedly have fanned the flames of nationalism, if not revolution, in many countries. But what would be regarded as intolerable when demanded by a major foreign power might, it seemed, be rather more acceptable if administered instead by an impartial multilateral agency with no ostensible interests other than the maintenance of international monetary stability. Likewise, the fund could apply pressures to banks, to maintain or increase lending exposure in debtor countries, that might have been resisted had they come from national officials. As the country with the largest share of votes in the fund (just under 20 percent), and as the source of the world's preeminent international currency, the United States still enjoyed unparalleled influence over IMF decision making—in effect, it had an implicit veto on all matters of substantive importance. Through its ability to shape attitudes at the fund, therefore, Washington could hope to exercise more leverage over debtors and banks indirectly than seemed feasible directly, and at lower political cost.

On the issue of policy conditions the fund had begun to tighten its standards even before the Mexican crisis, owing in good part to the Reagan administration's active disapproval of its earlier lending practices. By the summer of 1982 its institutional attitude had already shifted back toward more rigorous enforcement of domestic austerity measures. Thus once the storm hit, fund officials needed no persuasion to take on the role, in effect, of the "cop on the beat"—setting policy conditions for new or renewed credits and ensuring strict compliance with their terms. Following the Mexican crisis, nearly three dozen countries in Latin America and elsewhere fell into arrears on their foreign loans; and over the next year nearly two dozen of them found it necessary to negotiate debt relief of some sort with private and/or official creditors. In all these negotiations, the fund became a central arbiter of access to, as well as the terms of, new external financing. Creditors began to insist formally that a debtor country first conclude a lending arrangement with the IMF subject to tough conditionality as a precondition to their own financial assistance. Many reschedulings were also made conditional upon continued compliance with fund performance criteria; and on occasion disbursements of new loans were even timed to coincide with advances scheduled under fund stabilization programs.[53] The IMF spelled financial relief—and, as such, exercised considerable leverage over the policies of troubled debtors.

That leverage, however, was resented. Throughout Latin America and other Third World areas the slogan became, "The

IMF is a dirty word." And the hand of the United States behind the IMF was increasingly evident to many. In this respect, too, Washington's foreign policy gains proved essentially transitory. Initially, U.S. interests were served by letting the fund get out in front. But as the crisis persisted the veil tended to wear thin, and criticism more and more came to be focused on the perceived power behind the throne—the United States. Hence the widespread and growing dissatisfaction with what was viewed as Washington's miserliness and insensitivity toward the problems of debtor countries. It was no accident that Treasury Secretary Baker, in proposing his new Program for Sustained Growth in the fall of 1985, now chose to place most emphasis on the World Bank and regional development banks rather than, as previously, on the central role of the fund. By late 1985, IMF conditionality was being resisted or rejected by an increasing number of debtors.

The story is similar in the IMF's relationship with the banks. Initially, it seemed, U.S. interests might also be served by the fund's ability to apply effective pressure to banks. As already indicated, Washington's exhortations to banks to resume lending in Latin America and elsewhere fell largely on deaf ears. Not so, however, with the fund, which in several key instances successfully demanded specific commercial commitments as a precondition for its own financial assistance. In connection with its $3.9 billion arrangement for Mexico, for instance, which took some four months to negotiate, the fund refused to go ahead until each of the country's 1,400 creditor banks agreed to extend additional credit amounting to 7 percent of their existing loan exposure (amounting overall to some $5 billion in new bank money for Mexico).[54] Likewise, before approving a loan of $5.5 billion for Brazil in February 1983, a number of requirements were laid down for the banks: restoration of interbank credit lines to $7.5 billion; new loans of $4.4 billion; rollover for eight years of $4 billion in principal due in 1983; and maintenance of short-term trade credits at $8.8 billion.[55] Similar conditions were attached to agreements with other countries as well, most notably Argentina.[56] The IMF's message to the banks was clear. In the words of Jacques de Larosière, "Banks will have to continue to increase their exposures ... if widespread debt financing problems are to be avoided."[57]

Not all the banks were that eager to cooperate—not at first, at least. Many, pursuing their private interests, simply wanted to get their money out as quickly as possible. De Larosière had to "knock heads together," as one official phrased it.[58] But eventually the banks themselves came to recognize the crucial public interest in such involuntary lending in critical cases. Said one prominent U.S. banker, "It was clear that somebody had to step in and play a leadership role."[59] Said another, "The IMF sensed a vacuum and properly stepped into it."[60] Could anyone imagine the U.S. government taking such interventionist initiatives? In the first place, Washington had no jurisdiction over the banks of other countries (which accounted for well over half of total loan exposure). And second, even American banks would have been highly reluctant to take such direction straight from government officials. U.S. banks have traditionally placed great store in their arms-length relationship with the authorities and insist vehemently on their right, as competitors in the marketplace, to make their own commercial decisions. In this respect too, U.S. interests seemed to be served by letting the fund get out in front.

But here also the gain proved to be transitory. What the banks were willing to tolerate in certain critical cases, they said, would not be accepted as a general rule; this was conceded by officials of the fund itself.[61] Certainly bankers might again be prepared, should similar emergencies arise in the future, to surrender temporarily some of their traditional operating autonomy. But they would not, they insisted, accept a permanent role for the IMF in the management of private international credit flows, and they increasingly reasserted their right to do their own thing. Washington could not long rely on fund intermediation with the banks either. This too was evident in Secretary Baker's proposed Program for Sustained Growth, which, despite earlier limited results, returned to a policy of direct exhortations to banks to get them to resume lending in Latin America and elsewhere.

VI

Thus at mid-decade the Latin American debt crisis was still far from being solved.[62] Further efforts were needed to achieve the elusive goal of longer-term financial stabilization. (I shall return to this issue in chapter 11.) Whatever might eventually transpire in the region, U.S. diplomatic interests had by now become inextricably engaged. High finance posed a direct challenge to America's foreign policy.

Several lessons can be drawn from this complex experience. First, for all of the very real perils involved in the sudden threat in 1982 of a chain reaction of defaults south of the border, relatively few constraints appear initially to have been imposed on U.S. policymakers. Certainly the government could not ignore the risks to its own economic and security position in the hemisphere. Policy linkages could not be avoided. Yet at the outset at least, Washington's foreign policy capabilities in Latin America were actually enhanced rather than diminished by the difficulties of major debtors. The troubles of Mexico and others offered the government an opportunity to gain considerable good will and influence for itself in return for only limited financial concessions. This is in striking contrast to the Polish case (discussed in chapter 7). The difference lay in the state of U.S. diplomatic relations in the region at the time, which were essentially nonconflictual rather than adversarial. In Latin America, as in Poland, avoidance of financial disruption was treated as an important policy goal. When dealing with an enemy like the Jaruzelski regime, however, this tended to handicap realization of U.S. foreign policy preferences, since it undermined the credibility of other policy measures; whereas when dealing with its Latin friends, it meant that the government was able to help itself even as it helped others. The lesson seems evident. U.S. linkage strategies bred by foreign debt problems are more apt to be successful when the interest the United States shares with other governments in avoiding default is reinforced by other shared economic or political interests.

Even in Latin America, however, as we have seen, the

initial foreign policy gains proved essentially transitory. As the region's crisis wore on, and particularly as Washington's efforts to revive private lending in Latin America turned out to be largely ineffective, the government's ability to determine the course of events south of the border, whether directly or through the intermediation of the IMF, tended to decline significantly. Additional concessions, it appeared by 1985, would yet be necessary to preserve America's newly won influence in the hemisphere. A second lesson, therefore, also seems evident. Leverage in such situations is a wasting asset, requiring nourishment to remain effective.

A third lesson confirms two points I stressed previously: the importance of both unambiguous signals from the government and efficient channels of communication between the public and private sectors, to ease any potential for collision between commercial and political interests. The lack of contingency planning by the Reagan administration, despite signs of a gathering storm in Latin America, contributed to the severity of the crisis when it finally did strike; the contradictions in the government's subsequent signals to the banking community only threatened to make the situation worse. America's foreign policy position in the hemisphere would undoubtedly have been better off had Washington been able to define its objectives more clearly and spoken with a single voice.

Over the long haul, of course, America's position would have been best off had there been no crisis at all—which brings us to the fourth and final lesson of the Latin American experience: the importance of having a keener sense of history in international banking. Once again, given the green light by their home governments, financiers had risked all on the slippery path of sovereign lending; and once again, owing to a combination of increasingly lax management by debtors and unexpectedly severe shocks to the world economy, they came close to finding themselves sucked into the whirlpool. Future debt crises can be prevented only by curbing the banking community's recurrent proneness to disaster myopia. Improvements in both prudential supervision and monetary management are necessary, if not sufficient, conditions for long-term financial stabilization. As I suggested in chapter 4, high finance would benefit from more effective limits on its own excesses. So too, ultimately, would U.S. foreign policy.

Part III

CHAPTER 9

Diagnosis

Can there still be any doubt of the growing overlap of high finance and high politics? No longer. The four episodes I examined in part II clearly demonstrate how much, after the Incredible Quarter Century, international banking now encroaches on the traditional terrain of U.S. foreign policy. America's diplomatic capabilities are affected, and that influence is indeed significant. Nor can there be any doubt that the impact may at times be disadvantageous, despite the many economic benefits of international banking. The four case studies show that there are areas of potential friction between the government and banks that can in fact handicap Washington's ability to formulate and implement an effective foreign policy. None of the episodes, it is true, led to disaster; and in each case there were shared interests as well. Still, the margin of success most of the time was narrow. Must America always be skating on thin ice?

The fundamental challenge is to articulate a coherent public policy on international banking for the contemporary era that will ensure a broader margin of success in the future. The still evolving relationship between the government and banks must be managed in a manner that satisfactorily balances the legitimate interests of each, while at the same time enabling both sides to perform their respective functions more effectively.

At issue are the policy linkages generated by the internationalization of banking activity. Admittedly, four is a small sample; also, it may be noted that none of the four cases went beyond Third World or East European nations, where external financial considerations are bound to loom large, to focus on episodes directly involving more advanced industrial countries with developed banking systems and widespread cross-border relationships of their own. Valid generalizations, nonetheless, remain possible regarding some of the key circumstances in this issue area that affect linkage strategies in foreign policy. Valuable insights can be gained from a diagnosis of these examples, and these insights apply as much to U.S. relations in the industrial world as they do to relations with developing nations or the Soviet bloc. In total, nine generalizations are enumerated in the following discussion, all pointing to practical prescriptions for national policy in the future. I hope that these observations will contribute to a clearer definition of the public interest in international banking today. At the least, the chapter should help to promote a better understanding of the complex questions involved in bank–government relations in the foreign policy area.

I

Recalling the analytical distinction I introduced in chapter 3, we may begin by considering some of the indirect influences of international banking on the foreign policy process. The four episodes I examined in chapters 5–8 were selected to highlight two critical factors in the complex, continuing dialectic between high finance and high politics: (1) the immediate source of challenge to U.S. foreign policy; and (2) the net external balance-sheet position of U.S. banks. Each case represented one of four possible foreign policy contingencies, as initially outlined in table 1.2. Comparative evaluation of the sample as a whole suggests three broad asymmetries in the impact of international banking on the general foreign policy environment.

First, comparing intrafinance and extrafinance challenges to foreign policy, we see a distinct asymmetry in the way government officials react to issues of high finance and high politics—that is, what issues they regard as salient, and when. Call this the *policy behavior asymmetry*. In our sample, when serious diplomatic problems arose vis-à-vis Iran and Poland, countries with well-established banking ties to the United States, international financial questions became explicitly involved at the policy level in no time at all. The freeze of Iranian assets occurred just ten days after the seizure of American hostages in Tehran; Western government talks with Warsaw about a possible rescheduling of Polish debt to official creditors were suspended immediately after martial law was declared. In both cases, previously apolitical banking relationships were quickly raised from the merely routine and technical to become treated as matters of vital national concern. High finance was inextricably caught up in broader foreign policy conflicts.

By contrast, during the inflow of Arab bank deposits in the 1970s as well as during the Latin American debt crisis of the 1980s—both serious intrafinance challenges to U.S. foreign policy—explicit linkages to nonfinancial matters tended to develop far more slowly and to be far less intense or extensive. In both of these instances, fears of financial disruption were widespread, not only inside the government but also beyond it. Yet in neither case does there seem to have been much systematic effort to join international banking questions to otherwise unrelated policy instruments or issues. The Arabs, as indicated, did receive some concessions on disclosure and investment control; and the Latins did become a bit more accommodating on a number of issues of interest to Washington. But none of these influences was ever more than modest in scope; and in the case of Latin America, they did not even last very long. Problems originating in the banking area were not readily tied into other dimensions of foreign policy.

Such an asymmetry of policy behavior is understandable, of course, given banking's many positive contributions to the achievement of U.S. economic goals as well as traditional attitudes toward the role of markets in the society. U.S. pol-

icymakers, as a matter of principle, tend to resist explicit
political interference with the genuine efficiency gains of international banking, preferring instead, to the extent possible,
to maintain a wall of insulation between the respective realms
of high finance and high politics. No one wants to arbitrarily
restrain banking's capacity to help facilitate growth and prosperity, least of all for political reasons. So long as the competitive pursuit of profit in the marketplace does not obviously
conflict with other goals of foreign policy, therefore, problems
in financial relations are normally treated in strictly economic
terms, to be resolved solely by instruments of economic policy. Only when vital diplomatic or security interests appear
to be at stake is this attitude altered in practice. Then, as in
the Iranian and Polish cases, officials are tempted to look for
policy weapons wherever they can find them—even in private
banking relationships. The wall of insulation between high
finance and high politics is breached.

While understandable, the policy behavior asymmetry is
no longer easy to justify. Arguably, policymakers have no
choice once a diplomatic crisis has developed. At such moments, nothing can or should be excluded from the foreign
policy calculus—not even banking relationships. This is not
expediency: it is simply a matter of getting the job done.
Indeed, for officials to do any less at such times would be
tantamount to a dereliction of responsibility. But why wait
until a crisis has developed? We are entitled to ask, Why
ignore the fact that even short of an emergency, there are
salient tradeoffs between economic costs and benefits on the
one hand and noneconomic policy objectives on the other? In
other words, why pretend that international banking is still
a straightforward commercial activity? If the four episodes
demonstrate anything, it is that foreign policy is already involved whenever banks do a sizable amount of business with
sovereign governments. In substantive and functional terms,
there is no longer any insulation between the two spheres at
all. Traditional attitudes have gotten out of date.

A second asymmetry, stemming from contrasting net balance-sheet positions of U.S. banks, was highlighted at the end
of chapter 7. A comparison of the experiences of Iran and

Poland shows clearly that the impact of international banking relationships on America's foreign policy capabilities varies greatly depending on whether U.S. banks are net debtors or net creditors vis-à-vis relevant foreign states. Call this the *balance sheet asymmetry*. In the Iranian case, where U.S. banks were net debtors, Tehran's large concentration of assets actually expanded the available range of policy options, providing Washington with a new and powerful weapon to help secure the release of American hostages. A significant opportunity was created to help officials realize a key foreign policy objective. By contrast, in the Polish case, where U.S. banks were net creditors, Warsaw's overhang of debt tended to compromise American policy leverage after the suppression of Solidarity. High finance acted as a distinct constraint on U.S. diplomacy. The difference between the two episodes is striking.

We must draw our inferences carefully, however. It is tempting, on the basis of such a difference, to conclude simply that it is preferable always to be a debtor, never a creditor. To paraphrase Shakespeare's Polonius: Better a borrower than a lender be. But that, on its own, would be a naive and simplistic interpretation, even if there is evidently a core of truth in it. Other things being equal, it surely would be more attractive to government officials, in the event of an extrafinance challenge to foreign policy, to be able to wield the weapon of the International Emergency Economic Powers Act (IEEPA) rather than be forced to worry about the threat of default-induced banking failures. In the heat of a crisis, policymakers naturally want all the bargaining leverage they can get. But other things are not always equal: caveats are in order. Limits exist both to the usefulness of the IEEPA money weapon and to the dangers of a threatened default.

The IEEPA, for example, may appear to offer a convenient policy option to U.S. officials. But it is not one to be used lightly, owing primarily to the considerable costs that could be incurred in terms of efficiency, equity, or external relations. Quite special circumstances accounted for the success of the Iranian asset freeze, which might not be repeated frequently, if at all, elsewhere. Only one country was involved in that episode, and of course at the time the United States was still a net creditor in the world. Since then, following years of massive capital inflows, America has once again become a net debtor nation, for the first time since World War I—indeed, as before the Great War, the biggest single debtor anywhere. Now liabilities are owed, on balance, to many countries, seriously increasing the risk that another freeze might trigger a significant run on the dollar or U.S. financial institutions. Could a freeze this time be restricted to just one target country? And if not, could the economic or diplomatic costs be contained? The relevance of questions like these was confirmed in January 1986, when assets of the government of Libya were frozen following a particularly nasty terrorist incident which, according to the Reagan administration, had been directly supported and condoned by the regime of Muammar Qaddafi.[1] Such questions suggest that the money weapon really represents rather less of an opportunity for foreign policy than appears at first glance.

Likewise, while the danger of default may appear to pose inconvenient policy options for U.S. officials, here too caveats are in order. Net claims abroad matter only if a foreign debtor can make the menace of financial disruption seem truly credible. This requires not just that the endangered stock of claims be sufficiently large to constitute a genuine threat to the U.S. or Western banking system. It demands as well that the debtor be convincingly prepared to bear all the potentially serious costs of initiating a default (namely, isolation from world financial markets, possible seizure of its foreign assets or exports). These too are special circumstances, not apt to arise frequently. Accordingly, the danger of default really represents rather less of a constraint on foreign policy than appears at first glance.

Even so, the core of truth remains. From the government's point of view, there still is more advantage to being a debtor than a creditor in the event of an extrafinance foreign policy challenge. The key to the balance sheet asymmetry is moderation, on both the assets and liabilities side. Moderating foreigners' aggregate claims on the United States maximizes the IEEPA's usefulness in specific instances as a source of

leverage on others. Moderating aggregate claims abroad min-
imizes the leverage that others in specific instances may be
able to exert on us. Banks of course have a legitimate interest
in pursuing profit wherever they can find it. But the public
interest, it would appear, is not well served by too high a
degree of internationalization of their overall deposit-taking
and lending activities. Let high finance be high—but not too
high.

A third asymmetry, concerning situations in which U.S.
banks are net creditors vis-à-vis relevant foreign states and
stemming from contrasting states of diplomatic relations with
those states, was highlighted in chapter 8. A comparison of
the experiences of Poland and Latin America, both major
debtor areas, indicates that the foreign policy implications of
a threatened default may vary greatly depending on whether
relations at the time are nonconflictual or adversarial. This
may be called the *diplomatic relations asymmetry*. In the Polish
case, where relations were openly adversarial, Washington's
manifest concern to avoid financial disruption tended, as we
know, to handicap the realization of U.S. foreign policy preferences by undermining the credibility of other policy measures. By contrast, in the Latin American case, where relations
were essentially nonconflictual, efforts to maintain financial
stability actually yielded foreign policy dividends, at least for
a time. By helping others, the United States was also able to
help itself. The lesson was summarized at the end of chapter
8: linkage strategies bred by foreign debt problems are more
apt to be successful when the interest we share with other
governments in avoiding default is reinforced by other shared
economic or political interests. Put differently, when diplomatic relations are nonconflictual, the scope of available policy
options is expanded, and more opportunities are created for
linkages that are mutually advantageous (positive-sum
linkages).

II

The four episodes examined in chapters 5–8 also have much
to say about direct influences in the strategic interaction be-

tween banks and the government. Reciprocal attempts to alter behavior did take place in these cases, although with varying degrees of success. Comparative evaluation of the sample as a whole suggests three broad asymmetries here as well.

One asymmetry, not at all surprising in a world of "complex interdependence," focuses on the role played by implicit or explicit transnational coalitions in the bank–government strategic interaction (the *transnational coalition asymmetry*). Tensions between the public and private sectors developed, to a greater or lesser degree, in each of the four episodes in our sample. Attempts by either side to sway the decisions of the other, it seems, were most successful when one side's interests could be aligned with those of an influential third party (or parties), such as a foreign government (or governments) or a multilateral institution. In 1975, for instance, the large money-center banks were able to stave off congressional pressures for fuller disclosure of data on Arab bank deposits. At least in part, they succeeded because their case coincided with the preferences of key Arab governments. Though never formalized, the de facto coalition of bank and Arab interests was nonetheless strong enough to induce the executive branch to work out a compromise deal to preserve investor confidentiality. Conversely, during the first months of Latin America's debt crisis, U. S. officials were able to stave off bank overkill in the region at least in part because their efforts at persuasion were backed up by the leverage of the International Monetary Fund. This coalition of the government and the IMF was much more formal and was certainly effective in inducing increased, albeit involuntary, lending from the private banking community.

By contrast, when such coalitions could not be formed, reciprocal attempts at influence tended to be much weaker, as during Washington's confrontation with Poland after December 1981. Since few East European countries belonged to the IMF, less backing was available to the U.S. government from the fund to support efforts at curtailing the threat of regional contagion by banks. (Washington's influence in the Polish case was also weakened by the possibility that West European banks and governments might be provoked into negotiating a separate deal with Warsaw—another transnational coalition.) One exception proved the rule: in January 1983, the fund successfully pressured banks into providing some $1 billion of new money to member-country Yugoslavia as part of a comprehensive stabilization program,[2] in effect sustaining the line of policy that had been pursued by Washington since at least the time of Under Secretary of State Eagleburger's meeting with banks in April 1982.

And then there was the Iranian episode, which proved the rule by reversing it: if one side's influence could be strengthened by a transnational coalition, it could also be weakened by loosening an alignment of interests. That is exactly what the Treasury did, right after the asset freeze was first ordered, by permitting setoffs for deposits at foreign branches of U.S. banks. Other things being equal, American bankers could normally have been expected to oppose the extraterritorial reach of the freeze order, in effect joining them with the Iranian authorities in opposition to the U.S. government. But once setoffs were permitted, banking interests no longer coincided with those of Tehran but rather with Washington's. Banks now had an incentive to defend the freeze in foreign courts against Iran's attempts to get its money back, and an implicit coalition was formed with the U.S. authorities instead.

Another asymmetry, also not surprising, focuses on alignments and divisions of interests within the banking community (the *banking community asymmetry*). It is important to disaggregate in the context of complex interdependence, above all for equity reasons. The private sector is not a monolith: more or less serious rifts developed between differing groups of U.S. banks during all of the episodes examined— between institutions with and without large commercial interests in the Middle East, for example, during the congressional campaign for disclosure of Arab deposits; between banks with and without Iranian deposits during the period of the asset freeze; or between smaller local and regional banks and larger money-center institutions during the debt crises in Eastern Europe and Latin America. Although in each instance the rifts were eventually bridged over, what is striking is the extent to which, in every case, the outcome worked mainly even if not exclusively to the benefit of America's largest banks—continued confidentiality on Arab deposits; a favorable outcome of negotiations with Tehran; and a stemming of the retreat of smaller banks from Eastern Europe and Latin America, which might have jeopardized those with the greatest loan exposure. Evidently the giant money-center institutions do have easier access to the corridors of power, as I suggested in chapter 3. They can lobby more effectively at the highest levels of government in Washington, as David Rockefeller for one amply demonstrated during the Arab-deposit debate. They are more apt to be consulted by policymakers, as they were by the Reagan administration in early 1982 before its unconditional decision to waive formal default notification on Poland's maturing CCC-guaranteed debt. And they can even negotiate formally with sovereign governments abroad, as they did with Tehran after the asset freeze, and as they still do, through their ad hoc steering groups, with many debtor nations today. With size does come a differential ability to promote their own preferences, both negatively (for example, preventing disclosure of their Arab deposits) and positively (for example, full settlement of Iran's bank debts), albeit possibly at the expense of other interested parties in the private sector (for example, as charged by Iran's nonbank claimants).

A last asymmetry, perhaps the least surprising of all, focuses on alignments and divisions on the other side of the bank–government strategic interaction—within the government (the *policy coherence asymmetry*). The public sector is hardly a monolith either: it is important to disaggregate here too, though on this side more for reasons of effectiveness than equity. Bankers, it seems from our sample, have good reason to complain about the often mixed signals they receive from public officials. Frequently, Washington does fail to get its act together. And when it does, its diplomatic capabilities appear to be systematically impaired. The credibility of the Reagan administration's commitment to sanctions against Poland's martial-law regime, for instance, was perceptibly strained by known divisions between the Defense Department on the one hand and the Treasury and State Departments on the other, just as earlier public uncertainty over the purported Arab money weapon was undoubtedly exacerbated by open differences of opinion between the executive branch and Capitol Hill. And then there were the contradictions in the signals sent to bankers at the height of the Latin American debt crisis, which certainly threatened to make that difficult situation even worse. Conversely, the successful outcome of the Iranian episode was in no small measure directly attributable to the fact that officials at the time were able to speak clearly and with a single voice. Policy effectiveness tends to vary closely with the government's ability to maintain at least a semblance of coherence in its own objectives and preferences.

III

Finally, in addition to these diverse observations on direct and indirect influences in the bank–government relationship, three more common themes are suggested by the episodes I examined in chapters 5–8. These can be grouped under the headings of *information*, *communication*, and *moderation*.

One theme that comes through loud and clear from all four episodes is the importance of having the best possible information available. Neither bankers nor policymakers can be expected to perform their functions effectively without having adequate access to the relevant facts. Banks, for their part, need full data on the financial and economic conditions of their sovereign clients if they are to be able to assess intelligently all the risks involved in their overseas activities. Adequate information, by itself, does not guarantee prudence in international banking, of course. Facts alone are not a sufficient condition to avert, for example, the kind of "exciting" loan exposures that were built up in both the Polish and Latin American cases. As I suggested in chapter 2, even improved data might not have slowed banks very much in their drive to expand foreign lending in the 1970s; as we saw in chapter 4, a disposition toward disaster myopia recurs frequently in financial history. But adequate information, plainly, is a necessary condition for that proclivity to be corrected—or at least curbed. As a matter of probability, bankers are less likely to complacently discount risks if they can see clearly and accurately.

The government, likewise, needs full data on international banking relationships if it is to be able to cope successfully with challenges to foreign policy when they arise. In the Iranian case, as we know, much time was lost, after the freeze of Tehran's assets, just getting the numbers straight. Little could be done to develop an explicit linkage strategy for negotiating purposes until reasonably reliable information was obtained. Similarly, the 1970s debate over the purported Arab money weapon might have been less heated had more light been permitted to fall on the relevant statistics. Public apprehensions about the dangers inherent in large investment inflows were probably allowed to inflate needlessly, owing to the paucity of hard facts available at the time. In both cases, the government's own collection and disclosure policies were ultimately to blame. Policymakers themselves, in effect, were responsible for making their lives more difficult.

A second theme common to all four episodes is the importance of having efficient channels of commmunication between the public and private sectors in order to ease any risk of collision between commercial and diplomatic interests in specific instances. In both the Polish and Latin American cases, regional contagion might have been even worse had government officials been less successful in conveying their policy priorities to the banks. Likewise, during the Iranian hostage crisis, the outcome of the two separate tracks of negotiations with Tehran might have been far less favorable but for the close and frequent contacts between U.S. policymakers and bank representatives. Again, ensuring an adequate flow of information from Washington to the banking community will not guarantee an absence of areas of potential friction between them; to repeat from chapter 3, the divergences of the two sides' underlying motives and goals are too fundamental for that. Once more, it is a matter of probabilities—a question of reducing the likelihood of any misunderstanding by banks of the government's foreign policy intentions. Efficient channels of communication are a necessary, but not sufficient, condition for achieving greater convergence of public and private interests.

A third and final theme, probably the most crucial of all, concerns the aspirations of bankers and government officials. On each side, ambitions must be moderate if the legitimate interests of both the public and private sectors are to be well served.

On the banking side, the existence of a disposition toward disaster myopia has been repeatedly stressed; its dangers, not only for banks themselves but for the broader public interest, were underscored in particular, in our sample, in the Polish and Latin American cases. Improvements in information and communication might help to curb any recurrent tendencies toward reckless enthusiasm in overseas lending; so would enhanced prudential supervision and monetary management. But ultimately what is required is that each new generation of financiers have a keener sense of history—a greater appreciation of the risks of their own animal spirits. This is the sufficient condition. Prudent self-restraint in international banking is desirable not only from the point of view of the safety and soundness of individual financial institutions and markets. More generally, as suggested above (the balance sheet asymmetry), it is advantageous from a broad foreign policy perspective too.

However, any restraint on the banking side must be matched by comparable moderation by the government. Public officials also frequently exhibit a distinct tendency toward excess when, overcoming their traditional hesitations (the policy behavior asymmetry), they find reason to intervene politically in the realm of high finance. A case in point was the implicit encouragement of lending in Eastern Europe following the start of détente in the early 1970s. As I suggested in chapter 7, Washington (along with other Western governments) obviously overdid it, ultimately exacerbating the policy tradeoffs that were required once martial law was declared in Poland in 1981. And Washington came close to overdoing it with the Iranian asset freeze as well, which (as noted in chapter 6) could have proved very costly for the United States but for the unique circumstances prevailing at the time. A tendency toward excess on the official side too is well documented in financial history, from the Medici Bank's disastrous Milanese loans in the fifteenth century to the politically motivated lending of France and Germany in the nineteenth. Here too a keener sense of history is called for—a greater appreciation of the potential economic and political costs that may ensue from systematic manipulation of capital flows on foreign policy grounds. The wall of insulation between high finance and high politics may be thinner today than in the past, but that is no excuse for public officials to exercise their authority irresponsibly.

IV

Can this diagnosis be translated into practical prescriptions for policy? Admittedly, few of the nine generalizations just enumerated strike the eye as especially dramatic. Several, I have suggested, are hardly surprising at all; some might even be thought banal, little more than truisms. Yet often it is the most obvious truths that are the most easily forgotten. Even the simplest verities bear repeating if they come to be ignored in practice, as seems to have been the case here. One need not be apologetic. In the episodes we have examined neither bankers nor government officials appeared, in their actual behavior, to attach much importance to—or even to be conscious of—many of the asymmetries and themes I have identified. Spelling them out is the necessary first step toward defining the public interest in international banking today. The final step is to make use of this diagnosis to prescribe appropriate improvements for the bank–government relationship in the future.

CHAPTER 10

An Ounce of Prevention

One of the themes I emphasized in the previous chapter was the importance of maintaining efficient channels of communication between the public authorities and banks, in order to ease any risk of collision between commercial and diplomatic interests in the foreign policy process. This means that the still-evolving bank–government relationship can be improved, first of all, at the institutional level, by addressing the manner in which the two sides talk and do business with one another. For a new modus vivendi, it is necessary to find a better modus operandi. The growing interdependence of high finance and high politics must be explicitly acknowledged.

I

At present, hardly any systematic modus operandi exists in the foreign policy area. The working relations between banks and government on international issues can best be described by two negatives: unstructured and unplanned. In the first place, arrangements for communication tend to be mostly informal and ad hoc. Only when a crisis erupts, as during the Iranian asset freeze or the Latin debt storm, are contacts established on a regular, programmatic basis—and then, normally, only for the duration of the crisis. Over the long term. as I suggested in chapter 9, the wall of insulation between high finance and high politics tends to be preserved (the policy behavior asymmetry). The functional, substantive dialectic between the two spheres is given no formal, institutionalized content. And second, arrangements tend to be mostly short-sighted and improvisatory. Little attempt is made at forward planning or coordination on issues of mutual interest to re-duce or eliminate areas of potential friction in advance. The process is reactive rather than anticipatory—"problem-ori-ented rather than strategic," as one Federal Reserve official described it to me.[1]

Neither of these characteristics is accidental, of course. Quite the opposite, in fact. They are fully consistent with the most basic traditions of political economy in the United States, which have always been closer to the liberal concep-tion (as I described in chapter 1) than to either mercantilism or, needless to say, Marxism. In principle, for most Americans, politics and economics are separable and autonomous areas of activity: governments govern; the business of business is business. In practice, this translates into a determined ethic of distance in all dealings between the private and public sectors—an instinct for keeping business–government rela-tions in general, not just bank–government relations in par-ticular, to the extent possible at arm's length in order to maximize the efficiency gains of free markets. A wall of in-sulation between high finance and high politics is the Amer-ican Way. The burden of proof is on anyone who would propose to change that tradition.

Many bankers and government officials see no reason for any change at all. Unstructured and unplanned though it may be, the present method of operation seems to work tolerably well. Banks promote growth and prosperity; Washington runs foreign policy. As the old saying goes, "If it ain't broke, don't fix it."

For example, while relations may be informal, there is certainly no lack of dialogue between the private and public sectors. Indeed, conversations go on all the time, at all levels and through all sorts of channels. Bankers visit or telephone officials at the Treasury, Federal Reserve, and State Department to keep abreast of policy developments; policymakers try to stay in touch with banks in order to track trends in financial markets. When bank steering groups convene to review the progress of debt-rescheduling negotiations, a representative of the Federal Reserve System is usually present to provide background on official attitudes and actions. When major government decisions are in the offing, opinions in the banking community may be sounded out unofficially. Bankers and officials also come into frequent contact at a variety of public and private meetings, from the annual conferences of major trade associations to off-the-record study sessions at institutions like the Council on Foreign Relations. The two sides may be at arm's length, but neither is deaf or dumb.

Ostensibly, the purpose of this dialogue is educational—to exchange information and solicit views on matters of mutual interest. But that is hardly the end of the story. "It's not entirely innocent," realistically cautions one Washington official.[2] By its very nature, the process also offers opportunities for each side to influence the views of the other more or less overtly. Neither side is disinterested, after all. Both banks and policymakers have an axe to grind. As I emphasized in chapter 3, reciprocal attempts to alter behavior manifestly do occur. At a minimum, decisions may be subtly swayed, unconsciously if not deliberately, by the choice of information conveyed or by the channel selected to communicate it. Alternatively, ideas may be planted by knowing the right questions to ask—for example, what would you do if we did x? or what are your reasons for doing, or not doing, y? And at times efforts to persuade or cajole may become quite open, as we saw in each of the four episodes in our sample. Paul Volcker's well publicized speeches in the midst of Latin America's debt crisis could by no means be described as merely pedagogic.

Likewise, while bank–government relations may be improvisatory, there is certainly no lack of means for dealing with problems when and if they arise. An informal dialogue conducted through multiple, overlapping elite networks may not be to everyone's taste. Obviously this way of doing business lacks a certain abstract elegance. But for precisely that reason it tends to avoid tendencies toward petrification and rigidity that might otherwise result from more formal, institutionalized alternatives. Nothing is set in stone. What the process lacks in textbook attractiveness, it more than makes up for in practical flexibility. More than once during the episodes examined in our sample the pragmatic bank–government relationship was put to the test by unforeseen contingencies—and passed.

However, as any student (or professor) knows, there are ways—and ways—of passing. Financial disruption was successfully avoided in each of our four episodes. But that is scarcely enough reason to award current arrangements the highest grade. For all the many economic benefits of international banking, the episodes show that there may be disadvantages too in terms of limits on our ability to achieve agreed national goals. In the event of extrafinance challenges to U.S. interests, constraints may be imposed on the government's capacity to realize specific foreign policy preferences. In the event of intrafinance challenges, economic or even political costs may be threatened to offset banking's positive contributions to our national welfare. Again, the question has to be asked: Must America always be skating on thin ice?

In short, adaptability is not the only desideratum. Better foresight would also be valuable. More needs to be done to anticipate and if possible to avoid contingencies—to think and act strategically—rather than merely react hastily to an oncoming flow of events. Failure to plan ahead or coordinate on issues of mutual interest tends to limit policy options once a crisis hits (whether extrafinance or intrafinance in origin). Chapter 7, for instance, stressed that the sanctions imposed by Washington in response to Poland's suppression of Solidarity (an extrafinance challenge) might have been more effective had there been more anticipatory thinking in earlier years. Likewise, chapter 8 noted that the government's lack of a firm game plan to deal with Latin American debt troubles, despite signs of an impending storm (an intrafinance challenge), plainly added to the difficulty of resolving that crisis after the tempest finally broke. The present method of operation simply does not work well to reduce conflicts between private and public interests before they occur. The virtues of the process are ex post rather than ex ante. It ain't broke, but it ain't running so smoothly either. Performance could surely be improved. Another old saying applies: "An ounce of prevention is worth a pound of cure."

II

Can a better modus operandi be found? The practical question is how to reconcile the two desiderata of foresight and adaptability—a perennial dilemma of large-group dynamics. In practice, the one objective may be the enemy of the other. Strategic planning is usually thought to require a more structured process of contact and communication; but greater formality can easily reduce flexibility in the face of the rapid pace of real-world change. As dialogue becomes institutionalized, much of its substantive content often gets drained out of it. Agendas become rigid. The number of participants grows too large. And more and more time comes to be devoted simply to the defense of entrenched views rather than to a search for common interests. Can the Scylla of improvisation be escaped without veering too close to the Charybdis of petrification?

The answer lies in the level of the dialogue—in who does the talking. Large groups in the modern world tend to take the form of multilevel bureaucracies in which the temptation is always strong, given the severity of time constraints on "responsibles" at the top, to assign the task of external relations (that is, contacts with other groups) to figures lower down in the hierarchy. Low-level functionaries, however, normally lack the authority to make decisions or commitments— which is precisely why, over time, intergroup communication so often tends to become more a matter of form than of substance. To get the most out of any effort at strategic thinking, responsibles themselves must get directly involved. The higher the level of participation, the greater the likelihood that the process can truly become more anticipatory without losing the virtue of flexibility.

Ideally, what is needed is an opportunity for responsibles

to get together periodically for a session of stock-taking and brainstorming—in effect, a kind of retreat to commune and meditate on issues of mutual interest. At that level, numbers can be kept conveniently small and agendas can be kept deliberately informal. These limitations in turn would make it possible to focus more on future questions than on past ones— where we are going rather than where we have been. Alternative trends and contingencies could be reviewed, intended actions could be evaluated, and participants could be alerted to areas of potential friction. The highest level responsibles need not meet very often to ensure a more forward-looking modus operandi in practice. One or perhaps two sessions a year should not be impossible to fit into the schedules of even the busiest bankers and public officials. Nor is it necessary to plan in any formal, detailed sense in order to enhance the strategic dimension of thinking. Participants would need to commit themselves only to a process of mutual sensitization, not to coordination of specific operational decisions. The basic idea is to structure the relationship but not the discussion— a *structured dialogue*.

The keynotes of such a structured dialogue would be voluntarism and parity. Neither side would be compelled to participate in the discussion; nor would either be expected to take a position subordinate to the other. No coercion is implied, either by banks or by government officials. The procedure is not intended as a cover for dirigiste intervention in the banking industry (the mercantilist conception of political economy); nor would bankers now become the backroom directors of foreign policy (the Marxist conception). Each side would continue to act independently on the basis of its separate responsibilities and objectives. The difference is that now decisions on both sides could take fuller account of the two sectors' growing interdependence.

Can the ideal be turned into reality? Given the necessary commitment on both sides, practical difficulties could undoubtedly be ironed out. No formal legislation would be required; indeed, any statutory requirement would be in direct contradiction of the keynote principle of voluntarism. All that is needed is an appropriate, informal initiative by the executive branch to get the process started. Undoubtedly the biggest obstacle along the way would be the tricky question of representation.

On the banking side, the process would require participation by chairmen or chief executive officers (or, at a minimum, senior vice-presidents with international responsibility). But which ones? Not all internationally active U.S. banks could take part, if the number of participants is to be kept small; but neither, on equity grounds, could participation be limited only to the money-center giants that already enjoy significantly easier access to the corridors of power in Washington (the banking community asymmetry). Interested banks of every size, including foreign-owned institutions based in the United States, must be able to share equally in the benefits of improved communication. Agreement would be needed on a representative inner caucus of institutions to carry on discussions with the government on behalf of the American banking community as a whole.

One solution, perhaps, might be to rely on the good offices of the Institute of International Finance—whose mandate since its origin has included development of regular channels of communication with official bodies—to arrange for mutually acceptable representation on the banking side. Although institute membership includes foreign-based as well as domestic banks, the organization nonetheless seems well placed for a task of this kind. The institute already provides a forum for banks to exchange their experiences on international financial issues. Its Working Party on the Future of International Lending is reported to be especially useful as a mechanism for communication and consultation within the banking community.[3] This same forum could conceivably be used as well to work out consensus on the composition of the necessary inner caucus of institutions, with the institute itself taking responsibility for communicating the substance of discussions to nonparticipants. Alternatively, a purely U.S. trade group, such as the American Bankers Association (ABA) or the Bankers Association for Foreign Trade (BAFT), might be put to use for this purpose. Whatever the approach taken, of course, exemption from antitrust regulations would have to be assured in order to allow the process to proceed.

Conversely, on the government side, participation would be required of the heads of all relevant executive agencies (or again, at a minimum, their senior deputies with international financial responsibility). This means, of course, the Treasury secretary and Federal Reserve chairman, along with the Comptroller of the Currency and the chairman of the Federal Deposit Insurance Corporation (because of their regulatory responsibilities). No doubt the executive office of the president would also be represented, in the person perhaps of the chairman of the Council of Economic Advisors. And most definitely, the process must embrace as well the secretary of state (or his under secretary for economic affairs) to keep the foreign policy dimension clearly in view in all discussions. Inclusion of key members of Congress should also be considered where relevant responsibilities are directly involved (for example, the chairmen of the Senate and House Foreign Relations Committees and the Senate Finance and House Banking Committees).

Currently, working relations within the government on international banking issues—as on most issues of foreign economic policy—replicate all the worst features of Washington's relationship with banks, including its lack of much formal structure or forward planning. Multiple ad hoc channels of communication exist at all levels. However, these too tend to be mainly reactive rather than anticipatory in any serious sense. During the Reagan administration's first term, for instance, responsibility for coordination of policy in the international economic area was assigned to the so-called Senior Interagency Group on International Economic Policy (SIGIEP), comprised of cabinet-level officers from the Treasury, State Department, and a number of other key executive-branch agencies. Like the relationship with banks, though, SIGIEP remained essentially problem-oriented rather than strategic, meeting only when crises developed that unavoidably cut across agency lines. SIGIEP, said a well-placed State Department official in early 1985, "tends to be very concrete—

country-specific or issue-specific. It's a front-burner operation."[4] Nor was much changed when, in April 1985, SIGIEP
was merged into a new cabinet-level council on national and
international economic policy, the Economic Policy Council,
which like SIGIEP was to be chaired by the secretary of the
Treasury. Short of urgent problem situations, policy coordination on bank-related issues remains minimal. Here too the
virtues of the process are more ex post than ex ante.

Worst of all is the government's failure to keep the foreign
policy dimension in view. The major reason for this is the
determined resistance of the Treasury and Federal Reserve to
encroachment on their traditional bureaucratic turf—well illustrated by Treasury's objections to the State Department's
April 1982 meeting with banks to discuss lending to Yugoslavia. Says the same State Department official, "Treasury
has no interest, in institutional terms, in getting the advice
of State."[5] Retorts a high-level Treasury official, "Communication is poor because the others are not well informed.
They don't have a feel for the market."[6] Such attitudes help
to explain why, as we have seen, explicit linkages to nonfinancial matters tend to develop so slowly in the face of intrafinance challenges to foreign policy (the policy behavior
asymmetry): unless, or until, a crisis appears to become truly
threatening to U.S. diplomatic interests, the entrenched bureaucratic prerogatives of the economic agencies forestall formulation of systematic political strategies. And these
attitudes also help to explain why, even when consistent linkage strategies are formulated, effective implementation is so
frequently hampered in practice (the policy coherence asymmetry). Again, the need is to recognize that international
banking, even short of a crisis, is no longer a straightforward
commercial activity. Regular input from the State Department is essential if the growing overlap of high finance and
high politics is to be managed properly.

But of course not just any input: the State Department
must know what it is talking about when communicating with
the economic agencies or with private-sector actors on bank-
related issues. In other words, it must make itself less vulnerable to charges, such as the one cited above, that it lacks

sufficient knowledge or understanding of the business of international finance. Treasury officials are by no means alone in their criticism of the department on this score: the banking community as well expresses widespread skepticism about State's feel for the market. If the foreign policy dimension is to be kept clearly in view, State has an obligation, first of all, to ensure the quality of its own in-house expertise.

Practical difficulties of representation aside, the key issue in bringing bankers and public officials together is gaining the necessary commitment, a far more serious obstacle. A restructuring of the bank–government relationship along the lines suggested requires a considerable transformation of attitude on both sides—effectively, abandonment of the traditional ethic of maintaining distance in dealings between the private and public sectors in this most sensitive of issue areas. Instead of remaining at arm's length when doing business with one another, banks and government would now be expected to work more closely together to identify and pursue mutually acceptable objectives in the international arena. In place of antagonism and suspicion, they would be expected to substitute cooperation and reciprocal trust.

Dialogue does not mean collusion or corporatism. As already emphasized, each side would continue to act independently on the basis of its separate responsibilities and objectives. A structured dialogue does not demand shared views or a common approach to decisionmaking—only recognition of the two sectors' growing interdependence and mutual interest in avoiding conflict. The autonomy of each side can be preserved, even as it becomes more sensitized to the aspirations and intentions of the other. All that is called for is a willingness to accept the legitimacy of closer working relations than have existed until now.

Even this much change, of course, might be too much for most Americans to accept unhesitatingly. Social values, after all, are held with some tenacity. But that is precisely why I have written this book—in hope of promoting a better understanding of the complex issues involved in the bank–government relationship today. Following the Incredible Quarter Century, the old American Way is out of date. A newer and more coherent public policy on international banking is needed for the contemporary era. Other advanced industrial nations seem to have less difficulty in accepting the need for breaching the wall of insulation between high finance and high politics on a regular basis. In both Germany and Japan, for instance, according to a recent study by a U.S. banker, "highly sophisticated relations . . . have evolved between commercial banking and foreign policy [that] appear less antagonistic, more coordinated, and more consistently oriented toward the achievement of mutually accepted goals."[7] Even in Great Britain, where social values are closer to American conventions than they are in Europe, let alone in Japan, there is a long-established tradition of regular consultation between the public authorities and appropriate representatives of the private sector on matters of vital mutual concern.[8] The evidence presented in this book argues strongly for a closer bank–government relationship now in this country as well in order to accommodate more effectively the increasingly overlapping interests of each. The necessary commitment may not be easy to obtain, but it must be sought.

III

Can we be more precise about the content of that commitment? The purpose of close working relations between banks and government, I have said, is to encourage both sides to think more strategically about their multiple ongoing interactions—the ounce of prevention. But this is not just a matter of talking more often or more frankly: strategy cannot be made in a vacuum. There must also be agreement on basic goals and principles to keep the whole process on track. We are thus obligated as well to define an appropriate set of guidelines for a more structured dialogue between the public and private sectors. That is what the "structure" in the dialogue means.

Guidelines cannot be too specific, of course. Excessive detail would rob the bank–government relationship of the practical flexibility that is at present its greatest virtue. But neither can the process remain entirely ad hoc, as it is currently, if it is ever to become anything more than reactive and improvisatory. Once again, both the Scylla and the Charybdis must be avoided. Guidelines must be articulated at a level of generality sufficient to promote more anticipatory thinking without reducing adaptability in the face of the swift flow of events.

In fact, an appropriate set of guidelines can be readily derived from our comparative evaluation of the sample of episodes I examined in part II. The goal is to enable both banks and the government to realize their preferences in the international arena to the maximum extent possible. But that will depend on their ability to minimize any conflicts of interest that arise between them. The experiences in our sample make clear that areas of potential friction are most likely to be minimized if each side consciously accepts certain new responsibilities in their mutual relationship. In practical terms, this means attaching more importance than has been the case in the past to the themes of information and moderation. Both the private and public sectors have to recognize that they have a mutual responsibility to ensure the fullest possible availability of information relevant to their respective functions. Even more important, each must recognize that it has a responsibility in its international operations to take the fullest possible account of the legitimate interests of the other. In effect, a kind of bargain has to be struck that commits banks and government alike to the principle of reciprocal restraint for their joint benefit.

In formal terms, such a bargain corresponds to the standard solution of the so-called Prisoners' Dilemma of game theory—that branch of the social sciences that studies strategic interactions between players. In the usual game, players (like banks and the government in their strategic interaction) are assumed to share certain interests even as they compete against one another. (This is known as a "mixed-motive, non-zero-sum game.") The Prisoners' Dilemma is that while both players can benefit from cooperation and mutual trust, each separately might hope to gain more by acting on its own; but if both try to do so, the outcome is most likely to be inferior for all. To resolve the dilemma and maximize opportunities for joint gain, most studies of game theory stress the need both for better information and for a commitment to mutual accommodation.[9] It is precisely the absence of these prerequisites, owing to the traditional ethic of distance in dealings between the private and public sectors in this country, that accounts for the limited effectiveness of the present bank–government working relationship.

Good information is the sine qua non for improving that relationship. For the banks, this means prompt and comprehensive disclosure of all significant overseas activities. For the government, it means coherent and consistent communication of all important foreign policy priorities. On both sides, great strides have been made in recent years to provide fuller and more timely intelligence on matters of mutual interest. Nevertheless, much remains to be done to assure adequate reciprocal access to all the relevant facts.

On the banking side, there is now far more public disclosure of lending data than was once thought possible, or even advisable. Banks used to insist on almost total secrecy on competitive grounds: rivals might learn too much if numbers were released publicly. In 1977, however, under pressure from Congress, the government's three bank regulatory agencies—the Federal Reserve, the Federal Deposit Insurance Corporation, and the Office of the Comptroller of the Currency—instituted the so-called Country Exposure Report, requiring all banks to report semiannually on their outstanding foreign claims on a country-by-country basis. Data based on these individual bank reports were then made public in aggregated form by the Federal Financial Institutions Examination Council (the three agencies working together) in a Country Exposure Lending Survey.[10] And even more detail became available after passage of the 1983 IMF funding legislation, which included several new provisions designed to improve disclosure of bank lending (see chapter 8). Country-risk reports were made quarterly rather than semiannual, and individual institutions were required to identify publicly all countries in which their existing loan exposure exceeds 1 percent of total assets. Less detailed information was also mandated for exposures over 0.75 percent of assets, a provision

paralleling a tightened disclosure requirement enacted by the
Securities and Exchange Commission in August 1983.[11] All in
all, we now get a reasonably complete picture of the overseas
loan position of American banks. Earlier fears of competitive
disadvantage have, like reports of Mark Twain's death, turned
out to be greatly exaggerated.

Unfortunately, less progress has been made in keeping
track of the banking industry's burgeoning business in *contingent liabilities*—obligations such as standby letters of
credit, overdrafts, note-issuing facilities, bank-issued guarantees, and other commitments to make loans or purchase
and sell foreign exchange or securities. These are also relevant
facts. Such fee-based activities have increased rapidly in recent years, particularly on the international side, reflecting the
general deemphasis of asset growth as a key objective of bank
management strategies in the 1980s (see chapter 2). According
to the BIS, new contingent liabilities granted by banks in
international financial markets more than doubled between
1981 and 1984, at a time when syndicated credits were contracting dramatically.[12] At the end of 1984, such commitments
(domestic as well as foreign) by the fifteen largest American
banks, at $930 billion, actually exceeded their total recorded
assets by some $80 billion.[13] Although contingent liabilities
do not represent money already lent by banks, they do represent potential risks. Yet because they do not show up on
bank balance sheets, they are not easily captured by existing
disclosure requirements. Even private market analysts agree
that improvements could—and should—be made. Says one
securities broker: "This is a fast growing segment of the banking business that demands greater disclosure."[14] However, the
first regular reports from U.S. banks on these items were requested by Washington only in 1983. In 1985, government
regulators formed an interagency group to take a closer look
at the issue.

Similarly, on the government side, a strong case can be
made for more detailed disclosure, also on a regular basis, of
the authorities' own international programs and priorities, to
ensure greater accuracy in bank perceptions of the present
and future diplomatic environment. We know that banks are

sensitive to foreign policy considerations, both on a day-to-day basis and in terms of broader operational strategies. As both the East European and Latin American experiences underscored, commercial decisions can be quite dramatically affected by the flow of information from Washington. I argued in chapter 3 that the government has a growing responsibility to ensure that its overseas intentions are neither misperceived nor misunderstood in the banking community. The most appropriate vehicle for this purpose would seem to be the structured dialogue just outlined. Commitment to a new modus operandi implies, for the government, a commitment as well to adequate exposition and clarification of relevant diplomatic objectives.

However, not even good information is enough unless the two sides are sincerely prepared to act on it. Banks and government alike have an obligation, given the increasing overlap of high finance and high politics, not only to keep themselves constantly apprised of each other's needs and goals; they must also fully accept the principle of mutual accommodation of public and private interests as an inherent, legitimate ingredient of their reciprocal relationship. Both must keep firmly in mind the theme of moderation.

For the banks, moderation would be of value not just from the point of view of their own safety and soundness. As indicated, it would be advantageous from a broad foreign policy perspective as well. The public interest would be best served if, in pursuit of their private interests, bankers would not forget the possible impacts of their international activities on America's ability to achieve agreed national goals; that is, if they remember the indirect influence of their decisions on the government's own decision-making environment. At one level, immoderate behavior may result in intrafinance challenges to foreign policy (for example, the potential disruption of a Latin debt storm) that could more than offset the many economic benefits of international banking. At another level, constraints may be imposed in specific instances of extrafinance challenge to policy (for example, Poland's declaration of martial law) that could turn out to be quite damaging to U.S. interests. Sensitivity to foreign policy considerations must be more than merely a question of what such concerns mean for banks; it must also be a question of what the banks mean for foreign policy in its broadest sense. As a general principle, commercial strategies should be consciously framed, to the extent possible, to avoid compromising the effectiveness of foreign policy strategies. In practical terms, this would mean using two of the key asymmetries noted above, namely the balance sheet asymmetry and the diplomatic relations asymmetry, as informal guidelines in formulating and implementing the banks' operational policies.

For example, banks should always be cognizant of the significant disadvantages for national policy that may result from a sizable run-up of debt overseas—particularly in politically sensitive states where U.S. diplomatic relations are or might conceivably become unfriendly or adversarial. At the intrafinance level, this would mean limiting any tendencies toward general excess in lending that might at some point result in yet more debt storms abroad. At the extrafinance level, this would mean limiting lending in specific instances where such actions could result in undue leverage on the U.S. government in the future. Similarly, banks should recognize how a sudden retrenchment of lending, in the event of foreign debt-service difficulties, may pose serious intrafinance challenges to policy as well as possibly handicap Washington in its efforts to cope with specific extrafinance problems beyond our borders. Investor revulsion and regional contagion do not serve the public interest well.

Individual banks, of course, may view such matters differently. If all other institutions may be assumed to practice moderation, resisting temptations toward either overlending or (when debt troubles start) overkill, any one bank can hope to gain at the others' expense by acting immoderately—the classic "free-rider" problem of economic theory. And given the pressures of competition in the marketplace, as we saw in the Incredible Quarter Century, excesses by one can soon lead to excesses by all, making accommodation of foreign policy concerns difficult if not impossible. There is no infallible defense against the free-rider problem: its existence is one of the prices we pay for the benefits of open markets. But its incidence can at least be reduced insofar as it is possible to keep reminding each institution individually of the banking community's collective interests and how these relate to the public interest as interpreted by policymakers in Washington. That is precisely why a more structured dialogue between the banks and government is being recommended here. In effect, the process would help provide the needed corrective for the industry's recurrent proneness to disaster myopia. Regular consultation and sensitization to areas of potential friction can reduce the likelihood that banks will long ignore the broader public policy consequences of their private overseas activities.

For the government, moderation has the converse meaning—sensitization to the potential costs of putting too much emphasis on the public policy consequences of such activities. This concerns attempts to exercise direct influence over bank behavior on foreign policy grounds. Policymakers have temptations to resist too. The growing overlap of high finance and high politics in effect creates opportunities to deploy banks as part of the government's own linkage strategies; and as several of the episodes in our sample demonstrate, officials have not been above yielding to the temptation on occasion, despite traditional inhibitions on the subject. Even apart from possible diplomatic repercussions abroad, there are urgent questions of efficiency and equity to keep in mind. Bank profits and competitive positions, as we well know, may be seriously jeopardized by systematic political interventions in financial markets. This means that private interests cannot be forgotten either, as policymakers seek to promote their conception of the public interest in international affairs. Just as commercial strategies should, as a general principle, be consciously framed to avoid compromising the effectiveness of foreign policy strategies, so the reverse is also true. Legitimate interests of the private sector must also be accommodated, and public policy should properly differentiate between institutions that do or do not cooperate with government linkage strategies.

In practical terms, this principle might be most easily implemented by focusing on the element of risk (for banks) associated with alternative linkage strategies. Government attempts to shape bank decisions to suit foreign policy considerations are not, per se, irresponsible; to insist otherwise is to suggest that there is no public interest at all other than the private interests of banks—in effect, "what is good for Citibank is good for the country." As I argued in chapter 3, political and security objectives also matter to the nation, not just economics. But it would indeed be irresponsible for officials to try to push banks into accepting more risk than the banks themselves would consider prudent, unless suitable mechanisms can also be provided to assure an adequate degree of protection of some kind (insurance, guarantees, and the like) should institutions that choose to cooperate with the government eventually run into trouble as a result. An appropriate guideline, therefore, might be: Limit political interventions to forms that do not increase the commercial risks to which banks are normally exposed; or else be prepared to compensate cooperating institutions in some form for risks that they may, for foreign policy reasons, be persuaded or obligated to assume.

For example, under such a guideline, banks would not have been encouraged in the name of détente to increase lending to Eastern Europe in the early 1970s; or else even more of the banks' potentially risky exposure would have been covered by official guarantees than was in fact the case. (Whether Washington should have paid off Poland's guarantees unconditionally, on the other hand, is another matter entirely, as I argued in chapter 7.) Likewise, a strong case for compensation might have been created by the Iranian asset freeze had the damages to bank profits or competitive positions actually turned out greater than they did. However, under this guideline there would have been no such case for compensation in Latin America, where banks clearly got in so deep for reasons of their own rather than for reasons of state. Once the Latin debt storm developed, certainly, Washington had good cause to put its own money where its mouth was in an effort to dissuade lenders from regional overkill. But in this instance, it may be argued, it would have been quite proper to charge a higher rather than a lower price for any umbrella of public assistance. Banks have a claim to shelter from the government's mistakes, but not from their own.

Here too, of course, as with the free-rider problem on the banking side, there is no infallible defense—no absolute certainty that policymakers can be induced always to exercise their authority responsibly. But here too the incidence of irresponsibility can at least be reduced insofar as it is possible to keep reminding officials of the legitimate interests of banks. Again, that is precisely why a more structured dialogue between the banks and government is being recommended. Regular consultation and sensitization are necessary on the public sector side as well, to reduce the likelihood that officials will long ignore any risks to bank safety or soundness created by their foreign policy decisions.

IV

How well might the structured dialogue work in practice? That is difficult to say. Clearly, there would be pitfalls in relying on guidelines drawn at a level of generality as high as I have suggested here. Neither side, for instance, may be easily persuaded to share all relevant information on matters of mutual interest. Bankers may be reluctant to jeopardize their competitive positions by disclosing everything there is to know about their plans and activities abroad; policymakers may regard some of their foreign programs and priorities as too sensitive to be revealed, even behind closed doors, to private citizens. More fundamentally, neither side may be easily persuaded to accept the principle of mutual accommodation as an inherent, legitimate ingredient of their reciprocal relationship. That is another price we pay for preserving the basic autonomy of each of the two spheres of activity (the liberal conception of political economy). In an institutional arrangement based on voluntarism and parity, no absolute certainties or magic formulas exist. Even in the best of all possible worlds, it would be impossible to eliminate all risk of conflicting interest between the banking community and the government. As I have emphasized repeatedly, divergences of underlying motives and goals are just too basic for that.

On the other hand, consider the alternative. As compared with the presently unstructured and unplanned modus operandi in the foreign policy area, a structured dialogue at least holds out the promise of improvement in the management of bank–government relations without threatening coercion on either side or a loss of the many economic benefits of international banking. Assuming even a qualified commitment on each side, there seems little reason to doubt that potential collisions could be reduced significantly through regular use of the procedure and guidelines just outlined. Strategic thinking about possible contingencies should enable both sectors to perform their respective functions more effectively.

Certainly there has been no lack of contingencies to think about in recent years. The four episodes included in our sample were by no means unique, as subsequent events in nations as diverse as the Philippines and South Africa have amply demonstrated. Nor is the need for a structured dialogue apt to diminish in the future. The internationalization of banking will persist, I argued in chapter 2, despite the temporary retrenchment of the early 1980s. It takes little imagination to project from present trends the possibility of yet other foreign policy linkages of the sort examined in part II. None of the boxes in table 1.2 is empty. America would surely benefit from a more systematic effort by bankers and policymakers to look ahead together at their international activities. Failure to coordinate on issues of mutual interest can severely weaken the government's foreign policy capabilities.

Consider the Philippines, for instance. After the 1983 assassination of opposition leader Benigno Aquino, as I noted in chapter 3, U.S. policy toward the authoritarian New Society regime of President Ferdinand Marcos shifted significantly in favor of support for domestic reform and political liberalization. Previously, repression in our former colony had been tolerated, or even encouraged, so long as it seemed to assure the security of America's large military installations at Clark Air Force Base and Subic Bay Naval Station. But the force of this strategic rationale had been gradually eroded by President Marcos's declining popularity as well as by the rising success of the New Peoples Army insurrection. By 1983 it was clear that our strategic interests would be better served by promoting a return to democracy in that country to help fend off the possibility of a communist takeover. The Reagan administration switched course. Bringing pressure to bear on the Marcos regime became a key extrafinance challenge for U.S. foreign policy.

Unfortunately, matters were considerably complicated by the Philippines' status as a major international debtor—and a very troubled one at that. In 1983, the country owed some \$25.5 billion to foreign creditors, including more than \$13 billion to private banks (\$5.5 billion alone to U.S. banks). Even before the Aquino assassination, debt service had begun to fall into arrears, in part because of the general retrenchment of international banking activity after mid–1982. Bankers were cutting back on short-term credit lines to Filipino borrowers as well as on all forms of longer-term lending. Following the assassination, a full-fledged debt crisis forced the first of a series of formal reschedulings tied to IMF-prescribed austerity measures. Under the circumstances, a linkage between Filipino debt and U.S. strategic interests could scarcely be avoided. (The Philippines, in effect, fell into subset D in table 1.2.) The problem was that Washington never seemed to be able to make its foreign policy intentions clear to the banking community. Did the Reagan administration want to use the banks, in effect, as instruments of a linkage strategy to help reinforce the political pressure now being brought to bear on the Marcos regime? Or, instead, did it prefer that lenders play a more benign, or even benevolent, role? Late in 1985, while one source was suggesting that Washington was happy to see creditors "turning the financial screw on President Marcos,"[15] others were saying just the reverse. One New York banker commented: "The United States keeps saying to give without the reforms, for security reasons."[16] Said another, "The Philippines are such a political-economic problem ...the United States is pushing for more loans."[17] Such a confusion of signals could hardly aid the administration in realizing its policy preferences in the Philippines. A structured dialogue would have made it easier for policymakers and bankers to coordinate their respective approaches to this vital issue of mutual concern prior to Marcos's eventual fall from power in early 1986.

Or recall what happened in South Africa in the summer of 1985, when a financial crisis suddenly erupted as a direct result of decisions taken by a number of key American banks to stop renewing maturing short-term credits in that country. South Africa had already become a focal point of U.S. foreign policy, especially after Pretoria's declaration of a state of emergency in July following months of racial unrest. Under its policy of so-called constructive engagement, the Reagan administration had long been on record as committed to the objective of ending apartheid in South Africa. But it had shown no inclination to back up its policy with serious economic pressures of any kind, and it certainly had no desire to jeopardize the stability of Western financial markets in the process. Unfortunately, that is precisely what was threatened by the hasty actions of U.S. banks.

Between 1982 and 1985, a surge of borrowing from abroad —particularly by South Africa's private sector—had more than doubled the country's external debt, to a level near $24 billion. (South Africa too fell into subsector D in table 1.2.) Almost half consisted of short-term credit lines from foreign banks (including $3.5 billion from American banks), which until the summer of 1985 the banks had customarily rolled over more or less automatically. But then came word, toward the end of July 1985, that Chase Manhattan Bank had told South Africa that it would no longer make loans to the private sector (no loans had been made by U.S. banks to the South African government for years) nor renew any existing credits. Although Chase's outstanding exposure in South Africa was small—reportedly not much more than $400 million—its prestige in banking circles was enough to prompt other banks now to adopt the same policy, quickly calling in loans as they matured.[18] According to the *Economist*, this was a classic example of what it ironically described as a cardinal rule of banking: "If you're going to panic, be first."[19] The result was a run on the rand (South Africa's currency) and a massive drain on the country's reserves that could be stemmed, finally, only by a decision from Pretoria to suspend all debt repayments until some sort of rescheduling could be worked out with creditors. Washington was hardly pleased. In the words of one high-level Treasury official, the banks' actions, which were taken without benefit of consultation of any kind, were regarded within the Reagan administration as "precipitous ...not helpful."[20] Again, a structured dialogue might have made it easier to avoid a collision between private and public interests on a crucial foreign policy issue.

Future contingencies can also be anticipated. It is none too soon for bankers and policymakers to begin asking themselves appropriate questions about developing trends in high finance. Consider, for instance, the massive capital inflows of recent years, which have transformed America once again into a net debtor nation. Here, certainly, is a fit subject for discussion to highlight areas of potential friction. Already we are starting to hear comments reminiscent of the Arab money weapon debate of a decade ago. On the one hand are Washington officials and others emphasizing the numerous benefits accruing to the U.S. economy, not least the support provided to the Reagan administration's huge budget deficits. Admits Federal Reserve Chairman Paul Volcker candidly: "We are relying on that capital inflow to finance the deficit."[21] On the other hand are voices in the private sector and on Capitol Hill expressing concern about the dangers of financial disruption or worse. James Robinson, chairman of American Express Company, says, "The implications ...are very serious. Financial market volatility would be intensified, the independence of our monetary policy could be compromised and the danger of rapid dollar drops might well rekindle inflation."[22] Says William Proxmire, a ranking member of the Senate Banking Committee, "You lose some part of your sovereignty under those circumstances. You lose your independence."[23]

Are such apprehensions justified? Or is this yet another instance of alarmism, even hysteria, in public reactions to an essentially innocent financial development? Could foreigners' net claims conceivably become a source of leverage on policy instruments or issues of interest to the U.S. government? Could Washington's diplomatic capabilities be significantly influenced in the event of an extrafinance challenge to foreign policy? Could intrafinance challenges be threatened to offset the economic benefits of the capital inflows? These are the sorts of questions that a structured dialogue should be addressing now, drawing insights from the representative cases considered in chapters 5 and 6 (corresponding to subsets A and C in table 1.2).

In particular, attention might be focused on the role of Japan, which in the first half of the 1980s became by far the single biggest source of capital inflow into the United States (reflecting that country's exceptionally large and persistent surpluses in international trade). Although Japanese investors have a distinct preference for U.S. government securities, they have also accumulated a substantial volume of deposits in American banks, amounting in early 1985 to more than \$24 billion—half again as large as the total of Arab bank deposits at the time (and exceeded only by the recorded deposits of four overseas financial centers, the amounts of which are of course swollen by the inclusion of many assets held in nominee or custody accounts).[24] Are there dangers here? Like the Saudis and Kuwaitis before them, Japanese investors to date generally have tended to be cautious and conservative, little given to rash or "irrational" movements of their money. Moreover, like Iran under the shah, Japan has long been regarded as a solid and dependable ally of the United States. On the surface, therefore, there has seemed little reason for concern over Japan's emergence as one of America's principal creditors. Few warnings have been heard about a purported *Japanese* money weapon.

Yet circumstances can change, as the Iranian experience amply demonstrated. Within living memory, Japan was America's bitter enemy in a world war; logic does not exclude the possibility of a return to more unfriendly or even adversarial relations, particularly if persistent tensions between our two countries over such issues as trade and technology are allowed to boil over. Furthermore, for all their caution and conservatism in the past, Japanese investors are not incapable of a massive withdrawal of funds in the future, given their well-known inclination to act in concert in response to economic developments or to their government's "administrative guidance." It is not necessary to envision a serious deterioration of extrafinance relations to imagine a genuine intrafinance challenge to U.S. interests. The essence of the threat has been aptly summarized by New York investment banker Felix Rohatyn:

> I think it's scary.... Suppose we don't do very much with our budget deficit, and we're looking at a $300 billion deficit. The Japanese yank their money, the dollar falls and we're faced with a falling dollar and higher interest rates at a time of recession.
> We'd probably have some sort of banking crisis.[25]

Is the threat farfetched? Assessment along the lines of the analysis in chapter 5 might suggest that while exaggeration is certainly possible, some degree of apprehension probably is nonetheless justified, particularly in view of possible ripple effects that might be created in financial markets by a sudden liquidation of Japanese assets. Could the danger be contained by dusting off the counterweapon of the IEEPA? Assessment along the lines of the analysis in chapter 6 suggests, as indicated above, that the success of the Iranian asset freeze would probably not be easily replicated. How, then, can the danger be minimized? According to our earlier discussion of the balance sheet asymmetry, the key would be moderation by the government and banks alike in their solicitation of Japanese funds. The structured dialogue could be used to remind both sides of the risks of undue reliance on capital inflows from any one particular source.

Conversely, consider the continued high level of bank lending activity in selected areas overseas, such as East and Southeast Asia. Here too is a fit subject for discussion to highlight areas of potential friction. The risks of excessive foreign exposure have been amply demonstrated in the cases of Poland and Latin America as well as in the Philippines and South Africa. Yet for more highly regarded Asian borrowers (for example, Indonesia, Malaysia, Thailand), U.S. bank loans have continued to grow despite the more general retrenchment in international financial markets. Might these claims one day also generate foreign policy linkages of significance to Washington? Might the government's diplomatic capabilities or U.S. economic prosperity be influenced critically by the dangers of a threatened default? These too are questions that a structured dialogue should be addressing now, drawing insights from the representative cases considered in chapters 7 and 8 (corresponding to subsets B and D in table 1.2) as well as from the more recent Filipino and South African experiences.

For example, a case in point might be the People's Republic of China, where U.S. bank claims quadrupled to nearly $1 billion in the two years from December 1982 to December 1984. (Admittedly, the amounts involved are still small. But that is precisely the point—to think about possible contingencies before the numbers get big.) China was once America's adversary and could conceivably become so again. Both sides in the structured dialogue should therefore be asking themselves whether more lending to China over the long term is desirable or not. For its part, the banking community should be reminded of the diplomatic relations asymmetry. A rapid run-up of debt to a potentially unfriendly state may not be in America's foreign policy interest. For their part, government officials should be alerted to the dangers of political intervention in high finance. Private lending should not be encouraged simply in order to help cement U.S. relations with the current Chinese regime unless means are provided to compensate cooperating banks for any extra risks that may be incurred. Not all danger of conflicting interests would thereby be eliminated, of course. As emphasized repeatedly, underlying divergences in the bank–government relationship are too fundamental for that. But at least both sides would be better informed than before about the needs and objectives of the other.

V

My recommendations can be summarized in a handful of capsule precepts—Five Commandments for an Improved Bank–

Government Relationship. (Half a Decalogue is better than none.) These five precepts are:

1. *Talk together*. Like it or not, banks and government are now engaged in a strategic interaction that neither can afford to ignore. If the risk of conflicting interests is to be reduced, therefore, the substantive dialectic between the public and private sectors—between politics and markets—must be given an institutionalized form. The traditional ethic of arm's-length distance in bank–government dealings must be replaced by a more structured, cooperative dialogue than exists at present.

2. *Involve responsibles*. To preserve flexibility in the relationship, participation in a structured dialogue must be at the highest level from both sides. Among banks, representation could be arranged through the good offices of the Institute of International Finance. Government representation would have to include not only the relevant economic agencies but also the State Department, in order to keep the foreign policy dimension clearly in view at all times.

3. *Think strategically*. The purpose of a cooperative dialogue is to do more than just react to crises, if and when they occur. The object must be to look ahead, anticipate contingencies, and coordinate on issues of mutual interest, in order to ease the risk of collisions of interest before they occur. This is the ounce of prevention.

4. *Provide information*. A successful dialogue requires the fullest possible availability of information relevant to the respective functions of the two sides. Banks must agree to prompt and comprehensive disclosure of all significant overseas activities. The government must agree to coherent and consistent communication of all important foreign policy priorities.

5. *Accommodate interests*. To minimize areas of potential friction, each side must make a serious commitment to the principle of reciprocal restraint. Commercial strategies must be consciously framed to avoid compromising the government's foreign policy capabilities, using the balance sheet and diplomatic relations asymmetries as informal guidelines.

Linkage strategies in foreign policy must be deliberately designed to avoid increasing (or else to compensate for increasing) market risks for banks. The essential theme is moderation. The ultimate goal is maximization of joint benefits. If the relationship cannot be ignored, why not, then, make the most of it?

CHAPTER 11

A Pound of Cure

The aim of an improved bank–government relationship, I have said, is to enable both sides to think strategically—to look ahead, anticipate contingencies, and coordinate on issues of mutual interest. But that of course is advice mainly for the future: the ounce of prevention. What about the past and present? Something must also be said about the legacy that remains to us from the Incredible Quarter Century now—contingencies that have already occurred, as a result of the growing overlap of high finance and high politics, and that pose difficult problems for public policy today. We do not have the luxury of starting with a clean bill of health. We need a pound of cure too.

In this chapter, I return to the strictly economic component of foreign policy. I have previously made clear that the internationalization of banking activity, for all of its genuine efficiency gains, has left in its wake a number of intra-finance challenges to U.S. national interests, which call for remedies at the earliest possible moment. No discussion of contemporary bank–government relations in the foreign policy area would be complete without addressing, in this final chapter, the practical substance of these outstanding policy questions. As I suggested in the introduction, new approaches are needed to managing the potential costs of international banking, in order to maximize its many economic benefits. This too is part of defining the public interest in international banking for the contemporary era.

Three bank-related issues in particular stand out on Washington's current foreign policy agenda. These are global debt, prudential supervision of international banking, and the management of international liquidity. All three affect—and are affected by—the strategic interaction between policy-makers and banks here at home. But they also involve strategic interactions elsewhere between the U.S. government and other governments and multilateral institutions like the IMF and World Bank. The external-relations dimension cannot be ignored. In this sense, these are really systemic issues, since they bring into question different aspects of the international regime governing monetary relations across national frontiers—part of the ceaseless dialectic between politics and markets that I stressed in chapter 3. As I indicated there, the very success of international banking in the Incredible Quarter Century undermined the regime that helped get it started in the first place. Washington's intrafinance challenges today are best understood, therefore, in broad systemic terms. Can the government manage the dialectic between politics and markets in a manner that satisfactorily balances the interests of both the banking community and U.S. foreign policy?

I

Let me begin with some general principles. When it comes to systemic issues, I noted in chapter 1, the United States has interests that go well beyond the narrow pursuit of national advantage alone. As the largest and most influential state actor in financial matters, America has little choice but to concern itself with broader questions of systemic stability as well—support and preservation of the overall environment that contributes so much to U.S. as well as others' economic welfare. We have the biggest stake. Smaller nations may ignore the systemic consequences of their policy actions; likewise, they need not worry unduly about any feedback from the system to themselves that might result from those policy actions. In effect, they can afford simply to be free riders, concentrating on getting the best possible deal for themselves within the existing rules of the game (that is, the principles, norms, etc., that make up the prevailing regime) without concerning themselves unduly about possible adverse ripple effects of their individual behavior. The United States, however, cannot. By virtue of the country's size and importance, its actions almost inevitably have systemic consequences; and these consequences, in turn, almost inevitably feed back to affect the U.S. economy. This means that, like it or not, America has a vital responsibility for the stability and maintenance of the system as a whole. Equally, it also means that America's interests are affected directly by anything that influences the overall stability and maintenance of the system, including our own actions.

The singularity of America's systemic role was amply reaffirmed in the episodes examined in part II. For instance, when the U.S. money weapon was turned on Iran's ayatollahs in 1979, the free functioning of international financial markets everywhere seemed suddenly to be placed in jeopardy. Likewise, when the Latin American debt storm broke in 1982, Washington seemed the only place where penurious debtors in the region could go to find the necessary emergency assistance. Singularity does not mean hegemony, of course. The days are long gone when the United States had it in its power to mold a world monetary system largely to its own design, as it did at Bretton Woods in 1944. In Latin America, the financial difficulties of Mexico and others gave Washington leverage—but only for a time. America's power resources were insufficient to manage the crisis solely through its own efforts. (Likewise, why would Washington have accepted the indirect intermediation of the International Monetary Fund unless its capacity to act directly was limited?) Singularity, however, does mean predominance—primus inter pares, as it were, even if no longer primus motor. The United States still has a disproportionate influence on all aspects of the international financial regime and therefore a disproportionate interest in regime support and preservation.

The policy implications of this are subtle. On the one hand, if the United States cannot be a free rider, Washington's policy autonomy is necessarily constrained. Call this the responsibility constraint. True, it is an indirect, discretionary constraint, reflecting America's own conscious choices—a matter of voluntary self-restraint rather than some absolute limit directly imposed from the outside. U.S. policymakers themselves decide how much narrow national advantage is to be sacrificed, if necessary, for the sake of wider system maintenance; that is, how much the national interest is to be equated with broader international interests. Nonetheless, it is an effective constraint for all that. In reality, a narrowly self-interested pursuit of national advantage by the United States almost inevitably comes into conflict, to some degree, with wider systemic responsibilities, as we saw in part II. Washington's freeze of Iran's assets threatened serious economic costs worldwide; the impact of economic sanctions against Poland was critically compromised by concern about the risks to the United States as well as to others of a possible Western banking crisis. When such conflicts occur, delicate tradeoffs are required in the formulation and implementation of U.S. policy to keep the broader system functioning efficiently without risk of disruption or discord.

On the other hand, such tradeoffs need not necessarily be painful to the United States insofar as the results can be made mutually advantageous for all concerned—in other words, insofar as positive-sum linkages can be exploited in coping with key policy challenges. I have already indicated that prospects for such linkages (in contrast to zero-sum linkages) are greatest when dealing with international regime issues (chapter 3). In such instances, the responsibility constraint can actually become an opportunity to help lift all parties, governments and private banks alike, to a superior policy outcome. As I suggested in chapter 10, the general principle must be reciprocal restraint for joint benefit. Can this principle be put into practice for each of the three specific bank-related issues on Washington's current foreign policy agenda?

II

Consider the issue of global debt. The Senate Foreign Relations Committee staff proved prescient back in 1977 when it wrote that "the debt issue is likely to dominate U.S. relations with the Third World."[1] In fact, since Mexico's crisis in mid–1982, if not before, debt has come to head the agenda of the north–south dialogue. More international negotiating time has been devoted to the complicated and painful process of debt restructuring than to any other single question of interest to developing countries. While Latin American nations have been among the most prominent of troubled sovereign borrowers, they have been by no means alone. The problem is really worldwide, encompassing numerous Third World and, as we know, even East European states. As I indicated in chapter 2, the most serious debt-service difficulties have been encountered by those countries that relied most heavily on bank financing during the exuberant go-go years of the 1970s. As I indicated in chapter 8, at mid-decade the debt issue was still far from being solved. Further efforts would still be needed to achieve the elusive goal of longer-term financial stabilization.

At first, banks seemed to think that they could manage sovereign debt problems on their own, through rescheduling agreements negotiated by their own ad hoc steering groups. During the 1970s, "work-outs" of overdue or shaky credits became increasingly routinized and commonplace. But then came the Latin American debt storm, which was simply too big for private institutions, on their own, to handle. They sought assistance from official sources, including both creditor-country governments and the IMF. More and more, after 1982, it became clear that—for the biggest Third World borrowers, at least—purely commercial solutions simply were no longer feasible. The issues had become too contentious and politicized, as domestic resistance to prolonged austerity in debtor nations continued to swell. The challenge became diplomatic, not just financial.

The gist of the problem may be easily stated. It is a question of who should bear the burden of adjustment. What could be more political? Under the rules prevailing after 1982 (what may be called the standard debt regime), debtors themselves were obliged to shoulder most of the burden, through domestic austerity and reduced living standards. Despite lip service paid in the Reagan administration's early five-point debt strategy to the putative responsibilities of both banks and creditor countries (see chapter 8), in reality few concessions of any substance were made by either group. After 1982 most emphasis, in practical terms, was on IMF-sponsored programs of domestic stabilization, complete with tough policy conditionality and rigorous enforcement of internal and external performance criteria.

The short-term results of these programs were not unimpressive. By 1984, the aggregate current-account deficit of indebted developing countries was down to some $38 billion, reduced from $60 billion the previous year and a peak of $113 billion in 1981. Merchandise trade actually showed a collective surplus of $14 billion in 1984, as compared with a net deficit of almost $65 billion three years earlier. And domestic output expanded by about 4 percent, twice the rate achieved in either of the two preceding years. Foreign debt as a percentage of the group's exports of goods and services fell to a ratio of 151 in 1984 from a high of 158 a year before.[2]

Such a rate of improvement proved difficult to sustain, however. Already in 1985 it appeared that performance was once again faltering in a number of key debtor countries.[3] Even more important, the cost of the earlier gains was becoming increasingly clear to many. In fact, the bulk of the debtors' short-term trade improvement came through reduced purchases from abroad rather than through a rise of exports. Merchandise shipments did pick up in 1984, by some 11 percent, as compared with growth at half that rate in 1983 and with an absolute decline in 1982. But overall, exports in 1984 were only $20 billion higher than they had been in 1981, whereas imports in the same three-year span were compressed by three times that amount. As a result, living standards had been compressed as well: while recovering slightly in 1984, after several years of sharp decline, they remained

far below the levels achieved in the previous decade. Moreover, when compared with domestic output (rather than exports), foreign debt had not fallen but risen, from 29 percent
in 1981 and 33 percent in 1982 to a fraction over 36 percent
in 1984. Gains there most certainly were. But as the Bank for
International Settlements commented authoritatively in
mid–1985, "Despite this progress . . . the problems encountered by a number of debtor countries . . . can hardly be said
to have met with a lasting solution."[4]

In effect, the standard debt regime represented essentially
a piecemeal, short-term response to a much more fundamental, long-term problem. The domestic development of debtors
was retarded, or even postponed indefinitely, for the sake of
preserving creditworthiness in international financial markets. Formal default was avoided by rescheduling principal;
interest payments in most cases were maintained, albeit with
difficulty. Yet despite these determined efforts to honor outstanding debt-service obligations, very little new money
(apart from involuntary lending arranged in connection with
IMF financing) was forthcoming from private sources. As a
result, debtors found themselves transferring resources outward, as a group, to creditor countries and their banks. In
1981, debtors received net financing (external borrowing less
interest payments) approaching $50 billion. By 1983 that fig-
ure had turned negative, and in 1984 amounted to an outflow
of some $35 billion—equal to nearly 10 percent of the debtors'
aggregate export revenues, and 2.5 times their hard-won
trade surplus. Small wonder that tolerance for belt-tightening
was steadily declining. Again, to quote the BIS, "Inverse flows
of the order of magnitude witnessed in 1984 are clearly
unsustainable."[5]

The risk, of course, was that the pot might reach the
boiling point. Patience was the key, debtors were told: their
development would gradually resume if only they kept playing by the rules. Suppose they were in fact to stick to orthodox
stabilization programs as prescribed by the IMF. In that case,
according to a fund scenario developed in early 1985,[6] indebted developing countries could on moderately conservative assumptions expect their aggregate current-account

deficit to continue to decline over the remainder of the decade, their exports to continue rising, and their output growth to remain at or above 4 percent a year, gradually shrinking the relative weight of their foreign obligations. By 1990, their debt-to-export ratio could drop below the 110 percent recorded in 1980. And these improvements, in turn, could be expected eventually to spark some spontaneous new lending by banks as well. With perseverance, therefore, debtor efforts to preserve their creditworthiness would ultimately pay off.

But could the necessary patience be sustained by conditional promises of this sort? Annual output growth of 4 percent translates into per-capita increases of living standards well below rates of expansion recorded by many debtors before the crisis began. Worse, the IMF's projections implied years more of net outward transfers of resources for countries that, being less developed, are—or should be—natural capital importers rather than exporters. Seen from the popular perspective in the Third World, scenarios like these simply meant subsidization of the rich by the poor—painful sacrifices by debtors for the purpose of keeping banks from suffering losses—and all for the chimera of new market financing that, for all one knew, might never materialize. As this perception spread, the pot kept heating up, raising the risk of social or political disorder; and debtor governments came under increasing pressure to look for alternative solutions, up to and including moratoria on current debt service or even formal default of principal. Governing officials themselves might not regard such options as the height of economic rationality. But as I noted in chapter 2, personal and political considerations (for example, riots in the streets) could leave them with little effective choice. Throughout the first half of 1985, Fidel Castro struck a responsive chord in many Latin American hearts with his repeated calls for a suspension or even cancellation of all debt payments by hemispheric states.[7] In the summer, the presidents and foreign ministers of some twenty Latin governments renewed earlier regional pleas to banks and creditor countries to accept a greater share of the still-heavy burden of adjustment.[8] And in September, several Latin leaders used the forum of the United Nations General Assembly to publicize their dissatisfaction with the prevailing rules. Declared Peru's new president, Alan García Pérez, "We are faced with a dramatic choice. It is either debt or democracy.... We believe the objective must be the unity of debtor countries and a radical change of the current situation."[9] Commented one senior American banker, "We're moving back into the arena of confrontation.... We're not yet at the stage of rupture, but we don't know what's coming."[10]

The focus of dissatisfaction, as I noted in chapter 8, was the United States—the perceived power behind the IMF throne and acknowledged leader of the debt regime. It was not only in Latin America that the Reagan administration was increasingly criticized for what was seen as the miserliness and insensitivity of its original strategy. Throughout the Third World, America faced growing alienation and confrontation because of the debt problem. Our security and political, as well as economic, interests were clearly engaged. And that of course was the main explanation for Treasury Secretary James Baker's proposed new Program for Sustained Growth announced at the IMF–World Bank annual meeting in October 1985 (chapter 8). The central aim of his plan, Baker said, was to "strengthen" the administration's original strategy by supporting more growth-oriented policies in debtor countries as an alternative to the prolonged austerity measures of previous years. The key was to be some $20 billion of new commercial-bank lending to fifteen large debtors over three years (an annual increase of exposure of 2.5 percent), in addition to an extra $9 billion from the World Bank and regional development banks (representing a 50 percent increase over previous annual totals of about $6 billion). In effect, the heat on the pot in debtor countries was to be gradually turned down by a refreshing new flow of external finance.

Unfortunately, in the months following the unveiling of the Baker plan, it was not at all clear that the secretary's objectives could in fact be achieved. The change of tone coming from the Reagan administration was of course welcomed by many debtors. Commercial banks, on the other hand, even while endorsing the new plan in principle, expressed considerable reluctance in practice about committing themselves to

the additional lending sought by Baker.[11] Moreover, it soon
became evident that even should all the proposed financing
be forthcoming, the resulting impact on growth rates in most
debtor countries could be expected to be modest at best. In
fact, the administration's original strategy had been amended
only marginally, not fundamentally. The plan still failed to
go to the heart of the problem, which remains the question
of who should bear the burden of adjustment. The pot might
still reach the boiling point. The question remains, therefore,
whether any plausible alternative to the administration's
strengthened strategy can be devised. In the language of the
BIS, Is a lasting solution possible?

From a narrowly nationalistic point of view, of course, it
might be argued that there is no need for further fundamental
change of U.S. policy. Others now shoulder the burden of
adjustment, not us: why give up such an advantage? This
argument, however, ignores possible threats to the stability
of the broader international financial system should debtor
governments in fact be driven to extreme measures by the
rising tide of their own domestic discontents. America's foreign policy interests, as I have repeatedly emphasized, would
hardly be served by world financial disruption or discord. The
responsibility constraint obliges us to take systemic concerns
into consideration as well. The real issue is how much weight
to attach to the objective of system maintenance in formulating and implementing tradeoffs in our national policy. This
in turn is a matter of calculating the seriousness of any possible threat to international financial stability.

Such a calculus is necessarily subjective—another matter
of judgment (like the risks of other possible contingencies I
discussed briefly in chapter 10 or the purported Arab money
weapon evaluated back in chapter 5) on which sincere people
may sincerely disagree. Some would dismiss the threat of this
issue as close to negligible, even supposing that pure economic
rationality might indeed be overruled at some point by the
boiling up of resentments in one or a few debtor countries.
Just a handful of the very largest debtors—like Mexico, Brazil,
and Argentina—have the capacity to shake the system on their
own. They are the only true systemic threats. Yet none, at

least until now, has seemed convincingly prepared to bear
the potentially serious costs of initiating anything so drastic
as a default. The risk of world financial disruption does not
seem unduly serious. But can we ever be sure?

History suggests otherwise. As we saw in chapter 4, the
past gives us scant grounds for having confidence in the rational self-interest of sovereign debtors always to honor their
obligations under any or all circumstances. Quite the opposite, in fact. Political and economic conditions have a way of
changing—often quite dramatically—and as a consequence,
despite the best of intentions, debt payments have frequently
been suspended or even formally repudiated for reasons that
could not be easily anticipated. Moreover, once started, such
a process can easily snowball to include even the largest sovereign borrowers—the systemic threats—as both the nineteenth century and the interwar period eloquently testify. To
casually discount the seriousness of such risks is to engage in
the worst sort of disaster myopia: Russian roulette in high
finance. To refuse to play such a suicidal game is not alarmism
but simple prudence. Experience dictates a considerable degree of caution in the framing of public policy on international
debt. The justification for a more fundamental change of U.S.
policy is essentially an insurance incentive.

Two of the lessons of history outlined at the end of chapter
4 are relevant here—first, that once debt-service difficulties
do arise (as they surely have since 1982), there is no realistic
alternative to a negotiated settlement of claims; and second,
that when negotiations are in fact undertaken, a little give
and take on all sides helps to maximize the chances for a
successful resolution of outstanding problems. Recall that in
the nineteenth-century debt regime, sovereign borrowers anxious to preserve their creditworthiness—like their counterparts today—agreed at times to a measure of foreign
participation in the management of their domestic affairs.
Economic policy conditions were imposed by creditor consortia in a manner not unlike that of the IMF in our own era.
But it should be recalled as well that, in return, some form
of debt relief was typically conceded, with investors realistically accepting partial losses rather than stubbornly insisting

on terms no longer consonant with a borrower's capacity to pay. The burden of adjustment was shared rather than concentrated largely on debtors alone. And as a result, both the growth of borrowing nations and the flow of international credit were quickly and efficiently restored. The outcome, clearly, was mutually advantageous. The means, in effect, was a balanced positive-sum linkage of concessions by all concerned. Herein lies the key to devising a plausible alternative to the administration's current debt strategy.

The alternative, simply put, is to pay more than lip service to the responsibilities of both banks and creditor countries. More concrete concessions are needed from each group— concessions motivated not by some vaguely defined principle of internationalism or equity, but rather because, in the most hard-nosed terms, it would be to the benefit of all the parties concerned. This is not charity but common sense. A truly durable solution is in everyone's interest. The United States and other creditor countries would gain insofar as the risk of world financial disruption could be reduced. Banks and other private lenders would gain insofar as the capacity of debtors to service their debt obligations could be enhanced. And the debtors themselves would gain insofar as their development process could be speedily resumed and new external financing encouraged. Call this alternative a positive-sum-linkage strategy.

Debtors could not abandon their own efforts, of course. Stabilization programs would have to remain in place to guard against any repetition of the economic policy errors into which Latin American and other Third World nations were led by their easy access to market finance in the 1970s. Too many governments failed to ensure that their loans would be used to accumulate real or financial assets sufficient to generate the income streams needed to service their debt obligations in the future. Recall that another of the lessons of history noted in chapter 4 was the troubling penchant of sovereign borrowers to overcommit themselves owing to the twin exigencies of budget demands and balance-of-payments deficits. Some continuing discipline is therefore needed to ensure effective domestic economic management. But under a positive-sum-linkage strategy these internal efforts would now be supplemented by creative contributions from the other key actors in the drama as well, all designed to attain a superior policy outcome—a new debt regime, in effect. Collective action would be organized to deal with a common problem.

What would such a strategy mean in practical terms? Although space here does not permit a detailed blueprint for a new debt regime, the essential elements of one can be outlined briefly. Most important, such a strategy means that the U.S. government must take the initiative. Collective action does not organize itself. The festering debt problem is a typical example of a "market failure" caused by the unwillingness of any one actor or group of actors to take responsibility for the public good of system maintenance. No one wants to pay the costs: everyone wants to be a free rider. To overcome the stalemate of the prevailing regime and reduce the risk of international financial instability, leadership is required—and in these matters, in the contemporary era, there is simply no other obvious candidate. That is the price of still being primus inter pares in global monetary relations. America remains, as I said, the acknowledged leader. In the words of one prominent British scholar, "Nothing happens unless the United States leads."[12] Supplementary contributions will not be forthcoming, either from other creditor countries or from banks, until Washington shows the way. Treasury Secretary Baker correctly identified the proper objective of collective action in his Program for Sustained Growth—to ease the cash-flow problems of debtor countries in a context of renewed economic development. The challenge is to convert these good intentions into action.

To illustrate, nothing would help force down persistently high world interest rates and so lighten onerous debt-service burdens abroad more than a sustained reduction of America's own huge budget deficits.[13] Beyond that, Washington could make a significant contribution by substantially augmenting direct loan and guarantee programs designed to sustain essential imports of raw materials, spare parts, and capital goods into debtor nations. Adequate trade credits are vital to the Third World's long-term development process. At the national level, the guarantee and insurance activities of the Export-Import Bank should be further expanded, building on the precedent of the $2 billion package proposed for Brazil and Mexico in 1983. At the international level, other creditor countries should be encouraged to follow our example, and active support should be given as well to substantially increased funding (and also leveraging) for the multilateral development institutions, including both the World Bank and regional development banks. The direct budgetary costs of all such initiatives for U.S. taxpayers would not be great. The political and economic benefits could be considerable.

But even such concessions will not suffice if debtor nations are unable to earn the foreign exchange they need to pay their own way. Markets must be open to their exports: trade concessions are needed too, despite protectionist pressures in the United States. As I noted in chapter 3, there is an obvious linkage between import liberalization and debt. It does Brazil or Mexico, for instance, little good to receive new loan guarantees from the Export-Import Bank if they are then hit with new barriers to their exports of textiles or steel. Washington must ensure that what is given with one hand is not taken away with the other. It must not only avoid new restrictions on imports from Third World debtors, but also consider a permanent reduction of existing restrictions on a nonreciprocal and, if need be, unilateral basis. The Reagan administration has already demonstrated, in its Caribbean Basin Initiative, how an appeal to national security interests can be successfully used to achieve legislation of one-way import liberalization even in the face of strong domestic protectionist sentiment. Much foreign policy capital could be gained by extending that initiative to other strategically important debtors in Latin America and even in other parts of the world, such as the Philippines and Korea.

Banks too have their responsibilities and must be encouraged—or, if necessary, obliged—to make concessions for the sake of a positive-sum-linkage strategy. After 1982, banks argued that their high degree of loan exposure in the Third World prevented them from taking a more accommodating attitude toward troubled debtors. While they were in no im-

mediate danger, they said, their own solvency was plainly at
risk. Hence a short-leash approach was essential to ensure
that outstanding obligations were fully honored on a regular
basis. But much of the force of this somewhat self-serving
argument was effectively vitiated after the rescue in early
1984 of the Continental Illinois Bank, then America's eighth
largest banking institution, which had been teetering on the
brink of bankruptcy before being pulled back by the determined actions of Washington's three bank regulatory agencies. By that initiative, policymakers demonstrated their
determination to refuse to allow any large U.S. money-center
bank to fail, no matter how substandard its loan portfolio
might happen to be. Although Continental's problem loans
were in fact mainly domestic rather than foreign, most observers interpreted the rescue as effectively underwriting the
U.S. banking community's sizable investment in Third World
debt—in turn, obviating any excuse bankers may have
thought they had to avoid conceding some form of relief to
hard-pressed sovereign borrowers. The banks as well can afford to shoulder some of the burden of adjustment.

Again, to illustrate, banks might be encouraged to extend
to all debtor nations the precedent of multiyear reschedulings,
incorporating liberalized terms (lower spreads, longer repayment periods, smaller renegotiation fees), of the sort established for Mexico and Venezuela in the latter part of 1984.
Such concessions would not substantially loosen all reins of
discipline on debtors—the short leash—if they were formally
conditioned upon continuation of IMF stabilization programs
or, at a minimum, linked to regular fund or World Bank monitoring of their economic performance.

Even more fundamentally, banks could make a creative
contribution by agreeing to negotiate some form of debt relief
to reflect borrowers' altered capacity to pay. The most direct
approach would be to rationally relate debt-service obligations to some explicit measure of a country's foreign-exchange
availability, thereby ensuring greater certainty for future
planning for creditors and debtors alike. A cap could be
designed, for instance, limiting interest payments by pre-
arranged formula—preferably based on each country's his-

torical experience—to a stable percentage of current export receipts and nontied capital inflows. Any excess of market rates over the cap could be capitalized, perhaps with the addition of a "claw-back" clause to provide some immediate reimbursement for banks should either interest levels fall or export revenues rise unexpectedly. To ensure continuing discipline in domestic economic management, the cap too should be formally conditioned upon maintenance of IMF stabilization programs or regular fund or World Bank monitoring of economic performance. To encourage sustained growth policies (and also to discourage any temptation for debtors to underreport export values), a supplementary percentage of foreign receipts could by mutual agreement be set aside in a sort of escrow account, to be released gradually to debtor governments only when they are judged to be in compliance with overall development objectives.

Finally, in some of the worst cases, banks might agree by negotiation simply to write down a part, if not all, of the face value of existing debt—in effect, accepting as permanent the now altered circumstances of such borrowers. Banks must face the fact that a number of countries will have little or no payment capacity for years to come.

Bankers obviously dislike proposals of this sort, since any such concessions necessarily compel them to take a hit on current earnings. They have already been subsidizing borrowers, they complain, by the amount of difference between what debtors have actually paid in interest on rescheduled debts and what they presumably would have been obliged to pay (given increased perceptions of risk) had new loans been made with the money. Any disadvantage to current income statements, however, would be more than offset by the advantage of adding greater realism to their balance sheets, which have tended to carry even some of the most dubious of Third World debts at 100 percent of value. Banks could no longer be accused of demanding subsidization of the rich by the poor, and investors would no longer have an incentive to do the discounting of debt for them by writing down the value of bank shares instead. In any event, the losses contemplated here would be considerably less than might otherwise be the case should the pot be allowed to reach the boiling point in debtor countries. Bankers must be realistic about the fragility of the current debt regime: they too have an insurance incentive for making a contribution to systemic stability.[14] The losses contemplated here would also be considerably less than those implied by other, more draconian schemes for debt consolidation or forgiveness that have been floated by various commentators in recent years.[15] There is good reason for rejecting more extreme alternatives. Banks cannot be penalized too harshly if they are to be expected to retain any incentive for Third World lending in the future. Punitive approaches are not in the public interest. The object is to get the banking community to concede some form of debt relief, not to cut debtors off from the prospect of significant new financing. Bankers may have their systemic responsibilities, but they have legitimate commercial interests too.

Can those interests and responsibilities be effectively reconciled? Can banks be kept in the lending game even while they are pressed to make significant concessions to debtors? This brings us back to the role of the government, whose job it is to balance the interests of both the banking community and foreign policy. Nothing better illustrates the need to articulate a coherent public policy on international banking today. The balance called for here is delicate indeed. Incentives for new private financing, plainly, will be maximized insofar as the sharp edge of losses on old debt can be blunted by measures of official support—in effect, carrots to complement the stick of threatened financial disruption. Official support could be provided most directly—and with no need for new legislation—by rules changes or reinterpretations that are well within the scope of the bank regulators' present authority. Under existing accounting rules, for instance, when interest payments are capitalized, banks are required to reclassify the affected loans as "nonperforming" and to increase loan–loss reserves accordingly. This regulation could easily be rewritten to recognize the special characteristics of rescheduled sovereign debt. Likewise, extended periods could be allowed for writeoffs in order to cushion the shock to bank balance sheets. These steps should be regarded as an essential ingredient of a positive-sum-linkage strategy.

Such measures would not be without controversy, of course. As during the 1983 congressional debate on IMF funding, charges could be expected to the effect that an umbrella of public money was (mixing metaphors) being used to bail out private lenders, adding to taxpayers' share of the burden of adjustment. That would be true, however, only in a relative sense, not in absolute terms. Bank losses would be reduced or smoothed but certainly not eliminated or fully compensated. In any event, that is not the main issue. The essential point is that such measures can hardly be avoided if the responsibility constraint is to be taken seriously. Some umbrella (or some carrot) is needed to keep the banks in the game. The question is not whether there should be any public assistance but, rather, at what price: what should be the banks' quid pro quo? I have previously argued that after the excesses of the Incredible Quarter Century support should not come cheap. The excesses themselves suggest that the quid pro quo should take the form of effective limits on the possibility of any repetition of such behavior in the future—in other words, stricter prudential supervision of international banking activity. New lending should be encouraged but not excessive risk-taking. With this, we arrive at the second of the three bank-related issues on Washington's current foreign policy agenda.

III

Prudential supervision is a controversial subject, domestically as well as internationally. Regulation of financial activity at the microeconomic level frequently comes in for criticism, in principle as well as in practice, especially from the more conservative end of the spectrum of political opinion. Not only does regulation reduce the banking system's resiliency, critics say—that is, its ability to cope with sudden, unanticipated change. Worse, supervisory rules may actually encourage the very types of risky activity that they are ostensibly intended to prevent—the so-called moral hazard question. Regulation supposedly reduces efficiency, distorts incentives, and retards useful innovation. Such views, of course, have been highly instrumental in motivating the powerful deregulatory movement under way in the United States in recent years in the financial services industry no less than in other key domestic sectors.

For all its possible flaws, though, banking regulation continues to perform a vital function insofar as it safeguards the health of individual institutions and the stability of financial markets. Society has an undeniable stake in the safety and soundness of its banks. The banking industry, I emphasized in chapter 1, is both peculiarly vulnerable and exceptionally influential—in effect providing, I said, the oil that lubricates the wheels of commerce. The rationale for prudential supervision is that it reduces the probability that sand will ever get thrown in the wheels, endangering the stability of economic conditions in general. Even at some cost, say, in terms of banking resilience—and despite the recent fashion for financial deregulation—this is without doubt an objective in the public interest.

The rationale for prudential supervision is especially persuasive when it comes to the realm of international banking, where, as I have already observed, there is a particular penchant for reckless enthusiasm and willing suspension of disbelief. The excesses of the Incredible Quarter Century, we saw in chapter 4, were by no means exceptional. Yet another of the lessons of history noted in that chapter was the need for effective limits on the temptations and drives that naturally result from the intensity of competition in high finance. This too is a systemic issue, insofar as it calls into question the prevailing rules governing international banking behavior. And here too leadership is required from Washington, insofar as U.S. banks retain their place of preeminence in world financial markets. The practical challenge for U.S. policymakers goes back to the four e's outlined in chapter 3—how to make such limits truly effective at least cost in terms of efficiency, equity, and external relations.

Until recently, the evolution of Washington's supervisory

techniques lagged seriously behind the internationalization of private banking activity. Not until the latter 1970s were formal efforts of any substance made to catch up with the explosive growth in the overseas operations of U.S. banks. In 1977, for instance, at the same time that they instituted the Country Exposure Report (see chapter 10), the three bank regulatory agencies also implemented measures to tighten up supervisory procedures and ensure a basic uniformity of treatment of foreign lending practices. And in 1978 joint examination procedures were adopted aiming to encourage diversification of loan portfolios, identify problem credits, and evaluate the banks' own internal mechanisms for monitoring and assessing country risks. For the most part, however, these initiatives were another case of too little too late, failing to prevent American banks from becoming engulfed by the global debt crisis beginning in 1982.

Since 1982, by contrast, the pace of reform of U.S. supervisory techniques has accelerated, particularly following IMF funding legislation passed in November 1983.[16] Under Title IX of that legislation—known separately as the International Lending Supervision Act of 1983—disclosure requirements and examination procedures have been further refined, capital adequacy standards newly strengthened, and a system of mandatory loan–loss reserves initiated for certain categories of problem loans. The three regulatory agencies are now required to review loan portfolios regularly for evidence of "a protracted inability of public or private borrowers in a foreign country to make payments on their external indebtedness." All loans on which interest has not been paid for more than six months and for which "no definite prospects exist for the orderly restoration of debt service" are to be classified as "value impaired." Special reserves—so-called allocated transfer risk reserves (ATRRs)—equal to 10 percent of outstanding principal in the first year and in increments of 15 percent per annum thereafter as needed will then have to be established by banks out of current income. ATRRs may not be pooled with other reserves or be considered part of a lender's capital. In addition, banks must write down the affected loans themselves by the amount of the ATRRs set aside. The purpose of these reforms, of course, is to discourage excessively risky exposures in the future by obliging banks to value troubled loans on a more realistic basis. Nothing concentrates the mind of a banker so wonderfully as a hit on earnings.

Will this approach be effective? That depends ultimately on how it is applied by the regulatory agencies. The ingredients for success are there. At the end of 1985, however, ATRRs had been mandated for just six countries—Bolivia, Nicaragua, Peru, Poland, Sudan, and Zaire—all of which are commonly counted as being among the worst basket cases in the ranks of sovereign borrowers. The criteria for classifying loans as value impaired have thus been interpreted in the narrowest possible fashion. The reason is obvious: the authorities do not wish to err on the side of restraint. If fresh lending is not to be discouraged along with excessive risk-taking, they feel, the new system must be implemented with a considerable degree of caution.

While understandable, this attitude is questionable. Can we realistically expect to see prudence always observed in bank exposure levels if supervision remains so self-evidently timid? A more effective alternative would be to *draw a clear distinction between old and new debt in future reviews of loan portfolios*. Old debt should be given special consideration, along the lines suggested above, to soften the impact of prospective bank losses. This is the umbrella needed to keep the banks in the game. Any relaxation of accounting rules to permit capitalization of interest payments, for instance, should apply only to loans now outstanding rather than to possible future credits. Likewise, any writeoffs of old debts could be stretched out more generously than is presently permitted with ATRRs. New debt, by contrast, should be subjected to a much stricter interpretation of the meaning of "impaired value" in order to send an unambiguous signal to the banking community about what will—and will not—be tolerated in the future. This is the quid pro quo for the umbrella needed to keep the banks in the game. In effect, the distinction would permit government to pursue its two objectives simultaneously—encouraging new finance for debtor countries by offering lenders what amounts to a carrot on old debt, while discouraging any tendency toward renewed excesses in the banking community by holding a reinforced stick over new debt. Supervisors can use the structured bank–government dialogue I recommended in the previous chapter to make sure that their dual signal is clearly understood.

Assuming that supervision thus can be tightened, there seems little reason to expect that the efficiency of international banking operations would be adversely affected. Quite the contrary, in fact. Any enhancement of prospects for institutional and market stability should generate real economic gains through the greater certainty that would be provided for purposes of financial planning. Problems for public policy could be created, however, in terms of either equity or external relations. Stricter application of limits on a unilateral basis could put U.S. banks at a competitive disadvantage vis-à-vis their major rivals in Europe, Canada, and Japan. Alternatively, efforts by the U.S. government to maintain a "level playing field" for banks by pressing other countries to toughen their standards comparably on a multilateral basis could lead to serious diplomatic tensions and controversy. Supervisory arrangements in individual nations tend to differ substantially, reflecting distinctive institutional characteristics. Washington would be damned if it does and damned if it doesn't. Which way should policymakers go?

A strong case can be made for going the multilateral route, despite the risk the United States runs of becoming mired in conflicts of interest with other capital-market countries. At present, prudential supervision of cross-border banking activity on a global basis remains relatively unexacting, despite certain recent initiatives by a number of central banks. Indeed, the absence of strict regulation of foreign-currency-deposit business in key financial centers, as I noted in chapter 2, was responsible for the birth and, subsequently, the spectacular growth of the Euro-currency market in the 1960s and 1970s. Once banks discovered that they could successfully bypass domestic reserve requirements, interest-rate limitations, and capital controls, the domain of the market in effect outran the jurisdiction of states. Internationalization of banking was undoubtedly a good thing in broad economic terms, of course—but perhaps, it may be suggested, too much of a good thing, given the wisdom of hindsight and the reality of today's global debt crisis. Banks could never have gotten so deep into the risky business of sovereign lending had they been more effectively hemmed in by supervisory controls. As the international monetary regime became increasingly privatized, governments became engaged in a kind of "competition in laxity" in the hope of avoiding any competitive disadvantages for their national banking systems. Market forces did the rest.

Only in 1974 did the balance begin to shift, with the creation of a standing committee of bank supervisors—known today as the Cooke Committee, after its chairman, an official of the Bank of England—under the auspices of the Basle-based Bank for International Settlements. Owing to the traumatic financial difficulties of that year, including the failures of both Germany's Bankhaus Herstatt and the Franklin National Bank of New York (then America's twentieth largest bank), questions were raised about who, if anyone, was minding the store. Who was in charge of supervising the activities of institutions operating outside their home countries? Many observers feared that a lack of cooperation between the regulatory authorities of parent and host nations might permit some banks to escape supervision altogether. The stated aim of the Cooke Committee, which currently brings together supervisors from a dozen leading capital-market countries, was to help members coordinate surveillance of international banking activities and to share ideas about how to adapt their national supervisory systems to the evolving banking environment. In effect, the purpose was to restore some of the authority of politics in its ongoing dialectic with markets. The jurisdiction of states, it was felt, must catch up again with the domain of the market.

The best-known product of the committee's work has been the so-called Basle Concordat which, for the first time ever, attempted to lay down practical guidelines for the allocation of supervisory responsibilities among national central banks. First agreed to in 1974, the guidelines were updated and clarified in 1983 in the aftermath of the dramatic—and far-reaching—collapse of the Luxembourg subsidiary of an Italian bank, Banco Ambrosiano, in July 1982. In addition, great stress has been placed, since a formal committee statement was issued in 1978, on the need for supervision of internationally active banks on a consolidated basis; that is, on the basis of a single set of accounts for all of an institution's worldwide business. The intention is to prevent banks from increasing their risk-taking beyond acceptable bounds by shifting their operations to jurisdictions where supervision happens to be less stringent. Consolidation would permit all aspects of global risk, from capital adequacy to country exposure, to be assessed at one time. Since 1978, a number of major industrial countries have in fact moved to implement the recommendation for consolidated accounting, including most importantly the United States.

Nonetheless, gaps remain. The committee has regrettably failed to resolve the very critical problem of differing supervisory standards. Each country continues to enforce its own traditional norms, based largely on national historical experience and perceived domestic needs. The result, in practical terms, is still a very uneven playing field—a supervisory regime best characterized by one analyst as a "regulatory free-for-all,"[17] in which banks of different nationalities are still able to exploit existing disparities of treatment to gain competitive advantage in international business. The consequence of this is a continuing incentive for competition in laxity among governments, which effectively blocks genuine tightening of the current regime. Once again, we see an example of a market failure in which everyone wants to be a free rider. Once again, therefore, we see a need for some initiative from the United States, the acknowledged leader, to organize collective action to deal with a common problem.

The objective, to repeat, is to curb any tendencies toward excessive risk-taking in international banking, consistent of course with the legitimate commercial interests of banks themselves. The vehicle for collective action already exists in the mechanism of the Cooke Committee. What is required is a firm commitment from Washington to use that mechanism to push for coordinated reform of the prevailing rules, with the aim of achieving a higher degree of uniformity of standards at a more exacting level of application of limits. Uniformity of standards, to ensure similar competitive conditions between dissimilar banking systems, is essential to make reform attractive to governments from a narrowly nationalistic point of view; stricter application of limits, to ensure bank safety and soundness, would be consistent with a broader international interpretation of interests. This too could be described as a positive-sum-linkage strategy—reciprocal restraint for joint benefit.

Uniformity of standards does not necessarily mean uniformity of instruments. Governments need not use identical means to achieve a commonly desired end. Indeed, given the distinctiveness of institutional characteristics in each country, it is not realistic to expect that national regulatory authorities could be persuaded to subscribe to the same capital-asset ratios, loss-reserve requirements, or loan-classification schemes—or even to the same examination procedures. The objective must be not to suppress these differences but to accommodate them. How can that be accomplished?

The answer is: By broadening the surveillance function of the Cooke Committee to allow members to keep an eye not only on their banks but also on each other. Supervisory standards are apt to be applied most uniformly, despite institutional differences, if national techniques are subjected regularly to international discussion and evaluation. As in the structured dialogue I proposed in chapter 9, participants need not commit themselves to coordination of specific operational decisions so long as they remain committed to a process of mutual sensitization. In terms of a positive-sum-linkage strategy, therefore, highest priority must be given to the goal of reciprocal transparency. In practical terms, this could be accomplished most readily if all countries follow through on the recommendation for consolidated accounting. Here is where collective action in the area of prudential supervision now is most urgently called for.

IV

Beyond prudential supervision, finally, lies the issue of monetary management.[18] Prompt and timely regulation at the microeconomic level, I noted at the end of chapter 4, is only one way to temper the extravagant impulses that are so characteristic of high finance. Equally important is strict control at the macroeconomic level aimed at containing any tendencies toward prolonged periods of excess liquidity in the markets such as occurred in the 1970s. Ever since the Medici Bank conducted business in the Renaissance, foreign lending manias have been closely associated with an oversupply of capital in the aggregate. The Incredible Quarter Century was just the latest of a long history of episodes in which lenders "succumbed to the temptation of seeking an outlet for surplus cash in making dangerous loans to princes." Effective monetary management too is without doubt an objective in the public interest. That means effective management of international liquidity.

During the Incredible Quarter Century, as we know, the management of international liquidity—such as it was—in effect passed from public hands to the private sector. International liquidity refers to the means available to nations to finance balance-of-payments deficits, including not only their foreign monetary reserves but also their ability to borrow from private or official sources abroad. At Bretton Woods in 1944, the responsibility for making decisions affecting nations' access to international liquidity was, in principle, reserved to governments. But as the years passed, and particularly after the first oil shock in the early 1970s, banks, in practice, gradually took over much of the job themselves, in one of the most conspicuous manifestations of the increasing privatization of the global monetary regime. Through their role in helping to finance the swelling deficits of oil-importing countries, and later even those of some oil exporters, market lenders took over functions previously thought more appropriate to national and multilateral authorities. Effectively, the world monetary system took on some of the characteristics of a domestic credit system without a central bank. Private banking institutions, not official agencies, came to make many of the crucial decisions regarding access to international liquidity.

No one doubts the beneficial aspects of the banks' role in recycling petrodollars. As I noted in chapter 2, someone had to do it: neither oil exporters nor Western governments seemed eager to take up the responsibility; banks stepped in to fill the breach. However, the downside to this—of which we are now only too aware—was the risk that the resulting volume of financing might not always be consistent with stable performance of the system as a whole. In the years leading up to the Latin American debt storm in 1982, bank lending was excessive; since 1982, by contrast, it has seemed strikingly inadequate in relation to overall systemic needs. Few analysts question that if domestic credit creation were left entirely in the hands of private institutions, there would be a strong possibility of repeated periods like these of excessive or deficient lending in the aggregate, exacerbating cyclical instabilities. "Money does not manage itself" is the old adage. That is why we have central banks. The same argument evidently applies at the international level. More effective management of international liquidity is needed to help stabilize global macroeconomic performance, and this means reversing some of the privatization that has occurred in recent decades—in effect, as in the area of prudential supervision, it means restoring some of the authority of politics in its ongoing dialectic with markets. Here too it would be desirable for the jurisdiction of states to catch up again with the domain of the market.

In policy terms, therefore, collective action is once again called for to deal with a common problem. While a world central bank might seem a logical analogue to monetary management at the domestic level, such a radical departure would hardly be realistic as a serious political proposal. More practicable would be a joint effort by national governments to provide a substitute form of authority where no supranational agency can at present exist. Here too, however, such an effort must be organized to overcome the unwillingness of states separately to take responsibility for the public good of system maintenance (another market failure). And as before, one candidate for the necessary leadership stands out—the United States, the acknowledged primus inter pares among capital-market countries.

The objective of collective action in this context would be to encourage a volume of financing by the markets that is conducive to maintaining the stability of key macroeconomic variables, such as inflation, unemployment, and real income and output, in the broader global economy. The key to such an effort lies in the central role played by domestic monetary and fiscal policy in major financial centers in determining the overall pace of liquidity creation through international lending, a role that is a direct corollary of the inherently close functional relationship existing between internal and external credit markets. If domestic financial variables were genuinely under control in the leading capital-market countries, then so too would be the aggregate amount of credit (abroad as well as at home) created in their currencies. With international liquidity available from the markets in national currencies, the supply of finance for the world as a whole ultimately depends on monetary developments in a handful of issuing countries. As summarized by a special international report published a few years ago:

> What we have today is something that is moving toward what can perhaps best be described as a market-oriented or "federative" international system. Under this system the availability and terms on which official international liquidity can be obtained are determined in individual cases by private institutions. For the system as a whole, however, they are determined by the joint product of the monetary policies being followed in half a dozen or more major financial centres closely interconnected through the international financial markets....
>
> The overall level of lending activity in the international markets will depend on development in each of the major national markets to which they are closely related. If developments in these national markets are under the control of monetary authorities acting in consultation with

each other, the level of activity in the international markets will be brought under control as well.[19]

In short, governments in the major issuing countries already have it within their power to ensure effective management of international liquidity through appropriate coordination of their national monetary and fiscal policies. Without macroeconomic policy coordination, there is simply no bar at all to recurrent instability in international bank lending. With it, there is at least an enhanced probability that the amount of payments financing in the aggregate will remain roughly consistent with sound overall objectives for the system as a whole, thus reinforcing the broader stabilizaton objectives of coordination. This too could be described as a positive-sum-linkage strategy, based on the principle of reciprocal restraint for joint benefit.

Here also, as in the area of prudential supervision, coordination by no means demands harmonization of specific operational decisions. A positive-sum-linkage strategy does not require detailed integration of all aspects of macroeconomic planning in order to be successful. It is a uniformity of general goals that is at issue, not of particular instruments or policy mixes. The overall availability of financial resources to private lenders can be effectively controlled simply if each government takes more explicit account of international considerations in the formulation and implementation of its domestic policies—for example, if traditional definitions of money supply are widened to include net currency deposits abroad as well as at home, credit expansion targets are broadened to encompass foreign as well as domestic lending to final borrowers, and fiscal policies are managed with an eye to their effects on external as well as internal interest rates. That is all that policy coordination demands in practical terms; none of it is necessarily beyond the realm of political feasiblity. In essence what is called for, once again, is commitment to a process of mutual sensitization sufficient to remind participants of their collective responsibilities.

To some extent, of course, such a process already goes on

through a variety of existing institutional channels, ranging from private discussions among central bankers in monthly meetings at the BIS to the public exchanges among heads of state at the annual Western economic summits. National policies are subjected to multilateral review and evaluation; policymakers are aware of the interdependence of their domestic financial systems. Periodically, the importance of the objective of collective action is publicly acknowledged by government officials.[20] What tends to be missing, however, is the requisite commitment to do something about it all—to move beyond mere sensitization to the actual practice of coordination along the lines suggested. That is the lacuna in the management of international liquidity today.

Bridging the gap will require the leadership of the United States. Only Washington is in a position to persuade other major capital-market countries to resist the temptations of the free-rider role. The responsibility constraint gives the United States an incentive; its singularity in the system gives it the necessary influence. Not many governments need be involved, at least not at the start. Institutionally, a nucleus exists in the so-called Group of Five—America plus Britain, France, Germany, and Japan—whose finance ministers meet periodically, sometimes together with their central-bank governors, to discuss issues of mutual interest (much as I have proposed, in the previous chapter, for the domestic bank–government relationship). These five countries are crucial, since it is their financial markets, institutions, and currencies that at present provide the bulk of financing for the rest of the world. If they could be convinced to accept joint responsibility for international monetary stability, the system as a whole would no longer lack the equivalent of a central bank. In September 1985, a first step was taken when the Group of Five, meeting in New York, agreed to "cooperate more closely" to achieve a new alignment of exchange rates that would "better reflect fundamental economic conditions" (meaning, primarily, some depreciation of the dollar).[21] Can these countries now move on to broader and more effective coordination of their national monetary and fiscal policies?

Here is where collective action in the area of liquidity management now is most urgently called for.

V

In all three areas—global debt and prudential supervision as
well as the management of international liquidity—America
is confronted with difficult, interrelated challenges to its national interests. None of the issues, it appears, can be ignored;
yet neither does the United States have the capacity to cope
with any one of them, let alone all three, entirely on its own.
On the one hand, the responsibility constraint compels Washington to contemplate possible sacrifices of narrow national
advantage for the sake of wider system maintenance. On the
other hand, practical opportunities are generated for positive-
sum linkages that could lift America as well as others to a
superior policy outcome. Could anything more sharply illustrate the complex implications of international banking for
U.S. foreign policy today? For better or for worse, high finance
and politics are now wedded. The need for a coherent public
policy on international banking can no longer be avoided.

Appendix

Participants in 1983–84 study group, 1984–85 author's review group, and/or June 1985 meeting in San Francisco

C. Michael Aho—Council on Foreign Relations
Paul Applegarth—Bank of America
Nicolas A. Barletta—World Bank
Bo Baskin—First Boston Corporation
David O. Beim—Bankers Trust Company
Serge Bellanger—Crédit Industriel et Commerciel
Paul H. Boeker—Department of State
William Bolin
Lawrence J. Brainard—Bankers Trust Company
Ralph C. Bryant—The Brookings Institution
Russell K. Burbank—Thermal Power Corporation
Alexander D. Calhoun—Graham and James
Robert Carswell—Shearman and Sterling
Elaine Chao—Bank of America
Gary B. Christiansen—Pillsbury, Madison & Sutro
George J. Clark—Citibank
Elinor Constable—Department of State
William B. Dale—International Monetary Fund
Charles H. Dallara—Department of the Treasury
Carlos Díaz-Alejandro—Columbia University

William Diebold, Jr.
James Drumwright—Crédit du Nord
Johanes Esswein—German Consulate General
Albert Fishlow—University of California at Berkeley
Henry H. Fowler—Goldman Sachs and Company
Charles Ganoe—First American Bank of New York
Ian H. Giddy—Columbia University
Joanne Gowa—University of Pennsylvania
Philip Habib—World Affairs Council of Northern California
Edward Hamilton—Hamilton, Rabinovitz & Szanton
Bernard J. Hargadon, Jr.—McKesson International
H. Erich Heinemann—Shearson/American Express, Inc.
Robert H. Heller—Bank of America
Richard Herring—University of Pennsylvania
Cordell Hull—Bechtel Corporation
Barbara Insel—Council on Foreign Relations
Yves-Andre Istel—Lehman Brothers Kuhn Loeb, Inc.
Peter Jones—attorney
Miles Kahler—International Monetary Fund/Yale University
Henry Kaufman—Salomon Brothers
Nancy R. Kauppi—Bank of New York
David Kellogg—Council on Foreign Relations
Robert O. Keohane—Brandeis University
Paul H. Kreisberg—Council on Foreign Relations
Roger Kubarych—Federal Reserve Bank of New York
Thomas Layman—Crocker Bank
Karin Lissakers
Charles Edwin Lord—Prudential Bank and Trust
    Company
Winston Lord—Council on Foreign Relations
Angus MacNaughton—Genstar Corporation
Robert Marcus—Alumax
Charles F. Meissner—Chemical Bank
Alberto Mejía—Banco de Bogotá Trust Company
Martin A. Miszerak—Manufacturers Hanover Trust
    Company
William S. Ogden—Ogden Associates
Jesun Paik—Wells Fargo
Lionel I. Pincus—E. M. Warburg Pincus & Co., Inc.

John B. M. Place
Donald C. Platten—Chemical Bank
Susan Kaufman Purcell—Council on Foreign Relations
Jeffrey D. Sachs—Harvard University
Nathaniel Samuels—Lehman Brothers Kuhn Loeb, Inc.
William W. Sihler—University of Virginia
Paul Slawson—Getz Corporation
Robert Solomon—The Brookings Institution
Joan E. Spero—American Express Company
Helena Stalson—Council on Foreign Relations
Richard Sutch—University of California at Berkeley
Peter Tarnoff—World Affairs Council of Northern California
John Elting Treat—Bear, Stearns
Edwin M. Truman—Federal Reserve System
H. Anton Tucher—Bank of America
Andrés Velasco
Mikio Wakatsuki—Bank of Japan
Philip A. Wellons—Harvard University
Richard A. Wiley—First National Bank of Boston
H. David Willey—Morgan Stanley & Co.
John Williamson—Institute for International Economics
Gregory Wilson—House Banking Committee
Stephen Wilson—Dillon Read

Notes

CHAPTER 1

1. Adapted from R. M. Pecchioli, *The Internationalization of Banking: The Policy Issues* (Paris: Organization for Economic Co-operation and Development, 1983), Annex 1.

2. Technically, exceptions may be noted insofar as the interest rates on any of these transactions are determined in the domestic financial markets of the countries whose currencies are used, rather than in the Euro-currency market per se. Thus some of the transactions in subset D1 may be more akin to pure "domestic" operations, while some of those in subsets C, D2, and D3 may be more akin to traditional "foreign" operations, depending on the specific terms applied to them. See Pecchioli, op. cit., p. 130, nn. 1, 2.

3. See, e.g., Ian H. Giddy, "The Theory and Industrial Organization of International Banking," in *The Internationalization of Financial Markets and Economic Policy*, ed. Robert G. Hawkins, Richard M. Levich, and Clas G. Wihlborg (Greenwich, Conn.: JAI Press, 1983), pp. 195–243; and Ralph C. Bryant, "The Progressive Internationalization of Banking," Brookings Discussion Papers, no. 14 (April 1984), pp. 16–18.

CHAPTER 2

1. Herbert Feis, *Europe, the World's Banker, 1870–1914* (New York: The Council on Foreign Relations, 1930; reprint New York: Norton, 1965), p. xiii.

2. The literature on the history of the Euro-currency market

is voluminous. For useful primers, see, e.g., M. S. Mendelsohn, *Money on the Move* (New York: McGraw Hill, 1980); or Anthony Sampson, *The Money Lenders* (New York: Viking, 1980). For a more advanced treatment, see Gunther Dufey and Ian H. Giddy, *The International Money Market* (Englewood Cliffs: Prentice-Hall, 1978).

3. Alan R. Holmes and Fred H. Klopstock, "The Market for Dollar Deposits in Europe," *Federal Reserve Bank of New York Monthly Review*, November 1960, p. 197.

4. Oscar L. Altman, "Foreign Markets for Dollars, Sterling and Other Currencies," *International Monetary Fund Staff Papers* 8 (December 1961): 328; and Altman, "Recent Developments in Foreign Markets for Dollars and Other Currencies," *International Monetary Fund Staff Papers* 10, no. 1 (March 1963): 48–51.

5. The BIS data appear regularly in quarterly reports on "International Banking and Financial Market Developments," semiannual reports on "The Maturity Distribution of International Bank Lending," and its *Annual Reports*. More recently, starting in January 1984, the International Monetary Fund also began to publish comprehensive statistics on international banking activity in its monthly *International Financial Statistics*. Other useful data sources include the monthly *Financial Statistics* of the Organization for Economic Cooperation and Development and *World Financial Markets*, a monthly publication of the Morgan Guaranty Bank of New York.

6. To do this, most interbank positions between reporting banks (i.e., purely wholesale interbank transactions) were excluded in order to avoid doublecounting the same funds passing through several different institutions. With one major exception, sources were thus defined to include net loans in foreign currencies to nonbanks plus deposits placed in banks outside the reporting European area. The major exception was that reporting banks themselves were considered as original suppliers to the market, to the extent that they used funds obtained in domestic currency for switching into foreign currency; and, similarly, as users of funds to the extent that they switched foreign currency deposits into domestic currency. The advantage of including the banks' "own" supply and use of funds was that it automatically ensured that the two sides of the market would always balance. For a useful explanation of the BIS net size concept, see Helmut Mayer, "The BIS Concept of the Eurocurrency Market," *Euromoney*, May 1976, pp. 60–66. For a critical evaluation, see Dufey and Giddy, op. cit., pp. 21–34.

7. In fact, these totals still systematically understate the full extent of international banking activity insofar as they exclude (a) foreign currency lending by banks to domestic residents, and (b) all

international lending by banks other than those reported by the BIS. The resulting discrepancies can be substantial. To give just one example: one estimate of foreign loans outstanding in 1983 at banking offices, other than U.S. branches, in the five offshore centers listed in table 2.2, plus bank claims in two other centers, Bahrain and Netherlands Antilles, comes to some $270 billion. This represents an addition of more than 15 percent to the figure recorded in table 2.2 for the same year ($1,757.1 billion). See Paul Mentré, *The Fund, Commercial Banks and Member Countries*, IMF Occasional Papers, no. 26 (Washington: International Monetary Fund, April 1984), p. 3, table 1.

   8. R. M. Pecchioli, *The Internationalization of Banking: The Policy Issues* (Paris: Organization for Economic Cooperation and Development, 1983), p. 19, table 3.

   9. Mentré, op. cit., p. 6.

   10. Bank for International Settlements, "The Nationality Structure of the International Banking Market and the Role of Interbank Operations" (Basle: May 1985).

   11. The figures in this paragraph are drawn from J. Andrew Spindler, *The Politics of International Credit: Private Finance and Foreign Policy in Germany and Japan* (Washington: Brookings Institution, 1984), p. 187, table 7–2.

   12. The American expansion abroad was mirrored by a similar, albeit smaller, movement of foreign banks into the United States. By the end of 1981, 175 banks from 39 countries had established offices in the United States, with total assets equal to some $255 billion. See Betsy Buttrill White, "Foreign Banking in the United States: A Regulatory and Supervisory Perspective," *Federal Reserve Bank of New York Quarterly Review* 7, no. 2 (Summer 1982): 48–58.

   13. See, e.g., General Accounting Office, *International Banking Facilities Have Improved the Competitive Position of Banks in the United States*, Report to the Chairman, Board of Governors of the Federal Reserve System (Washington: August 7, 1984).

   14. Morgan Guaranty Trust Company, *World Financial Markets*, October 1982, p. 5.

   15. Maxwell Watson, Peter Keller, and Donald Mathieson, *International Capital Markets, Developments and Prospects, 1984*, IMF Occasional Papers, no. 31 (Washington: International Monetary Fund, August 1984), p. 23.

   16. Donald T. Regan, "Statement," *International Financial Markets and Related Matters*, Hearings before the House Committee on Banking, Finance and Urban Affairs, December 21, 1982 (Washington: 1983), p. 54, table 3.

17. James R. Waterston, "Statement on behalf of the American Bankers Association," *To Increase the U.S. Quota in the International Monetary Fund and Related Matters*, Hearings before the Subcommittee on International Trade, Investment and Monetary Policy of the House Committee on Banking, Finance and Urban Affairs, April 27, 1983 (Washington: 1983), p. 377.

18. As quoted in M. S. Mendelsohn, *Commercial Banks and the Restructuring of Cross Border Debt* (New York: Group of Thirty, 1983), p. 10.

19. Ibid., p. 11.

20. International Monetary Fund, *World Economic Outlook, 1983*, IMF Occasional Papers, no. 21 (Washington: May 1983), p. 204.

21. See, e.g., Jack Guttentag and Richard Herring, "Credit Rationing and Financial Disorder," *Journal of Finance* 39, no. 5 (December 1984): 1359–82.

22. As quoted in *Time*, January 10, 1983, p. 45.

23. As quoted in Sampson, op. cit., p. 144.

24. As quoted in *Time*, January 10, 1983, p. 50.

25. Lawrence J. Brainard, "More Lending to the Third World? A Banker's View," in *Uncertain Future: Commercial Banks and the Third World*, ed. Richard E. Feinberg and Valeriana Kallab (Washington: Overseas Development Council, 1984), pp. 34–35. Brainard is with Bankers Trust in New York.

26. As quoted in *Time*, January 10, 1983, p. 50.

27. Ibid.

28. OECD, *External Debt of Developing Countries, 1983 Survey* (Paris: 1984), pp. 34–35. *Short term* is defined as original maturity of one year or less.

29. See, e.g., Linda Sadler, "The Final Days of Offshore Banking," *Institutional Investor*, June 1984, pp. 61–66; and Michael R. Sesit and Daniel Hertzberg, "Internationalization of U.S. Banks Falters After Decade of Expansion," *Wall Street Journal*, August 7, 1984, p. 35.

30. As quoted in Neil Osborn, "Is International Banking Still in Fashion?" *Euromoney*, October 1984, p. 252.

31. As quoted in Daniel Hertzberg, "Big Bank Stocks Fall as Investors Challenge Worth of Foreign Debt," *Wall Street Journal*, June 8, 1984, sec. 2. More recently, a rough definition of the cost has been provided through development of small secondary market for Third World debt, in which a limited number of bank loans are swapped or sold outright at a discount from face value. In some of the worst cases, such as Bolivia and Nicaragua, discounts have run as high as 80–90 percent. See *New York Times*, July 7, 1985, p. D1.

32. See, e.g., *New York Times*, June 2, 1985, sec. 3, p. F1; and June 11, 1985, p. D1.

33. *New York Times*, May 23, 1985, p. D1.

34. As quoted in "A New Awakening, A Survey of International Banking," *Economist*, March 24, 1984, p. 23.

35. See, e.g., Office of Technology Assessment, *Effects of Information Technology on Financial Service Systems* (Washington: U.S. Congress, September 1984).

36. As quoted in Osborn, op. cit., p. 258.

37. Ibid., p. 255.

38. Ibid., p. 258.

39. See, e.g., *Economist*, August 27, 1983, p. 52.

40. Watson et al., op. cit., chap. 1.

41. See, e.g., Osborn, op. cit.

CHAPTER 3

1. Karin Lissakers, "Money and Manipulation,"*Foreign Policy* 44 (Fall 1981): 123.

2. Meyer Rashish, "Bank Lending Overseas Has Become Intertwined with Politics," *American Banker*, January 15, 1982, pp. 4–5.

3. Robert O. Keohane and Joseph S. Nye, *Power and Interdependence: World Politics in Transition* (Boston: Little, Brown, 1977).

4. Ibid., p. 26.

5. Ibid., pp. 30–32.

6. But see Jonathan David Aronson, *Money and Power: Banks and the World Monetary System* (Beverly Hills, Calif.: Sage Publications, 1977); and Janet Kelly, "International Capital Markets: Power and Security in the International System," *ORBIS* 21, no. 4 (Winter 1978): 843–74.

7. A case in point is a 1977 book by two American Marxists, Lawrence H. Shoup and William Minter, entitled *Imperial Brain Trust: The Council on Foreign Relations and United States Foreign Policy* (New York: Monthly Review Press, 1977). Ostensibly a history of the Council on Foreign Relations, the work argues that since its founding in 1921 the Council has served as the agent of "monopoly capital" in general and of the "New York financial oligarchy" in particular, secretly directing this country's foreign policy. "The Council on Foreign Relations...was designed to equip the United States of America for an imperial role on the world scene....The Council...plays a key role in molding United States foreign policy. ...[It] has been extremely successful in achieving its goals....The

Council is solidly based in the United States capitalist class" (pp. 3, 5, 50, 85). That Council leaders have often been in disagreement both among themselves and with various policies of the government is dismissed by the authors as of little practical significance; that the Council itself is as frequently criticized from the right as from the left is conveniently dismissed as "a reflection of certain intraclass divergencies.... The main conclusions should still be clear: the Council on Foreign Relations and the New York financial oligarchy, which it primarily represents, have a leading position in molding United States foreign policy" (p. 111).

8. J. Andrew Spindler, *The Politics of International Credit: Private Finance and Foreign Policy in Germany and Japan* (Washington: Brookings Institution, 1984), p. 7. Spindler was a vice president of Continental Illinois Bank at the time he wrote his book.

9. "State Department Calls in U.S. Bankers to Warn Against Cutting Off Yugoslavia," *Wall Street Journal*, April 22, 1982, p. 33.

10. Jack Zwick and Richard K. Goeltz, "U.S. Banks are Making Foreign Policy," *New York Times*, March 18, 1979.

11. Robert W. Russell, "Three Windows on LDC Debt: LDCs, the Banks, and the United States National Interest," in *Developing Country Debt*, ed. Lawrence G. Franko and Marilyn G. Seiber (New York: Pergamon Press, 1979), pp. 263–64.

12. Herbert Feis, *Europe, the World's Banker, 1870–1914* (1930; reprint New York: Norton, 1965), p. 468.

13. Charles P. Kindleberger, *Manias, Panics, and Crashes: A History of Financial Crises* (New York: Basic Books, 1978), p. 6.

14. See, e.g., Spindler, op. cit.

15. See, e.g., Stephen D. Krasner, ed., *International Regimes* (Ithaca: Cornell University Press, 1983), esp. p. 2. Principles are understood as beliefs of facts, causation, and rectitude. Norms are standards of behavior defined in terms of rights and obligations. Rules are specific prescriptions or proscriptions for action. Decision-making procedures are prevailing practices for making and implementing social choice.

16. See, e.g., Benjamin J. Cohen, in collaboration with Fabio Basagni, *Banks and the Balance of Payments* (Montclair, New Jersey: Allenheld Osmun, 1981), chap. 1.

17. Guido Carli, *Why Banks Are Unpopular*, The 1976 Per Jacobsson Lecture (Washington: International Monetary Fund, 1976), pp. 6, 8. Carli was governor of the Bank of Italy.

18. Charles Maynell, "How Chile Reappeared on the Tombstones," *Euromoney*, June 1977, p. 105.

19. Jim Leach (Rep., IA), as quoted in *New York Times*, November 11, 1982, p. D3.

20. "The Politics of Banking," *The Banker*, September 1977, p. 21.

21. Zwick and Goeltz, op. cit.

22. See, e.g., Robert D. Tollison and Thomas D. Willett, "An Economic Theory of Mutually Advantageous Issue Linkages in International Negotiations," *International Organization* 33, no. 4 (Autumn 1979): 429–49; and Arthur A. Stein, "The Politics of Linkage," *World Politics* 23, no. 1 (October 1980). For a slightly different typology of linkages, see Kenneth A. Oye, "The Domain of Choice," in *Eagle Entangled: U.S. Foreign Policy in a Complex World*, Kenneth A. Oye, Donald Rothchild, and Robert J. Lieber (New York: Longman, 1979), pp. 13–17.

23. U.S. Senate Committee on Foreign Relations, *International Debt, the Banks, and U.S. Foreign Policy*, A Staff Report (Washington, 1977), p. 7.

24. Rashish, op. cit., p. 6.

25. U.S. Senate Committee on Foreign Relations, op. cit., p. 7.

CHAPTER 4

1. The term *banchi* (singular, *banco*) derives from the table, or bench, on which early moneylenders customarily did their business.

2. John H. Makin, *The Global Debt Crisis* (New York: Basic Books, 1984), p. 38.

3. Raymond de Roover, *The Rise and Decline of the Medici Bank, 1397–1494* (Cambridge: Harvard University Press, 1963), p. 141.

4. Ibid., pp. 262, 272.

5. See Richard Ehrenberg, *Capital and Finance in the Age of the Renaissance: A Study of the Fuggers and Their Connections* (London: Jonathan Cape, 1928).

6. De Roover, op. cit., pp. 2–3.

7. Ibid., pp. 355–56.

8. Raymond de Roover, *The Medici Bank: Its Origin, Management, Operations and Decline* (New York: New York University Press, 1948), p. 66.

9. Anthony Sampson, *The Money Lenders* (New York: Viking, 1981), p. 27.

10. These data are restricted to long-term capital only, no reliable estimates of short-term capital movements being available. Of the totals shown, at most 10 percent represent direct investments. The vast majority of long-term flows in the nineteenth century consisted of acquisitions of fixed-interest securities (portfolio investments), as discussed below.

11. Herbert Feis, *Europe, the World's Banker, 1870–1914*, (1930; reprint New York: Norton, 1965), p. 17.

12. See Ralph Hidy, *The House of Baring in American Trade and Finance* (Cambridge: Harvard University Press, 1949).

13. Sampson, op. cit., p. 35.

14. For more detail on the Baring crisis, see Charles P. Kindleberger, *Manias, Panics, and Crashes: A History of Financial Crises* (New York: Basic Books, 1978), pp. 153–56.

15. Feis, op. cit., pp. 27, 57, 78.

16. Kindleberger, op. cit., chap. 7 and appendix.

17. David S. Landes, *Bankers and Pashas* (London: Heinemann, 1958), p. 52.

18. Leland H. Jenks, *Migration of British Capital to 1875* (New York: Knopf, 1927), p. 282.

19. Edwin Borchard, *State Insolvency and Foreign Bondholders*, vol. 1, *General Principles* (New Haven: Yale University Press, 1951), p. xx.

20. Clifford Dammers, "A Brief History of Sovereign Defaults and Rescheduling," in *Default and Rescheduling: Corporate and Sovereign Borrowers in Difficulty*, ed. David Suratgar (Washington: International Law Institute, 1984), p. 77.

21. See, e.g., Feis, op. cit., chaps. 12, 14, 16.

22. Borchard, op. cit., p. xxv.

23. Feis, op. cit., pp. 465–66. See also Jacob Viner's classic 1929 article "International Finance and Balance of Power Diplomacy," reprinted in Viner, *Studies in International Economics* (Glencoe, Ill.: The Free Press, 1951), chap. 3.

24. Feis, op. cit., p. 223.

25. See, e.g., John T. Madden, Marcus Nadler, and Harry C. Sauvain, *America's Experience as a Creditor Nation* (New York: Prentice-Hall, 1937), chap. 3.

26. Ibid., chap. 4.

27. Melvyn P. Leffler, "1921–1932: Expansionist Impulses and Domestic Constraints," in *Economics and World Power: An Assessment of American Diplomacy Since 1789*, eds. William H. Becker and Samuel F. Wells, Jr. (New York: Columbia University Press, 1984), p. 251.

28. Madden et al., op. cit., pp. 75–78.

29. Ilse Mintz, *Deterioration in the Quality of Foreign Bonds Issued in the United States, 1920–1930* (New York: National Bureau of Economic Research, 1951), p. 82.

30. Joseph S. Davis, *The World Between the Wars, 1919–39: An Economist's View* (Baltimore: Johns Hopkins University Press, 1975), pp. 148–49.

31. Derek H. Aldcroft, *From Versailles to Wall Street, 1919–1929* (Berkeley: University of California Press, 1977), pp. 259, 261.

32. Madden et al., op. cit., chap. 6 and Appendix 2.

33. Ibid., p. 288.

CHAPTER 5

1. U.S. Senate Committee on Foreign Relations, *International Debt, the Banks, and U.S. Foreign Policy*, A Staff Report (Washington, 1977), pp. 7–8.

2. See, e.g., Statement of Marc E. Leland, Assistant Secretary of the Treasury for International Affairs, in *Federal Response to OPEC Country Investments in the United States (Part 1-Overview)*, Hearings before the Subcommittee on Commerce, Consumer and Monetary Affairs, House Committee on Government Operations, September 1981, p. 127 (hereafter referred to as *1981 Hearings*).

3. Ibid.

4. Federal Reserve Board of Governors, Statistical Release No. E.11 (121), March 13, 1985.

5. Private estimates often run higher, sometimes much higher, though how reliable some of these sources may be is open to question. On matters like this, it is easy to be sensationalist. For a representative sample of such estimates, see the statement of David Toufic Mizrahi at the *1981 Hearings*; and the statements of Paul E. Erdman, Douglas F. Lamont, and Louis J. Walinsky in *The Operations of Federal Agencies in Monitoring, Reporting on, and Analyzing Foreign Investments in the United States (Part 2—OPEC Investment in the United States)*, Hearings before the same Subcommittee, July 1979 (hereafter referred to as *1979 Hearings*).

6. Richard P. Mattione, *OPEC's Investments and the International Financial System* (Washington: Brookings Institution, 1985), pp. 11–13.

7. See, e.g., Louis J. Walinsky, *Arab Investments and Influence in the United States*, with the cooperation of Robert R. Nathan (New York: American Jewish Committee, October 1978), p. 16; or Mattione, op. cit., p. 71.

8. Submission by the Secretary of Commerce, *1981 Hearings*, Part 1, p. 254.

9. Statement, *Multinational Corporations and United States Foreign Policy*, Hearings before the Subcommittee on Multinational Corporations, Senate Foreign Relations Committee, Part 15 (Washington: July–October 1975), p. 22 (hereafter referred to as *1975 Hearings*).

10. Statement, *1979 Hearings*, Part 2, p. 202.

11. Statement, *1981 Hearings*, Part 1, p. 128.

12. For more detail on these early projections, see Benjamin J. Cohen, "Mixing Oil and Money," in *Oil, the Arab-Israel Dispute, and the Industrial World*, ed. J. C. Hurewitz (Boulder, Colo.: Westview Press, 1976), pp. 197–98.

13. One of the best of these best sellers, published in 1976, was *The Crash of '79* by Paul E. Erdman, a former banker.

14. Statement of Henry C. Wallich, *1981 Hearings*, Part 1, p. 220.

15. Kevin Muehring, "Inside SAMA," *Institutional Investor*, November 1984, p. 64. SAMA is the Saudi Arabian Monetary Authority, which holds the bulk of the Saudi government's overseas portfolio. See also Mattione, op. cit., chaps. 5–6.

16. Statement, *1975 Hearings*, Part 11 (January–March 1975), p. 263.

17. Statement, *1979 Hearings*, Part 2, p. 206. See also *Are OPEC Financial Holdings a Danger to U.S. Banks or the Economy?* Report by the Comptroller General of the United States (Washington: General Accounting Office, June 11, 1979).

18. Reprinted in *1979 Hearings*, Part 2, p. 80.

19. Reprinted in *1979 Hearings*, Part 2, p. 78. Emphasis added. The Treasury even sent advisers to the Saudi Arabia Monetary Authority and established an Office of Arabian Affairs in Washington to work with the Saudis on financial matters.

20. See *1975 Hearings*, Part 15, pp. 28–29.

21. Ibid., pp. 64–65.

22. *1975 Hearings*, Part 5, p. 111.

23. Ibid., p. 112.

24. See *1979 Hearings*, Part 5, p. 161.

25. See *1975 Hearings*, Part 15, p. 75.

26. For more detail on this arrangement and how it was arrived at, see *1975 Hearings*, Part 15; and *1979 Hearings*, Part 5, pp. 160–88.

27. Most persistent was the late Benjamin S. Rosenthal, congressman from New York, who repeatedly used his position as chairman of the House Subcommittee on Commerce, Consumer and Monetary Affairs to attack the executive branch on its disclosure policy as well as on many other aspects of Arab investments in the United States. See *1979 Hearings* and *1981 Hearings*.

28. *1975 Hearings*, Part 15, p. 65.

29. This impression was confirmed in interviews with Karin Lissakers, formerly a staff member of the Multinationals Subcom-

mittee, and with former Assistant Treasury Secretary Fred Bergsten. At the time of Senator Church's 1975 inquiry, Lissakers told me in January 1985, "The Treasury and Fed both shared the banks' view. There is no danger, no threat, they said; but if you insist on asking for this information, you will set off the very crisis you want to avoid." During the Carter administration, Bergsten told me in July 1985, "We thought plenty about it. While we never had the slightest sense that they might withdraw their funds for political reasons, we were worried about what might happen if, in the event the dollar weakened, they might lose their nerve and convert into other currencies."

30. *1975 Hearings*, Part 15, p. 72.

31. Statement, *1975 Hearings*, Part 11, p. 264.

32. Statement, *1979 Hearings*, Part 2, pp. 209–10.

33. Executive Order 11858 (May 7, 1975).

34. *The Adequacy of the Federal Response to Foreign Investment in the United States*, Twentieth Report by the House Committee on Government Operations (Washington: August 1, 1980), p. 41.

35. See, e.g., Statement of the Securities Industry Association, *1981 Hearings*, Part 1, p. 8.

36. But not farmland: according to a 1981 Department of Agriculture survey, Arab acquisitions of U.S. agricultural land have been practically nil. U.S. Department of Agriculture, *Foreign Ownership of U.S. Agricultural Land* (Washington: July 1981).

37. For a summary of the existing federal legislation and regulations, see *1979 Hearings*, Part 5, pp. 129–46.

38. In fact, the degree of concentration may be even greater than suggested by table 5.3. According to Karin Lissakers, who as a staff member of the Multinational Corporations Subcommittee participated in the negotiations that led to the first release of these figures in 1975, the Federal Reserve had originally intended to provide the data in three-bank aggregates, grouped by size (three biggest, next three biggest, and so on). "When the Fed got the data, however, it discovered that the petrodollar deposits were so highly concentrated in the top three banks that it would be potentially embarrassing to the banks and their Arab clients to release even this aggregate number." See Karin Lissakers, "Bank Regulation and International Debt," in *Uncertain Future: Commercial Banks and the Third World*, ed. Richard E. Feinberg and Valeriana Kallab (Washington: Overseas Development Council, 1984), p. 68, n. 8.

39. In fact, such worries might even have been one of the motivating forces for Senator Church's inquiries. According to a former minority staffer for the Multinationals Subcommittee (off-the-record

interview, January 1985), there was a perception at the time among some circles in Washington of a "hidden agenda" in the campaign for disclosure of Arab deposits. Interest groups favorable to Israel apparently did fear the creation of a powerful pro-Arab lobby among America's biggest banks. Anything that might provoke a withdrawal of Arab deposits would thus have been welcome as a way of helping to forestall any erosion of U.S. support for Israel.

CHAPTER 6

1. Public Law 95-223, Section 202. For the legislative history of the IEEPA, see *Trading With the Enemy Act Reform Legislation*, Report of the House Committee on International Relations (Washington, June 23, 1977).

2. The only breach in this secrecy came in the fall of 1980, when a former Treasury official discussed his understanding of the figures involved. See *New York Times*, November 3, 1980, p. 19. Although the information then given turned out to be inaccurate, it was widely reported in Iran and, according to U.S. officials who were at the time still active participants in these events, "was not helpful to the U.S. negotiating position." See Robert Carswell and Richard J. Davis, "The Economic and Financial Pressures: Freeze and Sanctions," in *American Hostages in Iran: The Conduct of a Crisis*, ed. Warren Christopher et al. (New Haven: Yale University Press, 1985), p. 190, n. 30 (hereafter referred to as Carswell and Davis, "Pressures").

3. Ibid., pp. 176-77.

4. As quoted in Karin Lissakers, "Money and Manipulation," *Foreign Policy* 44 (Fall 1981): 112.

5. As quoted in Anthony Sampson, *The Money Lenders* (New York: Viking, 1981), p. 237.

6. As quoted in Lissakers, op. cit., p. 113.

7. *International Emergency Economic Powers Act Authority Taken with Respect to Iran—Message from the President of the United States to the Congress*, November 14, 1979 (H. Doc. No. 96-226), reprinted in Christopher et al., op. cit., Appendix A.

8. See, e.g., L. J. Davis, "Hostages for the Chase Manhattan," *Penthouse Magazine*, December 1980.

9. Carswell and Davis, "Pressures," p. 177.

10. House Committee on Banking, Finance and Urban Affairs, *Iran: The Financial Aspects of the Hostage Settlement Agreement* (Washington, July 1981), p. 6.

11. Carswell and Davis, "Pressures," p. 177.

12. As quoted in Sampson, op. cit., p. 245.

13. Interview, February 1984.

14. Carswell and Davis, "Pressures," p. 180.

15. Robert Carswell, "Economic Sanctions and the Iran Experience," *Foreign Affairs* 60, no. 2 (Winter 1981/82): 258 (hereafter referred to as Carswell, "Sanctions").

16. Ibid.

17. Interview, February 1984. Karin Lissakers, who also interviewed key participants in the Iranian episode, has a similar impression of motivations at the time. "In fact," she writes, "what triggered the freeze was not a desire to punish Iran for taking the hostages, but fear that a sudden withdrawal of those assets might set off a major currency and banking crisis for the United States." Lissakers, op. cit., p. 107.

18. See, e.g., the Treasury and State Department documents reprinted in *Federal Response to OPEC Country Investments in the United States (Part I—Overview)*, Hearings before the Subcommittee on Commerce, Consumer and Monetary Affairs, House Committee on Government Operations, September 1981, pp. 731–34 and 744–47 (hereafter referred to as *1981 Hearings*).

19. Carswell and Davis, "Pressures," p. 174, n. 1.

20. House Banking Committee, op. cit., pp. 6, 51. Emphasis added.

21. Carswell, "Sanctions," pp. 258–59.

22. Carswell and Davis, "Pressures," p. 182.

23. One rather tricky legal problem with the setoffs was that few of the deposits were in the name of an Iranian debtor or guarantor. It would clearly be difficult to set off the account of one entity against the debt of a separate, unrelated entity. Banks got around this by invoking the so-called Big Mullah theory, under which it was argued that as a result of the Iranian revolution and its subsequent nationalization programs, all elements of Iran's economy had in effect become parts of a single entity.

24. Lissakers, op. cit., p. 117.

25. Carswell and Davis, "Pressures," p. 193.

26. Ibid., p. 190.

27. House Banking Committee, op. cit., p. 17. Carswell and Davis acknowledge that to the very end information limitations "left Treasury ... with a shifting factual base from which to conduct the negotiations," but insist that these "were not significant enough to affect planning." See Robert Carswell and Richard J. Davis, "Crafting the Financial Settlement," in Christopher et al., op. cit., pp. 203, 205 (hereafter referred to as Carswell and Davis, "Settlement").

28. For more detail, see Carswell and Davis, "Pressures," especially pp. 184–89; and House Banking Committee, op. cit., chap. 2.

29. See Carswell and Davis, "Settlement"; and John E. Hoffman, Jr., "The Bankers' Channel," in Christopher et al., op. cit. (hereafter referred to as Hoffman, "Channel").

30. Communication between these two men was obviously facilitated by the fact that Carswell had been a partner of Hoffman's at Shearman and Sterling before his appointment as deputy treasury secretary (and has since returned to the same firm).

31. Interview, February 1984.

32. Hoffman "Channel," p. 252.

33. In fact, relevant deposit rates in the Euro-currency market had fluctuated wildly over the period of the freeze, ranging from 9 percent to more than 20 percent on some standard maturities. For more detail on this issue, see ibid., pp. 266ff; Carswell and Davis, "Settlement," pp. 220–24; and House Banking Committee, op. cit., pp. 17–20.

34. For more on the details of the final settlement, see *Iranian Asset Settlement*, Hearings before the Senate Committee on Banking, Housing, and Urban Affairs, February 1981.

35. Carswell, "Sanctions," p. 259.

36. Hoffman, "Channel," p. 235.

37. Gary C. Hufbauer and Jeffrey J. Schott, *Economic Sanctions in Support of Foreign Policy Goals*, Policy Analyses in International Economics, no. 6 (Washington: Institute for International Economics, 1983), pp. 74–76.

38. Behzad Nabavi, as quoted in Shaul Bakhash, *The Reign of the Ayatollahs* (New York: Basic Books, 1984), p. 149.

39. Carswell, "Sanctions," p. 262.

40. As quoted in Sampson, op. cit., p. 245.

41. See Kevin Muehring, "Inside SAMA," *Institutional Investor*, November 1984, p. 66; and Richard P. Mattione, *OPEC's Investments and the International Financial System* (Washington: Brookings Institution, 1985), p. 89.

42. Interview, February 1984.

43. Carswell, "Sanctions," pp. 262–63.

44. Carswell and Davis, "Pressures," p. 184.

45. House Banking Committee, op. cit., p. iv.

46. Warren Christopher, "Introduction," in Christopher et al., op. cit., pp. 15–16.

47. This was also the reason for limiting the freeze in foreign branches to dollar-denominated assets only, exempting holdings in

local currencies. As difficult as it was for U.S. officials to assert their right of jurisdiction over dollar deposits in, say, London, it would have been far more difficult to persuade the British government of their right of jurisdiction over sterling deposits there as well.

48. Christopher, "Introduction," p. 28.

49. Carswell, "Sanctions," p. 257.

CHAPTER 7

1. See, e.g., Emma Rothschild, "Banks: The Coming Crisis," *New York Review of Books*, May 27, 1976, pp. 16–22. According to Rothschild, a crisis was inevitable: "The question for the financial system is not whether these debts will be dishonored. Rather, it is an issue of when, and how, and where. . . . The choice will influence U.S. foreign relations" (p. 16).

2. U.S. Senate Committee on Foreign Relations, *International Debt, the Banks, and U.S. Foreign Policy*, A Staff Report (Washington, 1977), p. 7.

3. Lawrence J. Brainard, "Statement," *The Polish Economy*, Hearings before the Subcommittee on European Affairs, Senate Committee on Foreign Relations, January 1982, p. 35 (hereafter referred to as *1982 Hearings*).

4. Marcin Swiecicki, research director of the Polish government's Consultative Economic Council, as quoted in John Dornberg, "Poland on an Economic Tightrope," *Institutional Investor*, September 1984, p. 223.

5. As quoted in Charles Meynell et al., "Erwin Blumenthal is Zaire's Last Hope," *Euromoney*, February 1979, p. 11. Penn Central refers to the Penn Central Railroad, one of America's largest rail companies, which went bankrupt in 1970.

6. For more detail on these three episodes, see Benjamin J. Cohen, in collaboration with Fabio Basagni, *Banks and the Balance of Payments* (Montclair, New Jersey: Allenheld Osmun, 1981), appendix.

7. Darrell Delamaide, *Debt Shock* (New York: Doubleday, 1984), p. 74.

8. See, e.g., Richard Portes, "East Europe's Debt to the West: Interdependence is a Two-Way Street," *Foreign Affairs*, 55, no. 4 (July 1977): 751–82.

9. Brainard, loc. cit., p. 37.

10. J. Andrew Spindler, *The Politics of International Credit: Private Finance and Foreign Policy in Germany and Japan* (Washington: Brookings Institution, 1984), pp. 49–50.

11. Ibid., pp. 82–88. As an additional incentive, Bonn agreed to guarantee directly one-third of the total package.

12. As quoted by Karin Lissakers, who interviewed Schaufele in November 1981 for an unpublished paper on the Polish debt crisis that she prepared in February 1982, when she was a senior associate at the Carnegie Endowment for International Peace. Information on the interview was kindly supplied to me privately by Lissakers. I was also given much the same impression of the State Department's role in separate interviews that I had with two other high-level officials who had been involved in these events; these interviews were off-the-record. Of the $325 million provided by the American-led syndicate, only some $250 million actually came from Western banks. The rest was put up by banks of the Soviet bloc. See Spindler, op. cit., p. 86.

13. Off-the-record interview.

14. Interview, August 1984.

15. Robert Hormats, "Statement," *1982 Hearings*, p. 4.

16. Treasury and State Department Fact Sheet on Polish Debt, *1982 Hearings*, p. 12.

17. Ibid., pp. 11–12.

18. Peter Montagnon, "Eastern Europe: Is It Coming Back to the Market?" *Banker*, October 1983, p. 41.

19. Interview, August 1984.

20. "State Department Calls in U.S. Bankers to Warn Against Cutting Off Yugoslavia," *Wall Street Journal*, April 22, 1982, p. 33.

21. Interview, August 1984.

22. Interview, August 1984. One aspect of this fear was anything but inchoate: apprehension about the prospective loss of government revenues that would result if banks wrote off their Polish debt against tax liabilities. According to Scanlon, the Treasury estimated a tax loss of at least $1 billion over a two-year period.

23. "Polish Default: Bankers' Perspectives on the Issues," March 22, 1982, p. 4.

24. See, e.g., *New York Times*, February 1, 1982, p. 1. Strong support for a declaration of default also came from some surprising quarters outside the administration. See, e.g., Felix G. Rohatyn, "We Cannot Create a 'Municipal Assistance Corporation' for Poland. Let It Go Bankrupt," *New York Times*, January 11, 1982.

25. As quoted in *New York Times*, February 1, 1982, p. 1.

26. Marc Leland, "Statement," *1982 Hearings*, p. 7.

27. See, e.g., *New York Times*, June 8, 1982, p. D1.

28. Interviews with John Scanlon, August 1984; and Robert Hormats, February 1985.

29. William Safire, "Payoff for Repression," *New York Times*, February 1, 1982.

30. As quoted in *Financial Times*, March 2, 1982.

31. Gary C. Hufbauer and Jeffrey J. Schott, *Economic Sanctions in Support of Foreign Policy Goals*, Policy Analyses in International Economics, no. 6 (Washington: Institute for International Economics, 1983), pp. 74–76.

32. John Van Meer, "Banks, Tanks and Freedom," *Commentary*, December 1982, p. 17.

CHAPTER 8

1. *The Economist*, August 21, 1982, p. 11.

2. Jeff Frieden, "Third World Indebted Industrialization: International Finance and State Capitalism in Mexico, Brazil, Algeria, and South Korea," *International Organization* 35, no. 3 (Summer 1981): 407–31.

3. *The Problem of International Investment*, A Report by a Study Group of Members of the Royal Institute of International Affairs (London: Oxford University Press, 1937), p. 267.

4. Arthur F. Burns, "The Need for Order in International Finance," in *International Banking Operations*, Hearings before the Subcommittee on Financial Institutions Supervision, Regulation, and Insurance, House Committee on Banking, Finance and Urban Affairs, March–April 1977, p. 860.

5. International Monetary Fund, *Annual Report, 1977*, p. 41.

6. Benjamin J. Cohen, in collaboration with Fabio Basagni, *Banks and the Balance of Payments* (Montclair, New Jersey: Allenheld Osmun, 1981), esp. chaps. 4, 6.

7. See, e.g., Thomas O. Enders and Richard P. Mattione, *Latin America: The Crisis of Debt and Growth* (Washington: Brookings Institution: 1984), pp. 6–33; and Carlos Díaz-Alejandro, "Latin American Debt: I Don't Think We Are in Kansas Anymore," *Brookings Papers on Economic Activity*, no. 2 (1984), pp. 337–49.

8. Inter-American Development Bank, *External Debt and Economic Development in Latin America: Background and Prospects* (Washington: January 1984), statistical appendix.

9. Ibid.

10. See, e.g., *New York Times*, May 1, 1982, p. 1.

11. William R. Cline, *International Debt and Stability of the World Economy*, Policy Analyses in International Economics, no. 4 (Washington: Institute for International Economics, 1983), p. 34.

12. See e.g., *New York Times*, December 6, 1982, p. D9.

13. As quoted in *New York Times*, June 4, 1983, p. 29.

14. As quoted in Joseph Kraft, *The Mexican Rescue* (New York: Group of Thirty, 1984), pp. 4–5.

15. As quoted in ibid., p. 5.

16. Donald T. Regan, "Statement," *International Financial Markets and Related Matters*, Hearings before the House Committee on Banking, Finance and Urban Affairs, December 21, 1982, pp. 34–39.

17. Diáz-Alejandro, op. cit., p. 355.

18. Bank for International Settlements, *International Banking Developments, Fourth Quarter 1983* (Basle: April 1984), pp. 9–12.

19. Diáz-Alejandro, op. cit., p. 335.

20. Pedro-Pablo Kuczynski, "Latin American Debt: Act Two," *Foreign Affairs* 62, no. 1 (Fall 1983): 24.

21. Paul A. Volcker, "Sustainable Recovery: Setting the Stage," Remarks before the New England Council, Boston, November 16, 1982 (processed), p. 17.

22. *New York Times*, January 14, 1983, p. D1.

23. *New York Times*, November 5, 1983, p. 46.

24. As quoted in *New York Times*, May 13, 1984, p. 1.

25. *New York Times*, May 11, 1984, p. D2.

26. As quoted in *New York Times*, August 9, 1984, p. D1.

27. *Business Week*, August 27, 1984, p. 101.

28. As quoted in *New York Times*, August 18, 1983, p. 1.

29. Bank for International Settlements, *International Banking Developments, Fourth Quarter 1984* (Basle, April 1985), p. 7.

30. See, e.g., *New York Times*, September 8, 1984, p. 1 (Mexico); September 24, 1984, p. D7 (Venezuela); and February 2, 1985, p. 20 (Brazil).

31. *New York Times*, May 21, 1984, p. D1.

32. *New York Times*, June 23, 1984, p. 1.

33. As quoted in *New York Times*, May 21, 1984, p. D12.

34. See, e.g., *New York Times*, June 17, 1984, sec. 4, p. 2; and *Business Week*, June 18, 1984, p. 20. Coordination of the strategy was later reported to have been masterminded by a secret caucus of fourteen of the world's most exposed international banks—a so-called Group of 14. See *Wall Street Journal*, March 28, 1985.

35. Joint Memorandum, C. T. Conover, William M. Isaac, and Paul A. Volcker to Fernand J. St. Germain, "Program for Improved Supervision of International Lending," April 7, 1983. Conover was comptroller of the currency, Isaac was chairman of the FDIC, and St. Germain was chairman of the House Committee on Banking, Finance and Urban Affairs.

36. *New York Times*, June 14, 1983, p. D1.

37. As quoted in *New York Times*, February 9, 1983, p. D7.

38. Public Law 98–18l, Title IX. The entire piece of legislation is known as the "Domestic Housing and International Recovery and Financial Stability Act of 1983." Title IX is known separately as the "International Lending Supervision Act of 1983." For more detail, see below, chaps. 9, 10.

39. Interviews, U.S. Treasury, November 1983 and February 1984.

40. *New York Times*, November 15, 1982, p. D1.

41. *New York Times*, May 21, 1984, p. D1.

42. As quoted in *Wall Street Journal*, June 8, 1984, p. 25.

43. As quoted in *New York Times*, August 1, 1985, p. D13.

44. James A. Baker III, Statement before the Joint Annual Meeting of the International Monetary Fund and the World Bank, Seoul, Korea, October 8, 1985 (processed), p. 2. Emphasis added.

45. *IMF Survey*, February 6, 1984, p. 40.

46. See, e.g., *IMF Survey*, May 18, 1981, p. 152.

47. *IMF Survey*, March 19, 1979, pp. 82–83.

48. *IMF Survey*, November 23, 1981, p. 365.

49. As quoted in *IMF Survey*, October 4, 1982, p. 327.

50. As quoted in *New York Times*, December 12, 1982, sec. 3, p. 1.

51. The United States for a time held out for a slightly smaller quota increase to only SDR 85 billion but was unsuccessful. It was successful in preventing expansion of the GAB to the figure of SDR 20 billion favored by European governments. See *The Economist*, January 22, 1983, pp. 62–63.

52. Interview, January 1984.

53. E. Brau et al., *Recent Multilateral Debt Restructurings with Official and Bank Creditors*, IMF Occasional Papers, no. 25 (Washington: International Monetary Fund, December 1983), pp. 10, 26.

54. *Economist*, February 19, 1983, p. 89.

55. *New York Times*, March 1, 1983, p. D1.

56. *New York Times*, January 22, 1983.

57. As quoted in *New York Times*, January 9, 1983, sec. 3, p. 10.

58. Ibid.

59. Ibid.

60. Ibid.

61. Interviews, International Monetary Fund, January 1984.

62. This was clear despite temporary bursts of optimism from time to time in the financial press. Declarations of victory over the debt problem have repeatedly turned out to be unhappily premature. Compare, for instance, the headlines of two articles in *New York*

Times that appeared within three weeks of one another in February 1985: "Debt Crisis Called All But Over," February 2, 1985, p. D1; and "A Sudden Revival in Latin Debt Fears," February 26, 1985, p. D1.

CHAPTER 9

    1. *New York Times*, January 9, 1986, p. 1.

    2. See, e.g., *New York Times*, January 22, 1983.

CHAPTER 10

    1. Sam Y. Cross, Executive Vice President, Federal Reserve Bank of New York, interview, March 1985. Cross was U.S. Executive Director to the International Monetary Fund from 1974 to 1981.

    2. Charles H. Dallara, U.S. executive director, IMF, interview, April 1985. Dallara was appointed U.S. Executive Director in October 1984.

    3. See, e.g., *The Economist*, January 26, 1985, p. 76.

    4. Off-the-record interview.

    5. Off-the-record interview.

    6. David C. Mulford, Assistant Secretary of Treasury for International Affairs, interview, April 1985.

    7. J. Andrew Spindler, *The Politics of International Credit: Private Finance and Foreign Policy in Germany and Japan* (Washington: Brookings Institution, 1984), pp. 183–85. From his analysis Spindler concludes, as I do from mine, that a more cooperative relationship would be desirable in the United States too—but to be activated, according to him, "only during periods of international financial-political crisis," since it is necessary to "accommodate existing American values and institutional relationships" (pp. 203–04). Unfortunately, this fails to meet the desideratum of foresight: it would do nothing to help forestall crises. To achieve that—in other words, to think more strategically—existing values must be challenged, not accommodated. Spindler's recommendations are too timid.

    8. See, e.g., Benjamin J. Cohen, "Great Britain," in *Economic Foreign Policies of Industrial States*, ed. Wilfrid L. Kohl (Lexington, Mass.: D. C. Heath, 1977), p. 64.

    9. See, e.g., Robert O. Keohane, *After Hegemony: Cooperation and Discord in the World Political Economy* (Princeton: Princeton University Press, 1984), pp. 67–69.

    10. Statistical Release No. E. 16 (126), now published quarterly. Loan data in the Country Exposure Lending Survey are presented on a country-by-country basis collectively for all U.S. banks and

separately for the nine largest money-center institutions and for the next fifteen largest banks. For the origin of these groupings in multiples of three, see chap. 5, n. 38.

11. Securities Act Release No. 33–6478, August 11, 1983.

12. Bank for International Settlements, *Annual Report, 1985*, p. 124.

13. *New York Times*, June 24, 1985, p. D1.

14. As quoted in ibid., p. D5.

15. *Economist*, November 9, 1985, p. 79.

16. As quoted in *New York Times*, November 2, 1985, p. 38.

17. Ibid.

18. See, e.g., *Washington Post*, National Weekly Edition, September 2, 1985, p. 19; and *New York Times*, September 16, 1985, p. 1.

19. *Economist*, September 7, 1985, p. 83.

20. Off-the-record interview.

21. As quoted in *New York Times*, July 19, 1985, p. D2.

22. James D. Robinson, "Superdollars and Superdebt," *New York Times*, May 16, 1985, p. A31.

23. As quoted in *New York Times*, April 1, 1985, p. D1.

24. *Federal Reserve Bulletin*, July 1985, p. A59. The figures are for March 1985. The four financial centers are Bermuda, Britain, the British West Indies, and Switzerland.

25. As quoted in *New York Times*, April 1, 1985, p. D2. See also *Wall Street Journal*, June 10, 1985, p. 6.

CHAPTER 11

1. U.S. Senate Committee on Foreign Relations, *International Debt, the Banks, and U.S. Foreign Policy*, A Staff Report (Washington, 1977), p. 7.

2. The source of the data in this paragraph and in the one that follows is the International Monetary Fund's *World Economic Outlook, 1985* (Washington, April 1985). "Indebted developing countries" are defined to include all Third World countries except eight Middle East oil exporters (Iran, Iraq, Kuwait, Libya, Oman, Qatar, Saudi Arabia, and the United Arab Emirates).

3. See, e.g., IMF, *World Economic Outlook, October 1985*, Revised Projections (Washington, October 1985).

4. Bank for International Settlements, *Annual Report, 1985* (Basle, June 1985), p. 10.

5. Ibid., p. 138.

6. IMF, *World Economic Outlook, 1985*, chap. 3. Similar scenarios were also developed elsewhere, e.g., by the World Bank in its *World Development Report, 1985* (Washington, July 1985), part IV.

7. See, e.g., *New York Times*, August 1, 1985, p. D1.

8. *New York Times*, July 31, 1985, p. D11.

9. As quoted in *New York Times*, September 24, 1985, p. A15.

10. As quoted in *New York Times*, September 26, 1985, p. 1.

11. See, e.g., *New York Times*, October 30, 1985, p. D1.

12. Susan Strange, "The Credit Crisis: A European View," *SAIS Review* 3, no. 2 (Summer–Fall 1983): 179.

13. It is true, of course, that high interest rates, by attracting capital inflows into the United States and thereby contributing to a strong dollar, also have the effect of swelling U.S. purchases from debtor countries whose currencies depreciate in dollar terms, raising their export revenues. However, it is likewise true that a different macroeconomic policy mix—tighter fiscal policy and a more expansionary monetary policy—could produce the same import volume at a lower level of interest rates, thus unequivocally improving Third World debt-service ratios. This is only one reason among many why a reduction of Washington's budget deficits over the long term would be desirable.

14. A straw in the wind was the decision by Peru's Alan García Pérez, upon taking office in July 1985, to cap Peruvian debt payments at 10 percent of his nation's export earnings—in effect, a unilateral reform of the debt regime for one country. See, e.g., *New York Times*, July 30, 1985, p. D1. Banks obviously have an interest in participating in reform and thereby influencing its terms and conditions rather than in having it thrust upon them without their input.

15. See, e.g., Norman A. Bailey, "A Safety Net for Foreign Lending," *Business Week*, January 10, 1983, p. 17; Felix G. Rohatyn, "A Plan for Stretching Out Global Debt," *Business Week*, February 28, 1983, pp. 15–18; Peter B. Kenen, "A Bailout for the Banks," *New York Times*, March 6, 1983, sec. 3, p. F3; and Richard S. Weinert, "Banks and Bankruptcy," *Foreign Policy* no. 50 (Spring 1983): 138–49. For a comprehensive evaluation of these and a full range of other proposals for dealing with the debt problems, see C. Fred Bergsten, William R. Cline, and John Williamson, *Bank Lending to Developing Countries: The Policy Alternatives*, Policy Analyses in International Economics, no. 10 (Washington: Institute for International Economics, April 1985).

16. See chapter 8, n. 38.

17. Richard S. Dale, "International Banking Is Out of Control," *Challenge*, January–February 1983, p. 15.

18. This section draws heavily on the argument developed in Benjamin J. Cohen, in collaboration with Fabio Basagni, *Banks and the Balance of Payments* (Montclair, New Jersey: Allenheld Osmun, 1981), chap. 6.

19. *Towards Full Employment and Price Stability*, A Report to the Organization for Economic Cooperation and Development by a Group of Independent Experts, chaired by Paul McCracken (OECD: Paris, 1977), paras. 466 and 477.

20. For example, in a wide-ranging report on the international monetary system issued in the spring of 1985, a strengthening of the process of "multilateral surveillance" was advocated by deputies of the Group of Ten, an informal caucus of leading capital-market countries. Significantly, though, this specific recommendation was not explicitly endorsed by the group's ministers when they met to consider the deputies' report in June 1985. See *IMF Survey*, June 24, 1985, pp. 205–06; and *IMF Survey*, Supplement on the Group of Ten Deputies' Report, July 1985.

21. Statement of the Group of Five Ministers of Finance and Central Bank Governors, New York, September 22, 1985, para. 18, reprinted in *IMF Survey*, October 7, 1985, pp. 296–97.

Index